BUDGE ROGERS

BUDGE ROGERS

A Rugby Life

PHILIP STEVENS

First published by Pitch Publishing, 2017

Pitch Publishing
A2 Yeoman Gate
Yeoman Way
Worthing
Sussex
BN13 3QZ

www.pitchpublishing.co.uk
info@pitchpublishing.co.uk

A CIP catalogue record is available for this book
from the British Library.

ISBN 978-1-78531-133-8

Typesetting and origination by Pitch Publishing

Printed in the UK by TJ International Ltd Cornwall

Contents

RFU Injured Players Fund

IN addition to telling my story I want this book to support and raise awareness of a charity close to my heart, the RFU Injured Players Foundation.

The RFU Injured Players Foundation provides immediate and lifelong support for every rugby player across England who sustains a catastrophic spinal cord or traumatic brain injury while playing the game, and aims to help prevent future injuries through research and education.

Since it formed in 2008, over £8m has been spent directly supporting rugby players from every level of the game, amateur and professional, male and female, young and old.

The charity provides emotional, practical and financial support to newly catastrophically injured rugby players to enable each individual to achieve the best recovery they can. The Injured Players Foundation is committed to being there for catastrophically injured players for the rest of their lives, empowering them through access to home adaptations, disabled transport, vocational training and further education to enable independence in their daily lives.

As part of their work, they also fund and commission vital research with the aim of preventing catastrophic injuries from occurring, protecting every player who plays our wonderful game.

Please help the Injured Players Foundation continue its amazing work: find out how you can make a difference and get behind the charity to enable them to support and protect the rugby family.

For more information, please visit www.rfuipf.org.uk

Acknowledgements

IT is said that an author's time is mostly spent reading. In the preparation for this book, I have read countless match programmes, newspaper reports and many of the excellent books written about rugby in the post-war period. I have carried out dozens of interviews with Budge's family, friends and former teammates. In particular, I would like to thank the following for their kind co-operation: Chris Rogers, Roger Dalzell, Pat Briggs, the late David Perry, Gareth Davies, Rick Chadwick, Roger Bass and Brian Marshall, who had the original idea for the book.

Thanks also to Jane at Pitch Publishing, staff at the British Library and Gina Worboys of the Old Bedfordians. I would like to thank Bedford Rugby Club's archivist Philip Beard for checking early drafts of the book. I am particularly grateful to Bill Beaumont for taking the time to write the Foreword.

Lastly, thanks must go to Budge Rogers for his patience in spending hours in interviews when he would probably have rather been on the golf course. The project has been a genuine partnership, with Budge reading each of the draft chapters line by line, making comments and correcting my mistakes. It was a real honour to be trusted with his wonderful archive for 18 months. It has been a privilege to write the biography of one of the greatest rugby players of the past 50 years.

List of illustrations

Budge pictured in the back row of the Bedford School Under 11 cricket team (1950)
Budge on the right of his form tutor at Bedford School (1952)
The young Rogers waiting to receive a pass from teammate Roger Dalzell in a school match on a misty day at Bedford School (1957)
Captain of the school boxing team (1957)
Bedford School rugby 1st XV. Budge is pictured on the right of the middle row
During a visit to Goldington Road in 2016
A nostalgic visit to his former school in 2016
The old pavilion at Goldington Road in 2016
Victory shield marking Bedford's cup triumph hanging proudly in the old Scrum Hall bar at Goldington Road
Statue of Bishop Trevor Huddlestone situated in Bedford town centre. Huddleston spoke to the British Lions party prior to their controversial tour of South Africa in 1962
The British Lions 1962 party to South Africa. Budge pictured in the centre of the back row
Attempting a charge down during a match on the 1962 Lions tour of South Africa
Budge in support against the All Blacks in the 2nd Test at Lancaster on England's ground-breaking tour of New Zealand in 1963
The Barbarians squad for the 1963 Easter tour of Wales
The 1963 England Five Nations team
   Back row: K. Kelleher (referee), J. Roberts, L. Rimmer, R. French, F. Wright, W. Morgan, V. Harding, J. Horrocks-Taylor, W. Patterson, L. Boundy (touch judge). Middle row: P. Jackson, C. Jacobs, R. Jeeps, R. Robinson. Front row: M. Weston, D. Rogers

LIST OF ILLUSTRATIONS

A Bedford cricket club dinner in 1963

A proud England No. 7 shaking hands with Prime Minister Harold Macmillan before the 1963 Five Nations match against Scotland

The England team in the 1964 Five Nations at Twickenham

Phil Judd, ably assisted by Budge Rogers, tackling Welsh winger Davies at Twickenham in 1966

Receiving the award for the record number of England caps from previous holder Lord Wakefield

England team to play Ireland at Dublin in 1969, Rogers's comeback season

Budge and Greenwood at the England training headquarters before the match against France in 1969. Rogers replaced Greenwood as skipper when the latter sustained an eye injury playing squash the week before the game

Rogers showing his OBE with proud parents at the gates of Buckingham Palace in 1969

England and Japan teams on the 1971 tour of the Far East

A very happy Budge and Nanette with their families at their wedding in 1971

Budge, captain of the triumphant Bedford cup-winning team of 1975

Budge the family man. In the background is Rogers's cherished Jowett Javelin

Two England greats at the launch of Budge's new company

Two old friends in Australia for the 2005 World Cup. On the right is Phil Harry, former president of the Australian RFU

Budge with Cyril Gadney, past president of the RFU, at the centenary dinner in 1970. Gadney is showing the former England captain the centenary book, while Budge is holding the centenary sculpture he presented at the dinner to former president Bill Ramsey

Budge at the 1970 centenary dinner

Budge practising his public speaking skills

Budge at the BBC with Cliff Morgan and Jimmy Hill

Budge pictured with his first England selection panel in 1976. In the top row are Derek Morgan, John Curry, Budge and coach Peter Colston. In the front are Malcolm Phillips, Sandy Sanders (chairman) and Mike Weston

England's 1968 tour party to Canada

9

Foreword

BUDGE Rogers seems to have been around forever. As a boy growing up in the 1960s, I loved watching England play rugby. Budge stood out from the other players because of his name and his never-say-die attitude. Later, at the beginning of my career, I was fortunate to play against Budge when Bedford came up to play my club, Fylde. Back then, Bedford were one of the best sides in the country and Budge was their best player. He was a loyal one-club man who stayed true to his roots. As a player, I remember him as being extremely fit, fully committed and extremely strong defensively. He was a real team person. I came to know Budge much better after he was appointed chair of selectors in 1979. I was in the England team and Budge went out on a limb and appointed me as captain for the season, something that hadn't happened before. He had experienced the whim of selectors in his own career and wanted some stability in the England set-up. As an administrator, his enthusiasm and love for the game was an inspiration to the players. Budge and his coach Mike Davis were a great team and played a big role in England's grand slam triumph in 1980.

Budge was also a great tour manager. I was struck by the interest he showed in his players, not just on the field, but also in our work and family life. He was highly respected and kept his sense of humour, despite it being severely tested at times. On one occasion, in Singapore, the players arrived back at the hotel in the early hours. As they waited for the lift, the doors opened to reveal a very angry tour manager. 'Nice pyjamas, Budge,' joked Peter Squires, completely diffusing the situation.

For me, Budge Rogers was a rugby outsider who went on to become president of the RFU. As a player and administrator, he has been a wonderful ambassador for the game. In the amateur era, Budge was never paid for playing and gave an enormous amount of his time to rugby, while finding time to develop a successful insurance business. He was an extremely straight bloke. As a player, Budge played hard but was never nasty. Tremendously enthusiastic, he achieved everything the game had to offer. If there was ever a top person in the game of rugby, it was Budge Rogers.

Bill Beaumont

Introduction

He either fears his fate too much
Or his deserts are small
That puts it not unto the touch
To win or lose it all

James Graham, 1st Marquis of Montrose –
My Dear and Only Love

THE case for the first full-length biography of one of the greatest rugby players of the post-war period, Derek Prior 'Budge' Rogers, is easily made. Rogers is a rugby legend who captained Bedford RFC for five seasons, including the year they won the RFU club competition at Twickenham. Rogers made what at the time was a record number of England appearances, captained his country seven times, visited most of the world's rugby-playing nations and represented both the British Lions in two Tests and the Barbarians on 25 occasions. Budge missed just one international in six years when his troublesome shoulder injury prevented him playing against Scotland in 1962. Rogers's playing style and intense physicality, matched by supreme skills and unerring instincts, provided English rugby supporters with some of the most memorable moments of the 1960s. An exemplary playing career was followed by years in management and administration at the highest level as Rogers became a key figure in managing the difficult transition of rugby from its purely amateur status into the modern professional game we know today.

One of the most accurate and recognisable descriptions of Rogers appears in an article the journalist Victor Head wrote for *The Field* in February 1965.

It read: 'Rogers is lamb-like off the field, pragmatic, earnest, a serious student of the game. At 25, his grin is boyish, and the face under its fair thatch is that of a school history book Saxon.'

The 'thatch' remains, if a little grey in colour. Following retirement from playing in 1975, Rogers managed the England under-23 side and led England tours to the Far East and Latin America. He was appointed chairman of the England selectors in 1979/80, the season when England won the Five Nations grand slam. In 2000, the former open-side flanker became president of the RFU, the highest honour in the game of rugby. In the same year, Rogers was elected to the board of trustees of the Lord's Taverners. There are few people in the game of rugby who have had such a positive influence on the sport. In 1969, the Bedford man was awarded the OBE for his services to rugby union, the first person in the sport to receive such an honour. There is little doubt that Budge Rogers is one of the most influential sporting figures in post-war Britain and I was delighted when Budge agreed to co-author this biography.

I recognised Budge immediately as he strolled across the golf club car park. We had not met before but I had retained an image from the 1960s of a long-haired young man in a mud-spattered England rugby shirt. The shirt was cleaner but the hair remains intact and, at 76 years old, Rogers remains a commanding figure, liked and respected by the club members. We shook hands and settled over coffee and sandwiches to talk about the idea of a book on Budge's life in rugby. We talked openly for over an hour and I agreed to speak to the publishers and move the project forward. Then something extraordinary happened.

Our meeting over, Budge asked me to follow him to his car. He opened the boot and revealed six beautifully bound scrapbooks.

'Take them,' he said. 'They can be the basis of your research.' I had been introduced to Budge Rogers by a mutual friend and this was the first time we had met, yet he trusted a near stranger with his life story in six volumes, lovingly compiled by his mother, who was proud of her son's remarkable achievements. I was hooked. I thanked Budge and carefully carried the weighty volumes over to my car. Before I left, the former England captain explained the complexities of the course layout. We said goodbye and agreed that our next meeting would be preceded by 18 holes at Budge's beloved Royal Worlington and Newmarket Golf Club.

Any biographer presented with such a rich research bounty would feel both excited and full of anticipation. The scrapbooks contained more than I could have imagined – some real gems. Telegrams from the England selectors, press notices, letters of congratulation on Budge's astonishing achievements, confirmation of his appointment as England captain, election as president of the RFU and later his OBE. There were heaps of photographs graphically illustrating a remarkable sporting life. Contained within the covers of these six volumes was the life of one of England's greatest sporting figures of the post-war period. My one reservation on reading through this irreplaceable archive was the enormity of the challenge it presented. How was I to shape all this material into a coherent story of the life of one of the most outstanding rugby players of his or any era? I needn't have worried. Budge was immediately reassuring – a constant source of stories, clarifications and encouragement.

On my second visit to the Royal Worlington, we played a round of golf together. It was abundantly clear that the 76-year-old had lost none of his zest for life and competitive edge that fuelled his remarkable rugby career. Within a few weeks, we began the work that culminated in this book. I wanted to write a serious biography as befits a man of Rogers's stature in the game, but also one full of the rich anecdotes for which rugby is renowned. We very much hope you enjoy it.

Chapter 1

A giant among clubs

BEDFORD and Budge Rogers have become synonymous in the world of rugby. The success of this very local man can be understood in the context of the sporting history of the town. Set in the north of Bedfordshire, Bedford has enjoyed relative affluence for centuries. Its wealth was founded on wool and lace-making but following the arrival of the railway in 1846, brewing, engineering and brickmaking provided the main sources of employment for Bedford's growing population. But it would be wrong to think of Bedford as all brick and engineering works. Today, the large Italian community gives the place a real cosmopolitan feel, having introduced restaurants, shops and espresso bars in the period since the Second World War. The spacious park is one of the prettiest of the Victorian era and the gentle River Ouse, which flows through the centre, adds to the general appeal of the place. Today, like most towns in this part of the Midlands, Bedford has a multi-cultural population and enjoys all the amenities of a thriving urban centre.

Rogers comes from a long line of distinguished Bedford figures. Among the finest are John Bunyan, writer of *Pilgrim's Progress*; athlete Harold Abrahams; comedian Ronnie Barker; that wonderful golf commentator Henry Longhurst and, of course, our hero Budge Rogers OBE, who continues to live in the town that developed his talent and encouraged his competitive spirit. For Rogers, it was one of the local independent schools that provided the young Budge with the opportunity to excel and prepared him for the glittering sporting career that lay ahead. The Bedford School alumni include author John Fowles, politician Paddy Ashdown, England cricket captain Alastair Cook and numerous Nobel Prize winners and local dignitaries. Founded by the Harper Charitable Trust in 1552, Bedford School was nearly destroyed by fire in 1979, but today sits resplendent in acres of manicured grounds close to the centre of town. With its glittering Planetarium, magnificent library and music room, the school is every inch a model of contemporary independent education. Consistent with its charitable aims, the school offers scholarships and bursaries to bright, working-class boys, funded by a £7m endowment from the Harpur Trust and the Old Bedfordians. I visited the school with Budge on a damp December morning in 2015. Despite the weather the grounds looked wonderful, with the immaculate rugby pitch laid out behind the spanking new science block. Across to the left was the cricket ground where future England captain Cook once graced summer Wednesday afternoons with his prodigious run-scoring. The cricket pavilion is a classic of its kind and would sit comfortably at the boundary's edge on most first-class county grounds. As we wandered around the school, we were greeted by a sixth-former sporting his arts colours. Like Cook before him, the boy sang in the school choir and played violin and piano. Budge asked him whether he was going to pursue a career in music, but he replied: 'No sir, I'm going to read medicine at UCL.' A sign perhaps of how the school had adapted to the modern world. We wished him well as we left this oasis of calm in the centre of this busy town.

The sporting history of England's provincial towns and cities was usually created over the centuries by local dignitaries, charities and business people. Bedford is one such place. The town we know today has been shaped by a curious connection between a 16th century philanthropist, the town's two public schools, a local workhouse and the arrival of the railways in the mid-19th century. In 1566, Bedford-born Sir William Harpur, a former Lord Mayor of London, endowed Bedford Grammar School (later Bedford School) with 13 acres of meadowland in London's Holborn, creating a rich endowment for future generations of the local boys. In the 1840s the trust, set up to manage the generous gift, rented six acres of land along Goldington Road from the local workhouse, rather grandly named in the 19th century as the House of Industry. The newly acquired site was cleared and relaid, providing the town's two schools with their own sports fields, a naïve if well-intended idea that had disastrous consequences for all involved. Boys from the two rival schools strongly resented ground sharing and fighting often broke out during matches. Following one particular squabble on the cricket field in 1859, a fight spiralled out of control and what followed became known as the Bedford riot.

The Bedford riot remains the most serious social disturbance in the town's otherwise peaceful social history. A ruckus on the sports field involving boys and masters from the two different schools erupted into a full-scale punch-up when a young lad from the Commercial School was beaten up and badly injured by a 19-year-old from the grammar school. It is worth noting two things at this point. Firstly, in the mid-19th century, there were no laws regarding the number of players in a rugby team. International fixtures often involved 40 players on the pitch at any one time, with tripping and hacking legal and often actively encouraged. Many in the sport believed hacking was absolutely necessary to combat the increasing practice of 'mauling', making it extremely difficult to retrieve the ball. Secondly, teachers were almost always included in the school rugby teams, adding to the intensity of the local rivalry. Is it any wonder that fights were part and parcel of the game in those early years? Legend has it that the Rev. Septimus Philpott, brother of the grammar school headmaster, played for the school on many occasions. When matches got a little feisty, the good clergyman would stop play, call the players to one side and offer up a prayer. Matches thereafter continued without incident.

Rev. Septimus's prayers did little to quell the trouble brewing on this particular occasion. The day after the incident over 2,000 people, intent on justice, besieged a local solicitor's office where the youth and his headmaster were holed up. Stones were thrown and windows broken but heavy rain came to the rescue of the fugitives as the crowd dispersed into the local hostelries. The youngster recovered and the culprit was brought to justice and fined £5 for his bullying behaviour. The riot was the manifestation of a deep-seated division between folk who were loyal to the Commercial School, whose pupils were largely from the town, and supporters of the Harpur Trust-maintained grammar school, who were mainly sons of professional people, including a growing number of outsiders taking advantage of the excellent education offered by the trust. It is perhaps overstating the case to say that the Bedford riots were an example of an old-style class conflict – a feature of the turbulent years of the Industrial Revolution.

Bedford Rugby Club's biographers Neil Roy and Philip Beard claim that as a result of the activities of the Harpur Trust, education was Bedford's principle industry in the 19th century. The town's rapid growth and success, they argue, was 'almost entirely the result of the educational attractions of the Harper Trust'. This may or may not be true but what is certain is that the history of the two schools, Bedford Grammar and the Commercial School (later renamed Bedford Modern), is bound up with the history of the game of rugby in the town. It is a fascinating piece of social history that provides us with the context of the career of Budge Rogers, one of the most illustrious in the old amateur game. Bedford School dominated rugby in the region as its all-conquering team racked up huge scores in match after match. It was in this period that the reputation of Bedford School as a national force in schoolboy rugby was established.

It would be wrong to assume that the success of Rogers's club, Bedford RFC (known locally as the either the 'Blues' or the 'Town'), was built exclusively on players from the two public schools, or that rugby in the town was the preserve of the middle and upper classes. Far from it. The club welcomed building workers, farmers and workers from the local engineering and brickworks. One of the most impressive of the working-class lads at Goldington Road was 17-year-old former Bedford Modern pupil Gerald 'Beef' Thomas Dancer. In the 1930s, Dancer represented East Midlands and the Barbarians. He started his working life as a farmer before turning to bricklaying which, he believed, 'toughened me up for rugby'. Bricklayer Dancer was Bedford's first British Lion but never won a full England cap, an omission that surprised and disappointed his club skipper, the eminent broadcaster Rex Alston.

Farm workers provided a steady supply of front-row forwards for the club. Cattle farmer Dickie Furbank had his finest hour for Bedford when he took on the Percy Park pack single-handedly during an Easter tour. Furbank played like a human tank that day and would have earned his after-match beer. This particular tour achieved legendary status as the 'booziest Easter ever'. Rumour has it that one of the Bedford players consumed a staggering 18 pints during a particularly raucous post-match celebration. Somewhat hungover, the culprit came down for breakfast the next morning minus half of his previously impressive moustache. There are many such tales, most best left unpublished.

The early influx of working-class young men into rugby in the late 19th century resembles the classic stereotype in village cricket of the blacksmith discarding his apron for his white flannels and skittling out the opposition in a few fearsome overs. There was a further welcome influx of working-class boys into rugby in the 1970s due largely to the introduction of rugby-playing PE teachers from St Lukes, Carnegie, Loughborough and Brunel into comprehensive schools. But young men from working-class backgrounds often found it difficult to adjust to the ethos of public school-dominated rugby. Birmingham-born Nigel Horton was 20 when he was selected to play for England in 1969 and admitted developing a chip on his shoulder that led to him falling out with officials. When a selector asked the Moseley lock to put his jacket back on at an after-match dinner, Horton refused. He wasn't selected to play for England again for another two years. This may or may not be the reason Horton was left out but the story does suggest that players from poorer backgrounds often found the move to international rugby difficult. What is clear is that the public and grammar schools dominated rugby up to the 1970s. Very few of the grand slam team of 1980 were ex-pupils from the independent sector.

Despite the significant contribution to the success of the Blues by working-class boys in the town, independent schools historically remained the crucible in which the game of rugby was forged. For many in the game, this came as a relief. They may have admired the physicality of the local lad but believed he could never aspire to the qualities of 'true manhood and leadership' and, of course, the absolute values of amateurism fostered by the public schools, Oxbridge and the leading grammar schools of the 19th century. The entrenched attitudes in 'rugger' have in recent years come under extreme pressure, particularly with the introduction of professionalism in the 1990s. The social history of rugby is a fascinating topic and Rogers's Bedford provides us with a rich illustration of how rugby clubs have developed over the past 200 years.

In 1886 the Swifts, the major club in the town at the time, changed their name to the Bedford Rugby Union Football Club, with Goldington Road as its new and permanent home. The fixtures in the club's inaugural season included Northampton, Leicester, Bedford Grammar and Bedford Modern School. In effect, the club as we know it today was born on that day in 1886.

The Harpur Trust, the old workhouse buildings, two public schools and the two rugby clubs of the late 19th century are the historical roots underpinning the success of the Blues in the 20th century. The schools were critical to the success of the club and produced outstanding players, coaches and administrators.

'Up until its centenary, over half of its coaches, captains and presidents were either former pupils or masters at one or other of the two schools,' said Neil Roy.

As we have seen, the presence of the trust in Bedford attracted wealthy families into the town for the quality of its schools. Great players like Maurice Pugh arrived to give their children the best education available in the county. Both schools produced some wonderful players. Bedford School has 19 internationals on its roll of honour, including such luminaries as Andy Gomarsall MBE, Martin Bayfield and, of course, Derek 'Budge' Rogers. Rivals Bedford Modern can claim eight full internationals, including the legendary Dickie Jeeps, although the latter never played for the Bedford club. Both schools produced British Lions, Barbarians and countless county players.

In addition to the wonderful players mentioned above, the list of former coaches at Bedford is equally impressive and includes Pat Briggs who, with Rogers as his captain, won the RFU club competition for the town in 1975. Eminent administrators include the Rev. SV Hartley, Harry Bitton, and Bruce Willey, all past masters or pupils at Bedford Modern. The contribution of independent education to rugby in Bedford was crucial, particularly in the years prior to the professional game. However, sustained success would have been difficult without the intervention of the Harpur Trust and the Britannia Ironworks. It is a success story that combines charity, industry and education in a rather unique way.

Since those formative days 130 years ago, it is fair to say that the club has enjoyed its fair share of success while enduring moments best forgotten. Riots, exhilarating triumphs, miserable defeats and numerous financial crises have characterised the history of this great English rugby institution. But in the early years of the 20th century, as the dust settled, the club quietly accepted its new role as the county's premier rugby club. Both the quality of the players and the club's fixture list began to improve. The club's growing reputation even reached as far as New Zealand. In 1905, the legendary All Blacks came to Goldington Road. Schools, shops and factories closed for the afternoon to enable people to witness this defining moment in the history of their cherished club. The result hardly seemed to matter. A 41-0 defeat to New Zealand was no disgrace as the All Blacks rampaged across Britain's rugby grounds that season. The match announced the arrival of the Blues on the national rugby stage. As the town celebrated its hard-won status, the future looked very bright indeed.

During this time, an enthusiastic and energetic committee developed the club's ground and improved the fixture list. In the pre-war years, a new playing surface, a new stand at a cost of £1,760 and a splendid new pavilion were added to what was one of the most impressive rugby grounds in the country. The pavilion was built to such high quality and design that it has lasted right up until the present day – a tribute both to the ambition and far-sightedness of the club officials. We can safely assume that the pavilion's Scrum Hall bar must have witnessed some memorable post-match celebrations in its 100-year history. During the season World War, the army built Nissaen huts and field kitchens at the top of the ground but left the rugby pitch untouched so the club could resume business as usual after the end of the war. Most professional sports suspended their activities during wartime, although some amateur sports, including rugby, ran a limited programme. In any case, it was extremely difficult to raise a team of 15 men to play a regular game of rugby in the war years, and there was the added difficulty of travel. What we do know is that Bedford School and Beford Modern both maintained a full fixture list throughout the conflict, while the Bedford club ran a very restricted programme. This meant that from 1945 there was a steady supply of good young players keen and ready to play for the Bedford club once life returned to some sort of normality. The *Bedfordshire Times* rugby correspondent at the time wrote: 'Has there ever before or since been a period in which so many great players were coming out of our local school?'

Bedford's reputation had never been higher and the club officials were determined to regain the lost momentum. Blessed with a winning blend of talented teenagers and returning military personnel, the future looked promising. During this time, the Blues played in front of packed houses as sport across the country entered a boom period. Goldington Road heroes at the time included Rex

Alston, who captained both the rugby club and Bedford Cricket Club in the years after the war, England international Leo Oakley, rated one of the finest centre three-quarters ever to play for the club, Cambridge Blue and former Radley School pupil John Bance, Alan Towell, Geoff Kelly and the splendidly named former club captain St Lawrence Hugh Webb. 'Larry' Webb, the former Barbarian and England back row forward, was tragically killed in a helicopter crash at sea that also claimed his wife and daughter. Club legend David Perry said: 'Webb was a marvellous player and great captain. He would have made many appearances for England if he hadn't contracted flu when he was picked to play against Wales in 1960. Ron Jacobs took his place and Larry was never picked again'.

Oakley and Towell were a formidable midfield partnership. Towell made his Bedford debut while in the RAF, joined Leicester for three seasons before returning to Goldington Road and joining Bedford Modern as a PE master. He made his England debut against France at Stade de Colombes in 1948, a match the red rose jerseys won 15-0 – a record score at the time. Towell's club record was impressive, with 126 appearances and 96 points. The scoring feats of Oakley are the stuff of legend. Five times he scored three tries in one match and he is one of only ten Old Bedfordians in the club's 130-year history to score five tries in one game. Like Budge Rogers later, Oakley was also a champion boxer. His one and only England appearance was against Wales in 1951. Sadly, his career ended abruptly in 1953 following two broken legs in as many seasons. After Oakley died in 1981, the Bedford club named a memorial gate at the entrance of the ground in honour of this wonderful sportsman and loyal Bedfordian.

The club's success at this time led the *Daily Telegraph* correspondent to write: 'Bedford is a giant among clubs.' In the postwar period, the Blues gained a reputation as a club that put team ethos before individual glory, which may explain, despite the club's success, the relatively few internationals at Goldington Road during this period. One would think that great clubs would produce great players but this was not always the case, as Doddy Hay noted in the

March 1966 edition of *Rugby World:* 'Bedford has, to be sure, had their stars, but those who have received the accolade of international recognition are precious few. The real strength of the club has always rested on its teams – and this, surely, is the most admirable attribute of them all.'

Bedford was not a particularly fashionable club compared with some in the London area and in the west of England. Rather unfairly, Hay referred to Bedford as a 'trial horse among clubs' – a kind of back-handed compliment. 'A match against Bedford always serves to separate the men from the boys,' he continued.

There is no question that the 'Bedford character' was something the club had worked extremely hard to develop, but this character often failed to sufficiently impress the England selection committee. Hay's observations may have been true in the pre-war period, when Bedford were a hard physical team who ground out their victories. It was not so true in the post-war years, when a revolution in playing style, with an emphasis on mobile forwards and quick backs, took the Blues to another level. The day of great teams and great internationals was just around the corner for the Goldington Road faithful.

The Blues were particularly strong in the early 1960s, recording victories against most of the top sides of the day. When David Perry arrived from Harlequins in 1961, Budge Rogers had already made his England debut. Perry, one of the club's most distinguished former players, has clear memories of the team he joined.

'We had some great players in Lovell, Inglis, Webb and Rogers, to name just a few. It was great playing behind Budge. I just picked up the pieces he left behind.'

With 15 England caps, four as captain, Perry was one of Bedford's all-time greats and a wonderful No. 8. In the Blues's colours, he made 101 appearances, scoring 115 points. He scored two tries for England and on both occasions received try-scoring passes from his Bedford teammate Rogers. Perry was not a local boy. He was the fourth Old Cliftonian to captain England and, alongside his club teammate Fred Inglis (later a distinguished author and Professor of Cultural Studies), did his National Service in the Parachute Regiment before going up to Cambridge where, also like Inglis, he gained his rugby Blue. At the height of his playing days, the No. 8 was 6ft 3in and weighed 16 stone, much heavier than his back-row partner and fellow England captain. Inglis regarded Perry as one of his dearest friends and enjoyed playing under his 'benign and intelligent captaincy' at Bedford and Cambridge.

Journalist Victor Head described Perry as 'a tranquil giant who crashes through defences as irresistibly as a tank on an assault course'.

The back-row partnership Perry formed with Budge is legendary at Goldington Road and the former teammates were lifelong friends. David Perry made a great success of life outside rugby. He trained as a company salesman before becoming chairman and CEO of the board games company Waddingtons. In his time as CEO, the former England captain successfully fought off two hostile takeovers from the infamous Robert Maxwell. With Budge's energy and the gentle giant's 'tranquility of mind' in the heat of the moment, they formed a formidable partnership. David Perry died on 8 April 2017, aged 79, following a long illness.

In December 1963, the Blues hosted the England Probables v Possibles trial, which drew a capacity crowd to Goldington Road. Bedford's back-row forwards Perry and Budge Rogers both played in the match. The Blues enjoyed a wonderful spell in the mid-1960s, with three Bedford players regularly selected for the England team. In Rogers, Perry and Geoff Frankcom, Bedford had three players in the same England team for the first time in the club's history. Two of these, Perry and Rogers, were regularly chosen to captain their country as the club began to dominate the English domestic game. Rogers, Perry, Frankcom and Danny Hearn formed a distinguished list of internationals during this illustrious period. With such a formidable playing strength, honours were bound to come and in 1970 the Blues won the *Sunday Telegraph* English-Welsh rugby union merit competition. But the club's finest hour came in 1975 when, captained by Rogers, the Blues beat Rosslyn Park at Twickenham in the final of the RFU knockout competition in front of a crowd of 18,000. The club had become one of the most powerful in the land, able to compete on equal terms with the great London clubs and others like Leicester, Gloucester, Coventry, Northampton and Moseley.

It is true to say that in recent years Bedford's achievements have been more modest. Since that great day at Twickenham in the spring of 1975, the club have enjoyed only modest success and as a result have found it very difficult to hold on to promising young players. There have been some bright moments: promotion to Courage League 1 in 1989, the Allied Dunbar Premiership in 1997 and winning the Powergen Championship Shield at Twickenham in 2005 brought some joy to the club's supporters. A further bright spot for the fans was John Orwin captaining the England touring party to Australia and Fiji in 1988. When national leagues were introduced in 1987, the Blues were placed in Division 2 but were promoted to Division 1 in 1989. Sadly, success was short lived as the club were relegated the following season and endured a spell down in Division 3 – a real fall from grace for a club with such a distinguished history. Things were to get worse as the club struggled to cope with the advent of professional rugby driven by the Southern Hemisphere countries and the introduction of the World Cup.

In December 2015, I joined Budge on a visit to the Goldington Road ground. The club's former captain explained how the ground had hardly changed since the 1960s. The Scrum Hall bar remains intact, full of charm and memories. The pitch falls away down to the river, as it always did, and the main stand sits proudly with its back to Goldington Road. A host of temporary huts are scattered around the ground, painted in the club's bright blue. The place reeks of its history. Strolling around the ground, I am reminded of the words of the great football trusts pioneer Alan Lomax when he wrote: 'There is a sense of pilgrimage, of going to a sacred place; there is loyalty, sticking with something through good and bad times.'

Goldington Road, with its roots in the 19th century and its complicated historical links to the old workhouse and Bedford

School, certainly feels like a sacred place, if we can apply that word in a sporting context. Perhaps the most significant change at this distinguished home of rugby is the club's youth academy based on the former practice pitch, overlooked by the looming presence of the old workhouse. Like most serious rugby clubs, Bedford has a successful youth policy led by an experienced and well-qualified coach. It is perhaps indicative of the times that there are no more than a handful of boys from Bedford or Bedford Modern schools playing their rugby at Goldington Road. The academy draws the best talent from a relatively wide area and the schools' historic connection with this forward-looking rugby club is not nearly as strong today as it was when Rogers was a pupil.

It is clear to anyone who has visited the Goldington Road ground and spoken to former players that there is a deep sense of pride and loyalty in being involved with Bedford RFC. Many of the fans retain memories of Bedford as one of the top three senior clubs in the country. In recent years, their patience has been tested to the limit. The severity of the club's recent predicament inspired Stephen Jones, the eminent rugby writer, to include a section on Bedford's troubles in his seminal work *Midnight Rugby*. Jones argues that the players, despite the lack of direction and leadership off the field, remained loyal to the cause.

As the club struggled to adjust to the shining new age of modern rugby union, coaches Paul Turner and Rudi Straeuli, together with their players, kept their patience and believed they could weather the financial storm. Scottish international Scott Murray spoke for the players when he said: 'We had a few meetings and decided we should all stick together.' Marketing director Kathy Leather told of debts to the laundry and bailiffs appearing to remove items from the offices and clubhouse. She said: 'There was so much goodwill towards the club in the town, you'd go along and ask a sponsor to pay before he was due and they always would.'

Things were to get worse when boxing promoter Frank Warren bought the club in the mid-1990s. Unfortunately, Warren's assets were tied in a legal battle he was fighting with his American rival

Don King. Despite sometimes drawing crowds of over 6,000, the town struggled to compete with the big London clubs and others like Bath, Leicester and Northampton, who were prospering under the new professional era. On 23 April 1999, the day before Bedford were due to face Northampton, the club were hit by a bombshell from which it has only recently begun to recover. On the Friday evening before the match, Warren announced that he had sold the club to a group of financial speculators, Jefferson Lloyd International, for the princely sum of £1. The following season, Jefferson made their expected exit and left the club to sort out the mess they had left behind. That season, the Blues retained their Premier League status in a play-off, but the future looked bleak. Crisis was not too strong a word.

There followed an exodus of senior players as Bedford sank back into what is now National League One. The club have since consolidated under the steadying influence of local owners and have trimmed their ambitions, while retaining a core of around 3,000 committed supporters. In his book, Stephen Jones claims Bedford suffered from bad luck, while other clubs enjoyed success through good governance, careful handling of finances and expert marketing. Today, those in charge at Bedford, including 'old-style' local businessmen Geoff Irvine and David Gunner, plan to break even financially and balance the budget mainly through rights issues, sponsorship donations and the hire of a marquee adjacent to the main pitch. Oh yes – and pray for a good cup run. In 2001, the directors' report outlined the club's current position in the starkest of terms:

'During the last financial year, it had become very apparent just how disastrous a financial position we had inherited from the previous owners ... general incompetence has cost us dearly.'

After the near-demise of the club in 1999 and subsequent relegation from the Premier League, average home gates fell to below 1,400 in 2001, but had increased to an average of just under 3,000 by 2010, reflecting the team's improved results on the field. Today, the club has a strong chairman and a board that enjoys local confidence. The future of Budge Rogers's beloved Bedford RFC is back in good hands.

'The way forward is to invest in a part-time team good enough to play attractive rugby and to challenge at the top end of the table rather than put big money into major infrastructure projects,' Roy and Beard explained.

So this is the model. Bedford has supporters who are genuine stakeholders in the club and can be relied upon for support. There is a thriving junior section and academy and the club has learned from the bitter experience of 1999. Those running Bedford today are unlikely to put at risk 150 years of heritage which produced several England captains, one of whom was one of the greatest players ever to don the red rose jersey of England.

During our visit to Goldington Road, Budge introduced me to highly regarded Director of Rugby, former Bedford player and Welsh international Mike Rayer, and Old Bedfordian Howard Travis. Rayer certainly commands the respect of the players having been capped 21 times for Wales. The Welshman has the confidence of the board and a growing reputation across the country as an inspirational and forward-thinking coach. A retired police officer, Travis has been part of the fabric of the club for most of his life and spends much of his time today lovingly cataloguing the club's treasures, which include old shirts, photographs and other artefacts. The clubhouse walls are adorned with rugby jerseys, team photographs and an impressive honours board, most of which features their most decorated player, Budge Rogers. Howard tells a rather gruesome and perhaps somewhat embellished story of former club members being buried beneath the first-team pitch. If this story appears a little fanciful, we do know that ashes have been scattered across the pitch on a number of occasions through the years, such is the loyalty this famous old club attracts. Travis and Rayer represent the past and future of Bedford and share a real sense of pride and commitment to the club.

Bedford's players are drawn from across the county and beyond, although due to their busy training schedule all now live in the town.

On 6 March 2016, Bedford finished third in the championship and the mood around the old place has been much more positive. But modern professional rugby is a tough environment. The players need to be fitter, stronger and tougher mentally. The old era of refraining from beer and fags for a few days before a match is long gone, and with it primitive training sessions and inadequate coaching. The new world of rugby costs money and lots of it. The club exists financially on gates of 2,500 for home games, an annual subsidy from the RFU and the generosity of the sponsors. It doesn't help that the Goldington Road ground is owned by the local authority, which makes it impossible to attract the level of sponsorship required to regain their place in the top flight. It is the main reason why the Blues have no serious ambitions for Premier League status.

Bedford have found their level but it is a long way from the heady days of the 1960s and 1970s, when Rogers inspired his generation. The club are working hard to secure their future. A successful innovation is a partnership with London club Saracens. In September 2016, the link with the European and British champions brought five of Sarries's rising young stars to Goldington Road on a season-long loan. Two of the youngsters are current members of England's successful under-20s team. Both clubs benefit from the arrangement, which has seen the likes of Owen Farrell and George Kruis gaining valuable experience with the Bedford team before proceeding to make an impact on the game with their club and country.

The link is celebrated each year by a pre-season friendly under the Bedford lights between Bedford's first XV and a strong Sarries team. Mike Rayer is clearly enthusiastic about the partnership. 'Everyone is aware of the close links between Bedford and Saracens and I'm delighted that we will once again benefit from the arrangement,' he said. 'There are some very exciting prospects on the way to Goldington Road next season and we are looking forward to helping them accelerate their development by playing championship rugby.'

The Saracens Director of Rugby, Mark McCall, recently gave his club's view of the arrangement:

'The agreement between Saracens and Bedford continues to be of great service to both clubs. Many players have gained valuable experience within the championship before making the transition to the Premiership and we look forward to continuing this work.'

This is not what many of the older generations of Bedford supporters of the past 130 years would have imagined for their club, but those in charge have steered the Blues into a position in the modern game of which they can be proud. They are realists who understand that not owning their own ground will always be a barrier to attracting wealthy buyers. Maybe things are better the way they are down at Goldington Road.

Budge Rogers is unquestionably Bedford's greatest ever player. He made his first-team debut while still at school and went on to clock up 485 appearances, scoring 400 points that consisted of 126 tries and one dropped goal before he retired from playing in 1976. It was a remarkable career that had its roots in the 19th century on the muddy playing fields of the House of Industry, the Bedford Grammar School and funding from the Harpur Trust. For many years, when people spoke about sport in Bedford, they spoke about Budge Rogers.

Lord Wakefield of Harlequins, the most capped Englishman before Rogers relieved him of his record, paid tribute to his successor in words the good folk of Bedford would have appreciated. He said: 'There could not be a better guardian of our traditions on the field of play, nor a better exponent of the spirit and manner in which our game should be played.'

Bedford provided the platform for Rogers to build his international career and he always stayed loyal to his roots, remaining as committed to the success of his club as he was to the fortunes of England, the Barbarians and the British Lions.

Chapter 2

The early years

BEDFORD RFC historian Philip Beard remembers the young Rogers at the start of his career: 'At school I loved playing soccer and enjoyed boxing. But as soon as I made the switch to rugby that was it. I was in the school 1st XV and playing for the Colts at Bedford. At 17 I was in the Blues senior team. For a sports-loving youngster it was a wonderful time.'

'I travelled on the same 101 bus to school from Kempston to Bedford during the 1950s and well remember his father as the landlord of the King William and his mother's antique shop in Amphill.'

The culture of rugby as a sport has traditionally been associated, sometimes a little too closely, with excessive beer drinking, rowdiness and generally unwelcome behaviour. Bedford Blues's renowned Scrum Hall has hosted its share of cheery evenings fuelled by large quantities of the local brew. Participation in those evenings may have inspired some former players to enter the pub trade. In the early 1960s, the Blues's first British Lion Gerry Dancer kept the Griffin pub in Kempston before moving to the intriguingly-named Seven Wives in St Ives. Front-row legend Alan Lovell was the son of a former police officer and landlord of the Half Moon in Kempston.

Bedford's greatest ever player grew up in pubs around the area. Budge's grandparents were landlords of the Flower Pot before acquiring the license of the Swan in Bromham, a couple of hundred yards from Rogers's current home in the centre of the village. The Rogers's family home at the time was a small semi-detached house just across the road from the Swan. Budge was born in Bedford on 20 June 1939. When he was six months old, his parents took over the Chequers in Wootton, where the family stayed for nine years before moving to the King William IV in Kempston, a lovely inn that dates back to the 14th century. It says a great deal about the young Derek, later nicknamed Budge by his grandmother, that despite being brought up in a pub environment he remained a dedicated non-drinker throughout his playing career. Budge has vague memories of the Bedford players drinking in the family pub after matches and it may have been this that put off a young and exceptionally dedicated athlete from joining the long drinking sessions common amongst rugby players. Chris, Budge's young brother, also never touched alcohol as a young man. 'Beer was for selling,' the publican's son recently remarked.

It would be a mistake to think of the Rogers family as round-the-clock publicans with no time or inclination for interests outside the obvious restrictions of their trade. Budge's grandfather was a colourful character who loved his horses and had his own stables in Bromham. He often took one of his charges on the London train to Wetherby's auctions, where he sold it and brought back a new one on the return journey. Grandad Jackson was a gambling man who, Budge recalls, kept a stash of white fivers in a potty in his bedroom. Betting was an interest Budge's parents later inherited and he remembers his mother playing card games for money with regulars across the public bar, while his father enjoyed a bet and a drink with the best of them. Both were smokers, as most parents were in the 1950s, and Budge has boyhood recollections of smoke-filled rooms reeking of beer, perhaps another explanation for the future England captain's early aversion to alcohol and tobacco.

Budge and Chris spent their early years living at the Chequers. Being tied to the ever-present demands of running a pub meant that the family rarely took family holidays. This never particularly troubled the boys, both of whom hated being away from their friends and their beloved sport, to which they became increasingly dedicated. The one occasion the family did manage to get away was not a great success. Budge remembers a rain-sodden week camping in Jaywick on the Essex coast, at the end of which both parents and children were relieved to return to the sanctity of home and their different interests.

Neither of Budge's parents were ball game players, although Mrs Rogers was a keen horse rider in her youth. According to Budge, his mother was the driving force in this close-knit family. 'Brick', as she was known to family and friends, was a formidable woman. Not content with simply running a busy pub, Mrs Rogers also kept an antique business and a dress shop. Budge remembers their cramped pub accommodation full of furniture waiting to be moved to the shop. The energetic and extremely capable Mrs Rogers worked at the pub and her businesses until the ripe old age of 80. 'Mum was a dealer [sic], always looking to make money,' said Budge. 'Both Chris and I worked in the shop on Saturday mornings before we went off to play rugby.' This is not the privileged lifestyle we expect in a household with two boys at independent school without the financial cushion of scholarships or bursaries. The Rogers worked extremely hard to provide the right education for their two boys. It required financial sacrifices and a lifetime of hard work. But it was all worth it as they saw both boys grow and prosper and, in the case of their eldest son, captain England.

Budge was an intelligent boy but by his own admission never had academic aspirations. All his considerable energy and enthusiasm were directed into school sport. For a teacher taking team games, Budge must have been a joy to work with. His education began at the Crescent School and like many boys in the town he was expected to progress to Bedford School at the age of nine following the entry examination. However, things did not quite go to plan as Budge initially failed his entry test. His parents' response to their son's failure was interesting. Instead of blaming their son as many would have, mum marched into the school office, steam coming out of her ears, and with great force told the hapless headmaster what she thought of the school's behaviour towards young Budge. 'Just because my family are publicans and from a modest background, you have decided you don't want my boy at Bedford – I'm not having it,' roared an irate Mrs Rogers. As a result of mum's forceful intervention, Budge was allowed to retake the test and this time passed with flying colours and was allowed to progress to Bedford School.

Nine-year-olds entering Bedford School spent their first four years in the 'Inky', as it was known, where Budge settled happily into the life of the school. He was popular with staff and pupils and was soon to make a name for himself on the sports field. His teachers could not possibly have imagined just how far sport would take this talented and enthusiastic youngster. In the 'Inky', the boys played football rather than rugby and Budge went straight into the first XI as an industrious and tough-tackling inside right. He was devastated two years later to learn that the Lower School only offered rugby – he knew nothing about the game, but proved to be a quick learner.

In the first year of Lower School, Budge made the transition to rugby under coach Dickie Date, who played the youngster at wing-forward, the position from which he was later to captain his country. The following year, Budge moved to scrum-half, where he remained during his first three years in the Upper School. Murray Fletcher, an ex-Bedford scrum-half and rugby coach, was responsible for making a decision that was to have far-reaching implications. Fletcher found himself with a selection dilemma. Effectively, Budge was third choice at scrum-half.

Budge said: 'There were three of us competing for the position anyway and Murray Fletcher told me I was the worst of the three, and decided to give me a chance at wing-forward.'

When Budge played for a team made up of younger boys and masters against the first XV, he played so well that he was chosen at open-side flanker for the first school fixture. The coach's decision to switch Budge to wing-forward was an inspired move.

Budge later admitted: 'If he had demoted me to the second team, I would have struggled on as a scrum-half – and never been heard of again.'

The first XV at the time was no more than average, although four of the pack did go on to achieve greater things: Budge himself, wing-forward Roger Bass, a Blue at Oxford, where his fly-half was Richard Sharp, and John Hockey and Roger Dalzell at Cambridge. Budge and his friends loved their sport and like boys everywhere played together, laughed together and even suffered the cane together on the rare occasions they broke the school rules. Three of the first XV – Budge himself, Roger Dalzell and Roger Bass – were embarking on what was to become a lifetime of friendship. Dalzell, like Budge, was a day boy and his father was the art teacher at the school and a distinguished artist in his own right. A gymnast and schoolboy boxer, Dalzell later played for the Blues alongside Budge and his brother Chris.

Even at the height of his career, Rogers was not built like the giant forwards of today. As a 12-year-old he was quite small, standing just 5ft and weighing 6st 10lb, but he compensated for his lack of height by making the most of his physical fitness and determination, qualities that were to stand him in good stead throughout his England career and which kept him ahead of his contemporaries. Budge's mother described her eldest son's character as 'pugnacious', a quality that was probably decisive in teacher Mr Squibbs's decision to award the youngster five stars for his tenacious tackling.

It was in the Upper School that Budge really began to excel on the sports field and in the gym. He began to acquire a reputation in school rugby for his fearlessness and dogged determination. The physical side of his game often got the young scrum-half into trouble, particularly when facing older boys. In one particular match, Budge's tenacious tackling began to annoy the opposition fly-half, who out of the sight of the referee promptly laid out the Bedford youngster. The incident ended happily for Budge when, having recovered, he was given a lift home by Mr Wood in his 1930 Alfa Romeo, a journey that ignited Budge's lifelong passion for fast cars.

In their Upper School years, the Bedford boys played rugby for two terms and had the choice of cricket or rowing in the summer. Wisely, Budge chose cricket and his leg spin often troubled opposition batsmen, but as he admits: 'I was mainly selected for the school team because of my fielding – I couldn't bat to save my life!' Rogers was never a cricketer but does remember on one occasion later in life playing in a charity match with TV personality David Frost, who was a more-than-capable wicket keeper. From the list of minor sports at the school, Budge chose boxing, at which he excelled and, in the words of his coach, was 'one of the most vigorous and pluckiest boxers'. In 1953, to the delight of his parents, Budge won the coveted Junior Anderson Shield in the flyweight division at a gloriously named school event called the Assault-at-Arms. His great pal Roger Dalzell also excelled at the annual event, both at boxing and his chosen sport of gymnastics. Dalzell was an outstanding gymnast and in 1961, while up at Cambridge, he became the British Universities champion and an England international.

At Bedford, there was every opportunity for schoolboy adventure and the boys took every advantage. The school boxing coach, Jack Carlton, who lost a leg in the Second World War, took a specially invited group potholing in the Mendips, where they would undertake 300ft drops carrying no more than an old miner's lamp, all of which would horrify modern teachers bound by strict health and safety rules. If you were invited into the caving club by Carlton, you really were part of the school's sporting elite, although this wasn't enough for Budge's brother Chris, who actually turned down an invitation to join the select group. 'Just not for me,' he later confessed.

But Budge idolised Carlton, who was a huge influence on the teenager and an inspirational figure at the school. Roger Bass remembers the eccentric teacher, who was as hard as nails, sparring with the boys in the ring, held up by his walking stick. 'He had a stinging left jab,' recalls Bass. 'But we were terrified of hitting him and knocking him over.'

Bass tells an amusing story about a school caving trip to Priddy Pool in the Cheddar Gorge in their final year. 'Carlton insisted that the boys took an early morning swim in Pool's freezing water', remembered Bass. 'He took time to organise himself each morning due to his prosthetic leg, but his vicious corgi, Pip, rounded us up every morning'. On one particularly cold morning, fellow pupil Simon Murray said firmly: 'I'll sort this out.' He found a log nearby, dragged it to poolside and hurled it into the water, completely fooling Mr Carlton. Satisfied the boys were in the water, he called off his dog and the boys continued with their day. This particular incident reminded Roger Bass that the school 'was a wonderful atmosphere for growing up – they were very happy times at Bedford School'.

Fellow pupil Simon Murray enjoyed a highly successful career in the banking business in the Far East. He served in the Parachute Regiment of the French Foreign Legion for five years before undertaking a 1,200km trek to the South Pole with explorer Glen Haddow at the age of 63. Murray may have developed some of his considerable talents at his caving club's adventures in Priddy Pool.

Teachers like Fletcher and Cyril Fitt were an inspiration to their pupils and Budge thrived on their support and encouragement. The link between clubs and PE teachers has weakened in recent years with the expansion of academy rugby. But in the 1950s and 1960s, the link was crucial for developing young players. Budge's teachers were also good role models. Looking back, Rogers regards Murray Fletcher as one of the best scrum-halves in the post-war period never to be awarded an England cap, as was his playing partner at fly-half, Tich Haynes. Like many good teachers before and since, Fletcher encouraged his best players to go down to Goldington Road for training. Budge grabbed the opportunity and began training with Bedford in 1955, making his club debut in the annual Old Paulines fixture on Boxing Day 1956. In the team alongside him that day were his school chums Dalzell and Bass. The fixture was a match traditionally used for blooding promising youngsters and one the club were expected to win. Despite stiff opposition, they ran out 10-0 winners. According to Doug Bowker of the *Bedfordshire Times,* one player stood out. 'Rogers kept well with the ball and tackled keenly,' Bowker reported.

Playing for Bedford while at school proved a mixed blessing for Rogers. Uniquely, he was later selected to play against Portsmouth, but former Barbarian Fletcher stuck strictly to the rules regarding club versus school and rightly refused to allow Budge to play for the club when he was selected for the match against Leicester in December 1956. School commitments took priority. Youngsters can have split loyalties when there is a club versus school dilemma, but sense prevailed and there was no animosity between teacher and pupil. Budge accepted the explanation without question. The promising young wing-forward enjoyed training with the senior club players and soon caught the eye of the selection committee. His promotion came quickly. In season 1957/58, Budge played his first full season for Bedford. He was just 18 years old.

Popular with staff and pupils, towards the end of his time at school Budge was appointed head of Cuthbert House. Although he excelled at rugby and boxing, he enjoyed most extra-curricular activities. He participated in the annual independent schools' boxing tournament between Bedford, Haileybury, Dulwich and Eton, and in his final year entered the 100 yards sprint in the inter-house athletics meeting expecting to win – despite the field including the four fastest sprinters in the school. They might have underestimated the school's star rugby player, who pushed the quickest runners all the way to the tape. Chris recalled: 'Budge was not an athlete, but he was single-minded and determined. It was no surprise that he nearly won.'

As in most independent schools, Bedford teachers were strict. Budge flourished in this environment and never questioned the rules, although he did get into trouble from time to time. Of course, teachers in the post-war years were also strict in state schools, some brutally so, particularly with young men returning from the war.

I am reminded of the words of Francesca Kay, who touched on the issue in her novel *An Equal Stillness.*

> Many teachers in the immediate post-war period had been prisoners of war. Released into postponed adolescence after years of forced maturity, they were shaken bottles of champagne uncorked, profligate and fizzing.

Pupils, both boarders and day boys, were required to be in house or at home by 6.30pm in the winter and 7pm in the summer. One summer evening, Budge and a friend were watching a tense first XI cricket match and stayed until 6.50pm confident they could cycle home in ten minutes. Just as they were turning out of the school gates, a master stepped in front of the two miscreants. The dutiful master reminded Budge and his friend they were out after hours and would be dealt with in the appropriate manner. The next morning, Budge and his friend were beaten by the head boy, as was the custom at Bedford School. As a result of the incident, Budge's promotion to prefect was delayed for a year. Brother Chris remembers receiving the cane for breaking one rather arcane school rule. Pupils were required to wear the school uniform blue suit up until Sunday lunchtime, even though there was no school that day. Again, this applied both to boarders and day boys. Chris loved to go fishing early on Sunday mornings, so there he was in his blue suit at 5am surrounded by fishing paraphernalia on the banks of Kempston Mill.

If that were not enough, the boys were not allowed in Woolworths or Marks and Spencer, or most of the local shops. But again the rules, however ridiculous, were never questioned, either by pupils or parents. It does seem remarkable that some boys didn't rebel at the harshness of the school rules. On one occasion, Chris recalls studying for an exam in the library one break-time when he should have been out on the field. He was discovered and received his ritual beating from the head boy the following day. It is hardly surprising that Chris looks back on his schooldays with mixed feelings. 'I was never terribly keen on school,' said the younger Rogers.

Chris was a year or two behind his brother at school, where he played wing-forward in the same second team as politician Paddy Ashdown. Budge's younger brother was a good flanker who suffered from playing at the same club at the same time. Chris was good enough to make 15 appearances for the Blues first XV but played most of his rugby for the Wanderers, Bedford's second team. He certainly loved his rugby and played on until he was 36 before running the third and fourth teams at Goldington Road. The brothers played just once together in the Bedford first XV, against Wasps in 1960.

Budge remembers: 'Chris supported me throughout my career and was a very good wing-forward. We played once for the first XV together. We were away to Wasps and Chris travelled with us as a reserve. Our great prop Larry Webb went to Sunbury instead of Sudbury and missed the match, so Chris played.'

With his school days coming to an end, Budge could look forward to the next episode in his life. He had been an outstanding young sportsman and having made his club debut at 17 was a once-in-a-generation rugby player. On leaving school, headmaster Mr Brown wrote in young Budge's final report: 'A very keen performer at all games. I think he might have a future in rugby.' Another master wrote fulsomely of the young flanker's commitment and leadership qualities: 'His vigour and enthusiasm as captain of the form XV inspired his team to put up such a fine performance in the final of the form competition.'

The school magazine *The Ouzel* was equally effusive in its praise of its star pupil, reporting: ' ... he is fast, sometimes perhaps a little too wild. Tackles well and has enormous energy. In the loose, Rogers is everywhere.'

Murray Fletcher, not given to easy praise, made an exception for his young protégé in this valedictory statement: 'He is fast, a first-class tackler in defence, and in attacking can run and handle like a three-quarter. His covering and defensive kicking proved invaluable.'

Back in the Chequers, Mr and Mrs Rogers were undoubtedly proud of Budge's achievements. He had recovered from failing his initial entry test and went on to grab Bedford School by the scruff of the neck, carrying all before him. He left with his head held high, but even as a young man he was not one to look back for very long. Budge was now a promising teenager at Bedford RFC and could fully concentrate on his rugby, but first he had an important decision to make.

With two A-levels and a rare gift for playing rugby, Budge had to face the harsh realities of earning a living. He was aware there was no family tradition of going to university and knew his parents had made financial sacrifices to put him and Chris through a fee-paying school, and maybe didn't want to burden them further. There is little doubt that both Chris and Budge could have gone to Cambridge had that been their wish. For Budge, it is likely that his rugby career might have stalled at university. England captain Alastair Cook, a Bedford choral scholar, was strongly advised by Essex against going to Cambridge. They believed that his cricket would develop more quickly at the county academy – and how right they were.

School friend Dalzell recently remarked: 'Budge was far brighter than me and could have easily gone to Cambridge.' Dalzell was 364 days older than his friend and as a result was required to do National Service, something Budge missed by just under a year. Dalzell joined the Beds and Herts Regiment with Roger Bass, but spent most of his two years enjoying the sunshine of Jamaica. Many of the boys a year or two older than Budge joined up, including David Perry and Fred Ingles. Rogers and Dalzell kept in touch by letter throughout the latter's time out of the country, and was hugely disappointed to miss Budge's first England debut. With their school days behind them, Budge and Dalzell did not forget the teacher who was largely responsible for the sporting success of Bedford School, Murray Fletcher. They became very close with Fletcher's family and Dalzell was godfather to one of Fletcher's sons. The world of Bedford School was extremely close knit.

On leaving school, young Budge was undecided on a possible career and needed time to consider his future. Rugby, of course, was a purely amateur game in the 1950s, even at the highest level. The early Barbarian Bishop Carey's words that 'rugby football is a game for gentlemen of all classes but not for bad sportsmen of any class' remained the dominant ethos in the game, an ethos that was tested to its limits at both club and international level over the course of Rogers's rugby career.

After much thought, the 18-year-old decided to accept the offer of a position as a student with WH Allen, a local electrical engineering firm. Allen's was one of three large engineering firms in the town, all of which were major employers and provided first-class apprenticeships to local school-leavers. For the next four years, Budge spent six months at the works in Bedford and six months at a college of advanced technology in St John's Street, London. He was happy with his decision not to go to university, enjoyed living at the Chequers with the family, had an income of sorts and was free to concentrate on his rugby. Brother Chris was to follow a similar path two years later. If Budge was unenthusiastic about the prospect of becoming an engineer, Chris was the opposite. He chose mechanical engineering and became a highly skilled and innovative engineer working in the cable industry. While Budge chose Allen's to learn his trade, Chris joined Robertson's, one of Bedford's other engineering firms.

When Chris left school. he joined his brother on the journey to City University, where they studied their respective courses. The younger Rogers became a leader in his field and an extremely successful businessman. On retirement, he turned his considerable skills to agriculture on his farm deep in the Hertfordshire countryside. But back in the late 1950s, life was moving fast for the two boys as they put their school days firmly behind them. For the Rogers boys, life was becoming extremely busy with college, increasing rugby commitments and scrubbing and polishing the pub floor every Sunday morning.

The 1950s and 1960s were uncertain years for Budge's generation. Budge has often wondered how different life might have been had he joined his friends at Cambridge. Would he have been awarded his rugby Blue? Or would he, like Scottish international Ken Scotland, who was at Christ's College with Roger Dalzell, have been overlooked for his Blue, so fierce was the competition for places? In the 1960s, it was almost as difficult to get into the Christ's College first team as it was to be selected for the university side. At one England v Wales match in 1963, there were six Christ's graduates on the field, five in the white shirts of England.

Pat Briggs, a Cambridge Blue, schoolmaster and coach of the Cup-winning Bedford side of 1975, remembered: 'Dr Lucan Pratt was the rugby motivating force behind Christ's success on the rugby field. I played with Ian Balding and Tony Lewis and others. It was a difficult side to get into.'

Budge, with his strong family and local roots, might not have found life at Oxbridge to his taste. In his memoir, the historian Kenneth O Morgan, later Lord Morgan and from a similar background to Rogers, expressed his feelings about going up to Oriel College, Oxford as an 18-year-old:

'It was grim and unfriendly. The staff were arrogant … and the teaching was appalling.'

The great spy novelist John Le Carrè expressed similar sentiments about life at Oxbridge. Budge would not have dwelt long on the question of what might have happened had he gone to university, and in any case there was a more pressing issue to face. The government of the time was considering scrapping National Service. Going to university was a choice but with National Service there was no such luxury. As peace began to settle on Europe in the years after the war, Macmillan's government made a decision and decided to scrap it. A year or two younger than Dalzell and the others, Budge was kept waiting for a few months before he finally heard that he would not be called up.

Freed from uncertainty and with a secure job, Budge could focus on rugby and begin to indulge in what was to become a lifelong passion for motor cars. His first vehicle, a drop-head Austin 10, was acquired for just £40. Dad taught his son to drive but not well enough to pass his driving test first time. The test took place on a freezing cold day and Budge promptly removed the perspex from the car windows so he could make hand signals. The inspector was not best pleased to carry out his duties in arctic conditions and with little thought failed the chastened young man in the driving seat next to him. Further lessons with dad ensured Budge passed second time, leaving him free to enjoy his newly acquired automobile. A few years later, Budge was able to further indulge his love for the motor car by purchasing a speedy Jowett, which former Bedford teammate and England trialist John Cooley remembers well:

'On away games, Budge often picked me up in his Jowett,' Cooley recalls. 'It was hair-raising as he drove very fast, but somehow you always knew he was in control – he was a fantastic driver. He still drives fast today.'

On the rugby field, Budge went from strength to strength. In season 1957/58, he was established in the Blues's first XV and played 33 out of 37 matches, scoring two tries. There was no secret to the success of this audaciously talented young man. His friends emphasised his supreme fitness, exciting running and ability to think quickly. Cooley, who played with Budge for two seasons, has clear memories of the young Bedford protégé:

'He was the fittest player in the side by miles – the best tackler I have ever come across and always in the wars with cuts and having them stitched up and [sent] back into the action. We did not have coaches, so a lot of my rugby skills and attitudes were gained from playing with Budge.'

Cooley, currently secretary of the Former Bedford Players Association, is keen to stress the sheer amateurism of those early days:

'Budge often took the training and on one particular evening we wore running spikes to improve our speed,' recalled Cooley. 'He chased after me when I had the ball and his spikes went through the back of my Achilles tendon. I had to go off but nobody realised how bad it was until Budge found out the next day I was in hospital. He was very kind and visited me regularly.'

Fortunately, Cooley quickly recovered from his injury and suffered no lasting damage. Former Bedford captain David Jackson described Budge as 'an instinctive player', adding: 'At a 50/50 situation on the deck, while I considered for a second if it was worth it, Budge had already dived on the ball.'

Chris Rogers recalls his brother's approach to the game: 'He played his heart out for Bedford every week, never gave up and needed stitches after most games,' said Chris, who took a keen interest in his famous brother's rugby career.

'When I watched him play, I never followed the ball. I always watched Budge, not the match. Even in later years, he was not really that interested in the politics of the game – the team must win was his main motivation. Budge was utterly fearless, as he showed in life as well as on the rugby field.'

Budge's school friend Roger Bass echoed Chris's observation: 'He had this controlled ferocity in his play and no thought for his personal safety. You have to remember the Bedford first XV was full of thugs at that time – it was astonishing that an 18-year-old could hold his own in these games.'

Chris has a memory of his brother that neatly encapsulates Budge's attitude to his rugby. The boys would train together in the evenings with the Bedford teams, shower and head for the bar. Except Budge never made it to the bar – he would go back out on the field and repeat the session, only this time on his own. The first session was not enough for him. This drive and dedication to fitness explains why Budge achieved so much in the game over such a long period of time. The early work was done on those cold winter evenings at Goldington Road.

In his first season at Bedford, Budge was selected for the East Midlands in the County Championship. In his debut match, he was taught a salutary lesson when facing the future England cricket captain MJK Smith who, recalls Rogers, 'had the most wonderful sidestep I had ever seen – I didn't touch him the whole game'. Budge recovered from the lesson and turned in some outstanding performances for East Midlands, receiving his county cap at the end of the 1957/58 season. The members down at Goldington Road knew young Budge was a special player and they were soon to be proved right. In 1958/59, the Bedford boy received reserve cards for two England trials.

With his superb club form, Budge remained uppermost in the minds of the selectors and was duly chosen for his first full England trial at Banbury. Up against Budge that day was the great fly-half Bev Risman, recently returned from the 1959 Lions tour to New Zealand. Budge has less than fond memories of the occasion: 'Bev made a bit of a fool of me,' he said. 'After the game, I threw my kitbag into my parents' car and said: "That's the first and last trial I will ever play."'

He needn't have worried – his chance would come again. The next step in Budge's progress towards England selection came with the arrival of the formidable 1960 Springboks and his selection at No. 7 for Midland Counties against the tourists at Leicester. On a freezing November afternoon, the Counties held the tourists to a 3-3 draw, one of only two games the Springboks failed to win on their lengthy tour. After making a significant contribution in this game, Budge followed up with a brilliant performance in Bedford's 11-3 win against a strong Coventry side, inspiring the *Bedfordshire Times* to report: 'Budge was all over the field and to cap an outstanding afternoon he battered his way over for Bedford's last try.'

On the strength of these 'brilliant' performances, Budge was selected for the Probables versus Possibles match at Coventry, the first time in 30 years that a trial had been held at the Counden Road ground. In this his second trial, Rogers found himself up against Phil Horrocks-Taylor at fly-half and the current England wing forward Peter Robbins. After a disappointing display, Budge was demoted to the Rest for the third and final trial, in which he faced Richard Sharp in the first half and dominated him throughout. Sharp was replaced by Bev Risman for the second period and fared no better against the in-form Rogers. Budge had recovered from his disappointing displays at Banbury and Coventry, and the lesson he received at the hands of MJK Smith. He had learned from these experiences as his game began to improve and develop, along with his confidence.

As an England triallist, Budge's days of helping in the pub and mum's shop on Saturday mornings were well and truly over. But despite his early success, the youngster still lacked confidence in his ability. On the evening before the teams for the trial were announced, the 20-year-old told his parents not to get their hopes up as he had not been playing well. But the landlady of the King William IV knew better. 'I remember his brilliant performances and generally high standard in the early part of the season,' Mrs Rogers told the *Bedfordshire Times*. The next day, the teams were announced. Budge was in, along with his Bedford captain Larry Webb, who had played in all four England matches the previous season.

Budge received several congratulatory telegrams on his trial call-up, including one from his old school friend Dalzell, which read simply: 'Congratulations – Best of luck – Smash Risman – we'll be there.' Salford-born Bev Risman had an interesting rugby career and was a dangerous opponent. Son of rugby league legend Gus Risman, Bev gained eight caps for England between 1959 and 1961, during which time he appeared four times for the British Lions. In 1961 Risman switched codes, gave up his promising England career and signed for Leigh in Lancashire. He played full-back for Leigh, representing Great Britain (GB) five times and captaining the GB squad in the 1968 Rugby League World Cup. When he retired from playing, the former fly-half became a respected rugby league coach and was elected president of the Rugby League Football Union in 2010. In 2012, he was awarded an OBE for services to his sport.

Rogers's ability and resolve had been tested at divisional level and in England trials, but once again he rose to the challenge and gave the opposing fly-halves tough matches. The England selectors could no longer ignore the claims of the Bedford youngster. Here was a young man who loved rugby and had a deep pride in his performances, whether at the highest level of the game or back in

Bedford with his friends and teammates. Budge was something special and the selectors knew it – and were about to make their thoughts public. He later explained his meteoric rise up the rugby ranks: 'It all happened in a rush. I went straight from school into club rugby. I worked harder on my fitness than most young players. Once I made the switch to wing-forward my game improved dramatically. I was playing well, confident and seemed to make the transition to senior rugby without much difficulty. I was fortunate to receive lots of encouragement at home, from my teachers, and from Bedford. Two months later, I was playing for East Midlands and in my second season I got a reserve card for an England trial.'

As is often the case in sport, the emergence of a young player threatens the career of an established veteran. As Budge's fledging rugby career blossomed, others were left in his wake. Peter Robbins, one of Budge's idols, felt the pressure of the rapid rise of the young Bedford flanker. Robbins made his England debut as a student and went on to earn 19 caps between 1956 and 1962. The Coventry-born wing-forward captained both Moseley and Coventry, and appeared for the Barbarians on numerous occasions. Selected for a Lions tour, he was forced to withdraw through injury.

Donald Telford, in his obituary of Robbins wrote:

'He was an intelligent reader of the game, a talent that served him well later in life as rugby correspondent for the *Financial Times* and *The Observer*. He was an inspirational captain at Oxford but never led England, winning all his caps under Eric Evans and Dickie Jeeps.'

An Oxford Blue, Robbins was an inspirational captain of his university side. The flanker trained as a teacher at Oxford and through the 1960s taught at King Edward's School, Birmingham before he turned to journalism and later business. Interestingly, one of his pupils at King Edward's was the comedian and ornithologist Bill Oddie, who captained the first XV in his final year. After he retired from playing, Robbins became a respected journalist but suffered from the over-enthusiastic policing of the amateur game. The RFU barred their former player from any activities relating to the game while he held a paid job as a rugby writer. This was a theme that was to haunt Rogers later in his own time as an administrator. International rugby player, keen golfer, jazz musician and respected journalist, Peter Robbins died following a cerebral haemorrhage at Edgbaston Hospital in March 1987, aged just 53. Robbins wasn't just quick, he also had a tremendous instinct for the game. The England cricket captain and former teammate MJK Smith said of Robbins: 'I never saw him commit a foul in his life.' The Coventry flanker was an inspiration to Rogers, who displaced him in the England team. Robbins did continue to represent his country until 1961 but his young rival's emergence on the scene in 1960 signalled the imminent end of Robbins's England career. Donald Telford noted: 'Robbins went on to become the best open-side wing-forward since the war. Budge Rogers and later Tony Neary would be his closest rivals.'

Another distinguished international at the end of his career at this time was Northampton and England legend Don White. There were a number of similarities in the careers and lives of Rogers and White. Both played for top Midland clubs and both made a success of their lives outside rugby, although Rogers, unlike White, cannot claim to have been president of a male voice choir. They may have been from different generations but Budge had the greatest respect for his county captain and the Saints man had a lasting influence by taking the time to help Budge with technical aspects of his game, for which the younger man was grateful:

'He was really very helpful and most observant, and gave me lots of pointers,' Budge remembers.

White was a giant of English rugby during the golden amateur years. He made his debut for Northampton as a schoolboy and became the most influential player in the club's history, later becoming Saints's president. Gordon Ross, editor of the *Playfair Annual*, described his friend's style of play in the following way:

'Don, of course, who for most of his rugby life has positioned himself along the narrow line of demarcation between onside and offside with the cunning of a fox and the spirit of a buccaneer, has always been the subject of a referee's personal attention.'

The buccaneering White made his England debut as flanker against Wales in 1947, the first international after the war, and went on to play 13 more times for his country. During the Midlands Counties/Springboks match at Leicester, he was the unfortunate subject of derogatory remarks from the home crowd, mostly about his advancing years – although he was only 34. Although his best days were clearly behind him, by the end of the game he had silenced both the crowd and the opposition. It was one of White's finest games and his performance left a deep impression on young Budge. Outside rugby, White received the Queen's Award for Industry in 1990 after building up the family shoe business. Budge was thrilled to play in White's final match for the East Midlands – against the Barbarians in 1961. Donald Frederick White died in April 2007, aged 81.

Crucially, Budge had become a favourite of the local and national press, who were pushing hard for his selection. Richard Evans, in his *Evening Standard* column, was quite adamant:

'Two defeats for England ... could presage some changes. Robbins, for all his abilities, allowed the Welsh fly-half K Richards to dominate completely at Cardiff. Bedford's brilliant wing-forward DP Rogers would be a worthy successor.'

In the *News of the World* on 13 September 1959, rugby correspondent John Reason, highlighting Budge's modest background, reported under the banner headline 'Young Budge Won't Give 'Em An Inch': 'It is asking a lot of a 20-year-old without an Oxford or Cambridge University background to play Peter Robbins and John Herbert out of the England rugby team, but I believe that Derek Rogers of Bedford will do just that.'

Reason continued: 'Rogers was the most promising young English player I saw last year, just as Bev Risman was the year before.' Praise indeed. Rogers had enjoyed success in the trial matches and continued to show excellent form for his club. His performance for the Midland Counties against the Springboks brought him to the attention of the national press, and more importantly the England selectors. Budge was happily settled into his new life of college, work and rugby. The 1960/61 season was the young Bedford flanker's breakthrough moment. He was selected as a travelling reserve for the match against Wales in January 1961, a match that exposed the deficiencies in the England team. The future beckoned for the Bedford boy.

France had won the championship for the first time in 1958/59 and Les Blues shared the title with England the following year. That season, England achieved the remarkable feat of playing through the Five Nations unchanged and their attractive and exciting rugby made them a match for the previously triumphant French team. But this was an ageing England side, desperate for new blood. Following the defeat against Wales at Cardiff in 1961, the clamour for change became louder and louder as his old school and the town of Bedford waited in excited anticipation.

Chapter 3

England, my England

THE England career of Budge Rogers deserves a chapter on its own. Throughout his long career, Budge played in many memorable matches. For the British Lions in South Africa in 1962, for the England team on the pioneering tour of New Zealand in 1963, with the Barbarians at home and abroad, county games and important club matches for Bedford. From hundreds of games, Budge has drawn up a list of those that have meant the most to him.

The list contains some surprises. Among his 11 selections are a 0-0 draw with Wales, two county games, a Barbarians match, one for the British Lions and six with England. Here, we will focus on Budge's favourite matches in the white jersey of England and save the others for later in the book.

Rogers made his club debut at the age of 17 and represented his county the following season. The game of his young life for the Midland Counties against the touring Springboks in 1960 left little doubt in anyone's mind that the young Bedford flanker was ready for his England debut. Budge played well in the trial matches and was clearly ready for promotion to the full senior team. So it is no surprise that the first of his memorable England matches is his international debut against Ireland in Dublin in 1961.

As a young man, at the end of each college day young Budge would run the short distance from St John Street to the Angel tube station in Islington. From there, he'd take the single stop to St Pancras for the rush-hour train home to Bedford. As usual, he paused at the Angel to grab a copy of the *Evening Standard*. The team for the international against Ireland in Dublin on 11 February was listed in the stop-press. Budge was thrilled to see his name down as the new England No. 7. This was, of course, long before texts and e-mails became the preferred method of communication between the RFU and the players. Budge had first learned the news of his selection for his country on the back page of a London newspaper. Being a modest young man, Budge resisted the temptation to whoop with delight and dance around his carriage, but naturally he was excited and couldn't wait to get home to share the good news with his family.

In the office of the *Bedfordshire Times,* the news swept around the newsroom – 'he's in'. The paper had anticipated Budge's call-up the previous Friday but now the celebrations could begin. As Budge's train sped towards Bedford, down at the rugby club in Goldington Road members and officials began to drift into the bar to enjoy the moment with their friends. By the time the 21-year-old finally arrived home, news had spread quickly across town and the King William was ready to welcome home the Blues's latest international. In truth, few people in Bedford, and England supporters in general, were surprised by the selection of the young flanker. England had lost their previous two matches and the clamour for some new faces became irresistible.

The selectors had made six changes for the Ireland game, three of them positional. In came Price of Coventry, Willcox of Oxford University and, of course, DP Rogers of Bedford. Out went Budge's hero Peter Robbins, who had received unnecessarily harsh treatment from the press. Richard Evans, writing in the *Evening Standard* following the defeat against Wales in England's previous match, said: 'Robbins, for all his ability and experience, allowed the Welsh fly-half K Richards to dominate the game completely at Cardiff. Bedford's brilliant wing-forward DP Rogers would be a worthy successor.'

The *Bedfordshire Times* naturally focused on their local hero. Their correspondent believed Budge's success was due to his 'consistency':

'He never has a really bad game because he is properly grounded in the basic skills. He is no hanger-on in the scrums looking for the big chance … he has the energy and enthusiasm to collar the fly-half and quite often the centre as well.'

The reporter added that 'no one will wear an England cap with more modesty'. England selectors certainly recognised Budge's qualities which, he argued, would 'overcome his lack of experience'.

The congratulatory telegrams and letters flooded into the King William, including one from teammate Larry Webb, who wrote warmly: 'Well done Budge – the first of many.' A note from clubmate Barry Williams read: '… I am expecting to hear on Saturday evening that you played like a "bomb" – from all the boys at the club.' The secretary of the Old Bedfordians sent a letter wishing Budge well and, of course, his old school chum Roger Dalzell sent his best wishes. One of the most heart-warming and prophetic messages came in a letter from one old school friend, who wrote: '… all Old Bedfordians will be mighty proud of "Budge", and it has brought a much-needed boost to the school that means so much to us. I wish I could drop into the King Billy to toast this great feat. Let's hope you have a thundering good game and that in years to come the name of Rogers will become legendary in the world of rugby football.'

Another wrote that he looked forward to seeing Budge's first cap behind the bar in the King 'Billy' and many said how proud his parents would be of his achievement. An official at the Blues added the comment: 'I notice you have pulled out of the Old Boys game at home on Saturday – just as well, I think.' His boss at WH Allen expressed his own delight at Budge's selection. 'All of us in the electrical department would like to congratulate you – we look forward to reading in the Sunday papers you scored all the tries.'

More practical advice arrived from the artistic hand of his friend, club chairman Peter Perkins:

'The only things you need to watch are, one, your passing. Keep your shoulders nearest the man to whom you are passing out of the way. Two, the only kicking in attack that is worthwhile is the short grubber.'

And on and on it went, such was the young flanker's popularity at Bedford School, his club and around the county. The full postbag at the King William emphasised Budge's popularity. Local people had watched their young prospect progress from school rugby to the club's first team, the county side and now selection for the national side. They were extremely proud of their local hero. A member of Bedford RFC summed their feelings, saying: 'Not only am I pleased from your personal point of view at your selection to play for your country, but it also brings great honour to the club as well and I am quite sure will help to build a finer club spirit.'

Richard Date, one Budge's former teachers, took time from his new post at Wakefield Grammar School to compose the following message:

'It seems only yesterday that Mr Cobby was picking you up and dropping you on the scrum to see if it was binding properly. I can honestly say that back in those Lower School days a number of us predicted this event. I am sure all Bedford, both school and town will be most proud of you.'

His friend Lawrence Hall wrote simply: 'My hearty congratulations. No wavering!!'

Not much chance of that. To read these telegrams and handwritten letters today is a real privilege – they are fascinating historical documents that conjure up a sense of history and authenticity that an e-mail or text message could never do.

Budge and the family were overwhelmed by the response to his England selection. But the letter he waited for above all others was the one from Doug Prentice, secretary of the RFU. It duly arrived at Kempston on 31 January and confirmed what Budge had read in the *Evening Standard* a few nights previously. The final sentence requested of the excited young debutant: 'Please let me know by return if you are able or unable to play.'

Mrs Rogers read the pompous prose with a keen motherly interest. The RFU said that 'a jersey and socks will be supplied and white shorts should be worn. Travel expenses should be sent by Wednesday, 15 February. Please attach receipts to all expense claims'. Rogers later explained that one pair of socks was issued for the whole season and players were required to provide their own shorts for each match.

He tells an amusing story about England teammate Lewis Cannell, who gave his socks to teammates in his hospital rugby team. Within a couple of seasons, all the hospital players wore socks generously supplied by the RFU, until secretary Col. Prentice intervened. The Colonel issued Cannell with a warning: 'No more socks for you.' Cannell turned up for the next game without socks and proceeded to change into full kit, minus socks. Eventually, Prentice returned to the changing room, took one look at Cannell, shook his head and handed him a new pair of socks.

With the arrival of the RFU letter confirming the headline in the newspapers, Budge could begin to prepare for his England debut. The joining instructions soon arrived. He was to meet his new teammates at King's Cross Station on the Thursday before the game. The group travelled by train to Holyhead before taking the ferry across to Ireland. A young debutant, Budge had no idea what to expect but as an intelligent young man he did wonder why the team should undertake such an arduous journey two days before a major international. The reason soon became clear – the secretary had a fear of flying, although he did allow the players to fly home after the match. The idea that the travelling arrangements for a senior international rugby match could be decided at the whim of an official seems outrageous, but this was 1961 – the players considered themselves fortunate to be able to fly home.

Safely in Dublin, the party checked into the splendid Shelbourne Hotel, which more than made up for the rigours of the journey from London. As is the tradition, new boy Budge shared a room with

England skipper Dickie Jeeps. To relax, the young flanker spent the evening playing poker with Bev Risman and a few others – no video or laptop presentations from teams of coaches back in the early 1960s. On the Friday morning, the England players were presented with three beautifully printed cards in Ireland's colours, setting out the itinerary for the weekend. From the itinerary card, still retained by Budge, we see that both teams stayed at the Shelbourne and both teams practised on the Friday afternoon. Players were given free time until lunch on the Saturday morning prior to leaving for the ground. The second card invited the visitors to an after-match dinner in honour of the England team at the Royal Hibernian Hotel at 7.15pm sharp. The third and final card invited the players to a post-dinner-dance at the Royal Dublin Golf Club – formal dress, 9pm–2am. Entry to the dance cost 15 shillings per player.

Ireland 11 England 8
Lansdowne Road, 11 February 1961

On to the main business of the weekend. By the time the party reached Dublin, England's new young flanker would have recovered from all the fuss at home surrounding his selection. Settled in with his teammates, he had plenty of time to think about the game ahead. Rogers knew that selection was only the starting point – how he played in the match was what really counted. And matches didn't come much bigger than this. Budge knew that international rugby would be a huge step up. Former players have spoken about a 'cavernous border' between club rugby and playing for your country. Wearing the England jersey for the first time is a career-defining moment. In their book *Behind the Rose,* Stephen Jones and Nick Cain sum up the first cap experience perfectly: 'It is as if the difference between having no caps and having one is far wider than it is between having one and 100. It is a step into history.'

After spending a leisurely Saturday morning in their hotel, the players prepared themselves for the short trip to Lansdowne Road to face the formidable Irish. A long and uncomfortable journey from England, followed by just one training session, hardly seems adequate preparation for such an important match. But the young Bedford flanker would not have expected anything different. At the age of 21, he had received very little in the way of technical coaching since school, apart from bits of advice from his teammates. He knew he would have to think for himself during the game, and think quickly.

England had thrown away their chances of the triple crown in their previous match against Wales. But they had not been beaten by Ireland since 1950/51, when the Irish won the championship in the hugely successful Jackie Kyle era. The stage was set for a fierce encounter. The match programme notes sum up the atmosphere in Dublin that February weekend:

'Rain or shine there is electricity in the air – this is a very special occasion. The English match really starts on the Thursday night and has been known to continue until the following Tuesday.'

England debuts don't come much tougher than Ireland at Lansdowne Road. As the teams ran out in heavy rain in front of a crowd of over 50,000, including his father watching high up in the stands, Budge would have felt the tension in the stadium. But it helped that he never suffered unduly from pre-match nerves, so was able to relax and focus on his game. Rogers has a clear memory of his debut match: 'I remember from the start Jeeps screaming above the noise of the crowd throughout the entire 80 minutes: "Tackle, tackle, tackle". I was to hear the same words over and over again when Dickie and I sat watching an England international match many years later.'

The England flanker took his captain's advice as he harassed the Irish stand-off, Armstrong, throughout. Supporters back home in Bedford expected Rogers to have a good game but even they could not have anticipated what happened in the second half. Two crunching tackles helped to carry play to the Irish 25 and when the beleaguered Armstrong attempted a kick for touch, the debutant charged it down and ran in to score in the corner. It was England's second try of the match. Unfortunately, Budge's splendid interception did not prevent his team losing the match 11-8 on late penalties. Despite the defeat, the new England No. 7 had enjoyed a successful debut. However, it had been England's second defeat in succession and the result virtually handed the championship to England's next opponents, France. The match against England was to be Ireland's sole victory that season but one that the young Bedford forward was never to forget.

The teams on that wet Saturday afternoon were:

England: Willcox, Roberts, Weston, Risman, Young, Sharp, Jeeps (c): Jacobs, Robinson, Wright, French, Price, Rogers, Morgan, Rimmer

Ireland: Kiernan: McCarten, Hewitt, Walsh, O'Reilly: Armstrong, Moffett: Wood, Dawson (c), Millar, Mulcahy, Culliton, Kavanagh, O'Sullivan, Murphy

The next morning, following the previous evening's entertainment, young Budge might have had the opportunity to scan the Sunday papers as the England party prepared for their journey home. 'Alert and dangerous', 'extremely impressive', were the typical judgements of the debutant's performance at Lansdowne Road. Vivian Jenkins, in the *Sunday Times,* was fulsome in his praise, remarking: 'Rogers made an extremely impressive debut ... fully justified his selection being very quick on the ball.'

The *Sunday Telegraph's* Michael Melford, a great champion of Rogers, was equally effusive in his praise: 'Rogers's speed, which brought one of the two tries, gave the forwards new life in the loose. He has always looked an international wing-forward in the making and at 21 seems to have arrived.'

The *Sunday Dispatch* rugby reporter HLV Day added: 'DP Rogers certainly justified his selection by his energy and quick reaction to the needs of the moment.' The eminent sports journalist EW Swanton joined in the acclaim, commenting: 'Roger's speed and ball sense were in welcome evidence.'

Speed, quickness of thought, and ball sense encapsulated Rogers's performance against Ireland, qualities that epitomised the Bedford man's whole approach to the game of rugby. What a weekend it had been for the young flanker. Back home, the *Bedfordshire Times* correspondent summed up local feeling towards their new hero: 'All the press cannot be wrong and indeed yesterday came the news that Rogers was retained for England's next match against France at Twickenham on February 25.'

Of course, his family and friends were extremely proud, but keen to keep the 21-year-old's feet firmly on the ground. In the week following his debut in Dublin, Budge spent a quiet time in the college's half-term break, helping out in Mrs Rogers's shop and training at Goldington Road. For the moment, he had thoroughly enjoyed his first game for England and the whole Dublin experience. But the main question in Bedford that week was – would England's rising star turn out for the Blues against Moseley that Saturday? There was never any doubt. After all, what young player, international or otherwise, could resist another encounter with the great Peter Robbins?

Rogers gained his first cap in what was generally regarded as England's best game of the season, played well and fully earned the praise that came his way. More than anything, he had lived up to all the many hopes and expectations of everyone at his local club, old school mates, colleagues at work and his friends and family. They always believed that young Budge was something special – now they knew. Journalist Denzil Batchelor perhaps best sums up this extraordinary young athlete at that stage of his career: 'It is clear that rugby is his particular form of self-fulfilment. It suits the temperament of this sturdy young man with the fair hair hanging like a thatch over very blue eyes, a youngster who is modest and quiet off the field and a rampaging tornado on it.'

The 'rampaging tornado' was retained for the next international against France at Twickenham, which ended in a draw – frustrating for Rogers, who was desperate to cap his fine performances with a win. But he was learning all the time and enjoying the experience of being part of the England set-up. On the Friday afternoon before the France match, the England players had a gentle training session led by skipper Dickie Jeeps. After the match, they had tea at Twickenham before heading off to the Mayfair Hotel in Berkeley

Street for dinner. In the days before exclusive players' tables, the team shared their table with officials and other notables. Rogers remembers the after-dinner speech on that occasion being delivered by Tory Minister Ian McLeod. Budge enjoyed the dinner but has less fond memories of the sleeping arrangements at the team hotel that weekend. On his debut game in Dublin, Budge roomed with Dickie Jeeps, who entertained his girlfriend in the bedroom next door, while the youngster was banished to another room that he shared with six of his teammates.

Frustrated by the draw against France, Rogers was now desperate for a win in England colours. He didn't have to wait long. It came in his third game for his country, his second at Twickenham. Captained by Arthur Smith and with Gordon Waddell at fly-half, the Scots were determined to puncture England's new-found confidence following their determined showing in Dublin and the dour draw against France. A try by Roberts and penalties from Horrocks-Taylor saw England to a comfortable 6-0 victory in front of a passionate crowd of 82,000. Another low-scoring encounter would not have troubled England's young open-side. Once again, Rogers was impressive and made a significant contribution to the England victory. The Bedford youngster was making spectacular progress on the international scene.

Rogers's upward career trajectory continued the following season, which began with a draw against Wales in January and reached a high point in the February international against Ireland at Twickenham. When the same team was announced for the Ireland game, *The Times* rugby correspondent was a little sceptical, but with one exception. 'Rogers apart, it would be comforting to see a bit more speed and dash in the loose. Rogers, again accepted for he is five years younger than any of his colleagues, the rest of the pack on Saturday average a fraction under 30 years.'

The England forwards had a hard slog in front of them but at least one of them rose to the occasion. This was the performance that signalled the England No. 7 was something very special. Rogers's reputation had begun to extend out from Bedfordshire into the wider rugby world. During the Ireland match of 1962, TV's Peter West described England's open-side as 'an absolute terrier'. In *The Telegraph*, Michael Melford wrote: 'Rogers … had a big hand in the success of England's forwards.' Rupert Cherry confirmed Rogers's great potential: 'Rogers once again showed what an acquisition he is to the England pack.' But the greatest tributes appeared in the *Daily Mail* and *The Observer* following England's victory over Ireland and confirmed Rogers's status as a truly world-class player. 'Rogers and Sharp are the only two players of world class in Britain,' argued HB Toft in *The Observer*. The following day in *The Mail*, Terry O'Connor described Rogers as 'a world-class loose forward'.

With this kind of rapid progress in the game, conversation at the Scrum Hall bar in Goldington Road turned to the future of England's celebrated new No. 7. What next? they speculated. The Barbarians? The British Lions? All things now seemed possible given Budge's sudden burst on to the international stage. A few days after the victory over the Irish in 1962, Rogers was in the East Midlands team to play the Barbarians in the traditional Mobbs Memorial Trophy at Northampton. The county beat their distinguished opponents by the impressive score of 32-9. If the Barbarians were a little disappointing, the hundreds of noisy schoolboys present would have been thrilled to see their local hero produce another impressive performance. He was not alone. Ashby, Underwood and Coley all enjoyed outstanding games as their team racked up the points. Rogers and Underwood combined to produce a stunning try. Coley sold a dummy near his own line, Rogers handed off Hosen on the halfway line and Underwood took a 'scissors' pass and beat the covering Hurst to the touchline. It was indeed what *The Guardian's* Christopher Ford described as a 'memorable try'. The young Rogers was now keeping very good company and more than holding his own. In fact, he was producing performances of the highest class in almost every game. The England selectors knew they had found a player who could take English rugby to another level.

In contrast to Rogers's individual excellence, England as a team were disappointing through the 1960s, winning the Five Nations

Championship just once. This is a recurring theme in Rogers's England career and one to which we shall return. England won the championship in 1963 but not again until 1973, when the title was shared between England, France and Ireland. So Rogers, despite his own exemplary performances in a white shirt, was never part of a great England side. At this time, there were constant team changes and very little evidence of the attention to detail and team-building that we see in today's professional game. In addition to his outstanding debut against Ireland in Dublin, Rogers is very clear on what he regards as the other standout matches of his long England career. We would not expect to see a 0-0 draw against Wales in Cardiff as one of them.

England 0 Wales 0
Twickenham, 20 January 1962

This comes as a bit of a shock. The choice appears odd – a 0-0 draw with Wales at Twickenham in January 1962. But as we shall see, there was more to this match than the dull scoreline might suggest. The 1962 Five Nations was the 68th series of the championship and was notable for low scores, very few tries and a smallpox epidemic in South Wales that caused the match between Wales and France to be postponed until later in the year. It was to be the only match France lost that year as they took the championship by one point from Scotland. England finished a lowly third with victory against Ireland in February their only positive result.

The results show that perhaps the 1950s and early 1960s were not a great time to be a fan of international rugby union:

Wales 0 England 3 (1957)
Scotland 3 England 3 (1958)
France 3 England 3 (1960)
Scotland 3 Wales 0 (1961)

Low scoring reached an all-time low in 1962:

Scotland 3 England 3
Wales 3 France 0

Ireland 3 Wales 3
England 0 Wales 0

Changes in the rules relating to line-outs and offside were considered in the light of these dire results, but it took some years before the RFU accepted the inevitable. Meanwhile, England's shared championship win in 1960 proved to be a 'false dawn', as Jones and Cain argue: 'The 1960s slowly descended into a frustrating decade of under-performance, missed opportunities and poor selection, punctuated with seemingly random moments of brilliance, either individual or collective.'

Even the relatively successful tour of New Zealand and Australia in 1963 produced little in the way of sustained improvement. From 1961 to 1965, England were involved in seven low-scoring draws. One match sums up the sleepy malaise into which the Five Nations had descended. When Wales beat Scotland in 1963, there were 111 line-outs in the match. The following season, England played out another 0-0 draw, this time against Ireland (allegedly the worst game of rugby ever played). It is not difficult given these scores to conclude that the game was in deep trouble, with defences in complete control and very little space for the more creative players to influence matches. Following the 0-0 draw with Wales at Twickenham in 1962, *The Guardian*'s Denys Rowbotham was pitiless in his criticism: 'England and Wales are bankrupt of ideas – the game is all but insufferable monotony – [and] nimble backs who might have produced fireworks were reduced to damp squibs by immediate suffocation. One of these days, defensive, characterless rugby will empty grounds.'

Rugby union would not be shifted from its diehard belief in 'amateurism'. That Micky Steele-Bodger was employed as a touch judge during England's 1963 tour of New Zealand and Australia is an indication of the amateur approach to the international game. It is worth remembering that this was a time without coaches, squad training, dieticians, sports psychologists and directors of rugby. There were just selectors, players and the odd sponge-man – it was the same for everybody. Of course, there were moments of sheer brilliance at this time when the skill of certain players shone through the darkness. There was no shortage of outstanding footballers, inventive players like Jeeps, Risman, Sharp, Underwood, Duckham, and Rogers who would have graced any era.

Muddy pitches didn't encourage running rugby and endless, pointless kicking nullified the more skilful players. Rogers remarked about the 0-0 draw with Ireland in 1963: 'I can't remember a single incident from the game ... it was a wet and horrible day ... and the Irish kicked practically every ball. I don't suppose our backs touched the ball much, if at all.'

Rogers has tried to rationalise the depth to which rugby had sunk in the early 1960s. He continued: 'We were under no obligation to entertain in those days ... I don't think we thought about the game as a spectacle. We turned up to play and people paid to watch or they didn't.'

As Rogers points out, rugby was a different sport back then, with no lifting in the line-outs and no crooked feeds at the scrum. 'It was not unusual to get six or seven heels against the head,' he remarked recently. One of the major contributory factors to a decade of negative rugby was not the old line-out rules or the chaotic free-for-all, but the monotony of touch-kicking. You could kick to touch from anywhere at this time, leading to a line-out every couple of minutes. Scrum-halves would kick to touch to gain ten yards, showing a 'cynical disregard for any sort of open play'. Three-quarters and stand-offs looked on in frustration, as did most of the crowd.

Rogers remembers: 'I looked at the match programme for that 0-0 game against Ireland and I see Drake-Lee propping and he weighed 12 stone, so don't forget how much smaller everyone was. The heavy ball made a massive difference – it was almost impossible to hold on to. It was like a bar of soap.'

The new restrictions on kicking introduced in 1967 made for a more open game. Rogers offers another reason for the negative rugby of the early 1960s, which takes us to the heart of the problem.

The players were less fit than today, playing on heavy pitches, and had never heard of dehydration. In fact, they were told not to drink water on match days because it would mean carrying extra weight around. Neither were there any replacements, which often meant people playing on through injury with dire consequences for their careers. The career of Budge's friend David Perry was ended at the age of 27 through playing on with a serious injury, when today he would have been quickly replaced and his problem treated. Despite all these brakes on free-flowing rugby, crowds of 70,000 still flocked to Twickenham for Five Nations matches.

Outdated laws, lack of proper coaching and poor quality of balls and pitches all contributed to the poor results of the England side during the early part of Rogers's career. But on reflection, a major contributory factor was inconsistency of selection. Players were called up and discarded seemingly on a selectorial whim. The trial system was an ineffective way to arrive at the best team, with three matches of increasing importance arranged at various provincial grounds around the country. England full-back, and later captain, Bob Hiller joked that for the players 'Probables v Possibles' soon became 'Improbables v Impossibles'. Those in charge of the game were as much responsible for negative tactics as the players, with their illogical, often random selection procedures. Why would a new cap gamble on running with the ball or play his natural club game when this might be his only chance?

Teammate Mike Davis echoed Hiller's views on the England set-up: 'All those selectorial changes didn't help … you meet up with the team and look around. You think: "Yes, he's a good player, I'm glad he's on board". And in a few cases I would say: "What's he doing here?"'

Torquay's Davis, a schoolteacher and England coach in the grand slam year of 1980, made his England debut against Wales in 1963 and was a victim of quirky selection, as he explains: 'There was no TLC in those days with phone calls and quiet chats ahead of selection. If you were dropped, it was pretty brutal and pretty random as well. I heard on the radio that I had been dropped.'

Rogers recently reflected on English rugby in the 1960s. 'The way rugby was organised in England was fragmented,' he said. 'The choice of captains seemed arbitrary – there was not the same accent on winning the championship as there is today, or the structures that were introduced later. There was far less media attention for one thing. English rugby was a game for the players even at international level. Grounds were full – we could sell out Twickenham for 0-0 draws, so there was no incentive to entertain.'

International rugby was frustrating to watch in the 1960s, with the low scores and endless kicking. Rogers has admitted recently that his contemporaries say they preferred watching rugby in the 1960s to that of today. Similarly, as a player, he doesn't remember matches being dull. However, most agreed changes were needed, but even when they were introduced traditionalists still yearned for the old days, when things always seem better. The 'voice of rugby' Bill McLaren spoke for many purists when he wrote in 2004:

'There were some wonderful battles in the old game when you had two big line-out men who could jump vying for the ball. I miss seeing the spectacle on a regular basis. I make no apologies for saying that I loved the game as it was. Maybe it's just that I am too old to welcome change … everybody had their place under the old amateur laws.'

One can imagine McLaren loving every minute of a match played out on a muddy field when the fly-halves kicked all afternoon and the line-outs were contested by real men. But in the late 1960s, a process of change began and gained momentum over the following 30 years until the game had changed almost beyond recognition. Old romantics like McLaren did wonderful things for the game of rugby. But with the advent of television and sponsorship rugby union needed to move on, and did so with huge enthusiasm.

Initiatives to encourage attacking play in the mid to late 1960s had the desired effect as scores began to climb, but the players took time to adapt. So amidst all the negative rugby and amateur outlook at this time, why would Budge choose a 0-0 draw with Wales as one of his memorable matches? Saturday, 20 January 1962 was a filthy day – low temperatures and freezing rain. Adding to the gloom, Jeeps and Williams kicked from everywhere all afternoon. Despite the awfulness of the day, the match stands out for Budge because of an incident late in the second half that should have won the match for England. In the final seconds, Budge broke through the Welsh line with just Coslett left to beat. He chipped the ball neatly over the full-back, who late body-checked the England flanker, damaging the clavicular joint in his shoulder. Budge lay in the mud at the end of the match as the national anthems rang around the stadium. Today, the foul would have led to a penalty try and Wales would have been beaten.

Budge missed the next match against Scotland, the only game he would miss in a five-year spell. The 0-0 draw would not have pleased the Twickenham crowd but both teams' tactics sparked a discussion in rugby about direct kicking and its effects on the game. Still, the necessary law changes were not introduced until 1968, when direct kicking into touch from the 25-yard line was banned. The new law, known as the Australian Dispensation, was a direct response to Clive Rowlands's kicking in the Scotland v Wales match the previous season.

Budge remembers the day of the 0-0 draw for another reason only loosely related to rugby. That evening, his shoulder safely strapped up, Budge drove his open-top Jowett Jupiter with his one good arm in the direction of Mayfair for the after-match dinner. Unfortunately, the usually reliable Jowett broke down on the Hammersmith flyover. Luckily, a friend of Budge's was following in his own car and stopped to help push the stricken Jowett on to the central reservation. The AA was informed and the pair continued their journey in one car. Budge later retrieved his beloved sports car the following morning.

The teams in that dire encounter were:

England: Willcox, Underwood, Wade, Weston, Roberts, Sharp, Jeeps (c), Judd, Hodgson, Wright, Harding, Currie, Rogers, Taylor, Syrett

Wales: Coslett, Bebb, Price, Jones, Morgan, Rees, Williams (c), Jones, Meredith, Cunningham, Price, Davies, Nash, Morgan

Wales 6 England 13
Cardiff, 19 January 1963

This match at Cardiff Arms Park is an obvious choice as one of Budge's favourites. That season, England won the championship by three points and came close to a grand slam only to be thwarted by Ireland, who held the eventual champions to a 0-0 draw in Dublin. It was a glorious year for captain Richard Sharp.

The winter of 1963 was one of the coldest on record. Snow began falling in January and didn't stop until early spring. There was little or no professional sport played between January and March and rugby was no exception. At Bedford, the players trained throughout the winter in Budge's old school gym, not always to their advantage. On one freezing evening, David Perry trod on a medicine ball and had to miss the England game against Wales. But somehow, despite the arctic conditions, the match between England and Wales at Cardiff Arms Park on the traditional third Saturday in January survived. England had prepared well for the match, switching their final trial to Torquay, where the Recreation Ground was the only playable pitch in the whole country. For the match weekend, the England team stayed at the Esplanade Hotel in Porthcawl and trained on the beach.

On the Saturday morning, the match was given the go-ahead largely thanks to the sterling efforts of hundreds of Welsh volunteers, who cleared the ground of snow and kept dozens of braziers burning throughout the freezing temperatures of the previous nights.

The ground staff covered the pitch in straw so the game could go ahead. Skipper Sharp gave a graphic account of the conditions: 'The weather in Cardiff was so bitter we were offered extra underwear, which was fairly unusual for those days. One journalist described it as the coldest, craziest international ever played. That summed things up pretty neatly, but at least we had a win to keep us warm.'

Of course, like most players, Rogers spurned the kind offer of extra undergarments. The two teams included a total of 13 new caps – six for Wales and seven for England. The players took the field in the knowledge that Scotland had beaten France in Paris earlier the previous week, so for England it was everything to play for in Cardiff. The England team included eight Oxbridge players in Willcox, Roberts, Phillips, Sharp, Clarke, Owen, Dovey and Drake-Lee, while the Welsh had Thomas and Michaelson. This was the great era of Oxbridge rugby. Rugby-playing students often arrived two years late at university following their time on National Service and were mature for their years, which definitely helped their rugby.

Back in Cardiff, with some clad in mittens and thermal underwear to combat the cold, the players took the field. It was so cold that the teams were kept in the changing rooms while the national anthems were played, much to the annoyance of Clive Rowlands, who was not only making his debut at scrum-half but had been appointed the Welsh captain. Rowlands was livid, recalling: 'We couldn't hear the anthems in the changing rooms and they are a big moment for a player winning his first cap.'

The Guardian's aptly named David Frost described the scene as the players ran on to the pitch: 'There was a motley collection of farm implements, three tractors, harrows and other agricultural paraphernalia parked throughout the match between the River Taff and the West goal. There were high banks of snow encroaching to within a few yards of the goal line.'

The near-arctic conditions were the setting for one of the biggest matches on the international calendar. Welsh half-back Dai Watkins recalls teammate Robert Morgan sporting a 'wide, raw frost weal that began at his temple and disappeared under his jersey'. Clive Rowlands remembers the sound of players' studs on the frozen pitch sounding like a 'herd of cattle'. Debutant Roger Michaelson believed that the bitter weather did have one advantage, remarking: 'It was so cold that even Clive Rowlands stopped talking.' Perhaps for the only time in his career.

In the freezing weather, England scored two tries that afternoon. The first was by the Coventry lock John Owen, who ran the length of the pitch after Rogers kicked ahead. The first two players to get to the ball skidded yards past before Owen recovered to score. The second try was nothing short of miraculous. From a line-out on the 25-yard line, England threw long, releasing centre Mike Weston, who slipped the ball outside to Malcolm Phillips. He exchanged passes with Peter Jackson, leaving the England centre clear on the halfway line. Jackson went over in the right-hand corner, to the delight of his teammates. Phillips later recalled: 'Into the freezing wind it was a long haul to the Welsh line at the river end of the ground, but for me the defenders were covering as well and I was able to round off a move in which the ball must have travelled more than 100 yards.'

Skipper Sharp converted both tries and added a dropped goal, while Wales scored a very late consolation try and England ran out 13-6 winners. The match had added significance in that the Welsh took the wooden spoon that season for the first time since 1949, while England just missed out on the grand slam and the triple crown as a result of their scoreless match in Dublin. England's win that year was to be their last in Cardiff until 1991, leading Welsh skipper Rowlands to remark: 'Every two years I was asked what it was like to have been the captain of a Welsh team that lost at home to England. Mind you, I always pointed out that I'd started the winning sequence in 1965.'

Budge admits to playing well in the match and the win must have been satisfying for the England players. The match has lingered long in Rogers's memory largely because of the exceptional conditions and an England victory in Cardiff. The win took England's points tally to seven, enough to win the championship by three points. The Welsh would gain their revenge in the years to come and England had to wait a very long time before they achieved another victory in Cardiff.

England: Willcox, Roberts, Weston, Phillips, Jackson, Sharp (c), Clarke, Drake-Lee, Thorne, Dovey, Davis, Owen, Manley, Wightman, Rogers

Wales: Hodgson, Morgan, Jones D, Davies, Bebb, Watkins, Rowlands (c), Jones K, Gale, Williams, Thomas, Price, Pask, Michaelson, Haywood

The best seat in the house

There are two other England matches in the early 1960s that Rogers remembers with great affection, but do not appear in his most memorable list. By the middle of March 1963, the snow had melted to reveal early spring flowers, a sight that warmed the heart of every sports lover in the land. At long last, they could venture out to watch their favourite team. Later that season, Richard Sharp scored one of the most spectacular and stylish tries ever seen at Twickenham, helping his team clinch the Calcutta Cup.

Sharp remembers the response: 'There was a thunderous roar from the crowd but in typical rugby tradition the reaction on the pitch was very understated – but Malcolm Phillips did give me a pat on the back.'

The try has entered rugby folklore. Before the match, Harold Macmillan was introduced to the players on the pitch. Rogers treasures the photograph of him shaking hands with the Prime Minister. It might have been the only rugby match Macmillan ever attended.

Thanks to the wonders of technology, we can view Sharp's magnificent try over 50 years later as the unmistakeable blonde figure glides through the blue shirts to score. Three sidesteps at blistering pace saw the fly-half cut open the Scottish defence in his wonderful languid style. Sharp remembers the try with great clarity: 'It wasn't easy to make breaks from set scrums because in those days the defence was allowed to line up level with the front row and not be offside.'

The Times rugby correspondent wrote a delightful piece about Sharp at the time, observing: 'There is a languid grace about this modest young man which is fascinatingly deceptive ... opponents only realise this after he has passed them – lissom and beautifully balanced, he glides like a silent wraith through gaps nobody else has spotted. Even when punting, he does not kick the ball, he elegantly persuades it to do his bidding.'

Rogers had one of the best seats in the house: 'Sharpy's try was a great moment and I was lucky to have the best view in the house, tracking behind him doing that old flanker's banana run. Runs like that were Richard's genius. He wasn't a stepper. He had great speed and could beat anybody on the outside. He was a glorious player, such speed.'

Mike Davis also remembers the try well. 'I only caught a glimpse of that final dummy and touchdown – he was a special bloke,' said Sharp's England teammate. If the try has become the stuff of legend, Sharp's career never again reached the dizzy heights of that moment in 1963, as he explains: 'The simple truth is that my career as a serious rugby player ended there that day with my try in the Scotland game.'

Sharp had made himself unavailable for the New Zealand tour in 1963 so he could sit his finals at Oxford. The England skipper married soon after he graduated and needed to find a job and earn some money. 'To a certain extent, the party was over,' he said. Sharp secured a job teaching at Sherbourne School and was lost to rugby, apart from a brief recall a couple of years later. Cornishman Sharp was the greatest natural talent of his era and, for Rogers, a real privilege to play alongside. It is worth noting that Richard Sharp was just 24 years old when he scored that famous try

If the 1960s world of rugby was lit up by Richard Sharp's try in 1963, a second candidate for try of the decade was scored two years later by Northampton winger Andy Hancock. The match against Scotland at Twickenham in 1965 was Hancock's second England appearance. He was called up for the previous game against France on the evening before the match, so regarded the Scotland game as his proper debut. The pitch was dreadful and hardly ideal for running rugby. But Hancock ran the length of the touchline, handing off at least three Scots' attempts to bring him down, before scoring the try of his life. He has fond memories of his great day: 'Iain Laughland was a little unlucky when he slipped as he tried to tackle me... Budge Rogers was running hard in support and I think he distracted Stewart Wilson. The try line seemed miles away but I kept going ... Laughland tackled me around the ankles but I was over the line.'

Rogers remembers Hancock's heroics just as clearly: 'For the second time in two years, I had a ringside seat for one of the great England tries. Andy Hancock was an interesting player. He elevated himself to a level of strength and fitness that was almost unsustainable as an amateur. It was a tremendous, heroic run that late in a gruelling old muddy game. In the last minute of the match, Mike Weston opened up to Andy in our 25 – he ran the length of the pitch, beating off three attempted tackles. I ran in support as he went over for the try.'

Despite his heroics that day, Hancock had a brief international career and confesses the try was a 'complete one-off'. He admits receiving just two passes that rainy afternoon: the first one he dropped, the second is the stuff of legend. Reflecting on his famous day, Hancock remembers: 'There was no team practice. David Perry, our captain that day, said a few words in the dressing room but the first time we all got together was for the team photograph.'

Injury problems the following season hampered Hancock's development and, in the days before replacements, he was another victim of staying on the pitch for 80 minutes when he should have been taken off at half time. This, he admits, 'did untold damage – it was madness'. Hancock recovered but dropped down a few levels and had great fun playing for the wonderfully named 'Chelmsford Undertakers' veterans side. Hancock's famous try was played every week as the introductory clip to the BBC's *Grandstand* programme. His fame was brief but well deserved. Rogers continues to relish these great tries and the part he played in two marvellous moments in English rugby history.

A step into history
Unlike many elite performers, Rogers appears to be without ego and always judged his personal contribution to a match by the

overall team performance. So it should come as no surprise that he omits from his list of memorable matches arguably the most notable of his career. In January 1966, Budge Rogers was appointed captain of his country, an achievement that merits attention in his biography. In some senses, his promotion was inevitable. At the age of 24, Rogers was made captain of his club and thoroughly enjoyed the experience – Bedford, of course, were one of the top English clubs at the time.

Rogers's outstanding performance against Scotland in 1961 epitomised his attitude and had not gone unnoticed by the selectors. Since his debut that year, the Bedford flanker had impressed everyone with his outstanding displays for his country and emerging leadership skills. The years between 1961 and 1966 had seen Budge rise from raw debutant to established international star. He had been an ever-present in the Five Nations teams for four seasons, enjoyed a successful England tour to Australia and New Zealand in 1963, and played two Tests for the Lions in South Africa in 1962. The one glitch in his career was not being selected for the Lions tour of New Zealand in 1966 – 'the greatest disappointment of my career,' he admitted later. The frustration Rogers felt at being left at home by the Lions was eased when he was named England captain that same year – although the disappointment of not going to New Zealand remained with him for years.

The call from the selectors came as a complete shock but no player deserved it more. In 1966, his time had come. Rogers's first match as England skipper was against Wales at Twickenham on 15 January 1966. He had taken over the captaincy from his old friend and teammate at Bedford, David Perry. The *Bedfordshire Times* described Budge's elevation as 'fabulous'. Why? Because, they argued, he was 100 per cent a local boy living at the King William pub, was educated at Bedford School and a member of just one club throughout his career. When the local paper rang the pub to give them the news about Budge's promotion, Mrs Rogers exclaimed: 'Captain? I spent last night worrying whether he would get in – after all, there had been so much talk about Taylor this season.'

Mrs Rogers was overjoyed at the news of her son's promotion and her worries were unfounded. Taylor, the promising young Northampton star, was in the team but as blindside flanker. Perry retained his No. 8 jersey but Bedford teammate, Geoff Frankcom was passed over for the match. Clubmate Danny Hearn was named as a travelling reserve. Rogers impressed as skipper of the Rest in the trial game leading up to the match at Twickenham and must have harboured thoughts of captaining his country. Uncharacteristically, he said after the trial: 'I thought I did play well. I knew I had to keep Taylor out.'

The national press was enthusiastic in their praise for Rogers, with one radio commentator demanding that Budge not only be selected for the match against Wales but also be made captain. The *Bedfordshire Times* was steadfastly loyal to their man and promoted his cause shamelessly: 'To the captaincy Budge will bring several qualities; integrity, personal drive and, above all, experience as the most capped player of the side gained from 22 internationals.'

In the days leading up to the news of Budge's promotion, dozens of letters and telegrams of congratulations arrived at the King William pub, where Budge continued to live with his parents. He was held in great affection by Bedford folk and his promotion to the top job gave him almost godlike status in and around Goldington Road. His family, friends, old boys from school and colleagues at Bedford had been fully supportive throughout his career, for which the new England captain was eternally grateful. The England captaincy had seemed Budge's destiny from the moment he made his club debut at the age of 17. His early promise was confirmed two years later by his break-out performance for the Midland Counties in the match against the Springboks. These were years of consolidation in Rogers's playing career, underpinned by total confidence in his ability and a growing understanding of his game.

With real insight into Budge's personality, Barry Newcombe in the *London Evening Standard* wrote of his latest honour: 'Derek Prior Rogers talks rugby non-stop. He plays it non-stop. He thinks it non-stop. And he is very good at the game as 23 caps in five years amply testify. He has played rugby in every country where it counts.'

Among the congratulatory messages to arrive at the family pub was a typewritten letter from Bill Ramsey, the treasurer of the RFU. After warmly congratulating Rogers on his 'richly deserved' honour, the letter goes on to inform the new England captain that he is to be allocated the sum of £30 for 'refreshments to be served either in the team room or in the captain's private room at the Hilton after the match'. But Ramsey proceeds to politely warn his new captain that this figure 'should not be exceeded'. According to the previous skipper David Perry, the privilege was 'appallingly abused'. In the letter, the treasurer points out that in England's previous game over £200 was spent on bottles of whisky removed from Perry's room by 'hangers on' and warns this should not happen again. It is certain Ramsey's letter was received with much amusement at the King William.

Rogers had succeeded his Bedford teammate David Perry as national captain but would have been delighted that the selectors had retained his old friend at No. 8 for the match against Wales. Perry was a wonderful player and the pair exchanged captaincies of Bedford and England during the 1960s. With Perry alongside him, the transition from outstanding player to England captain should not have troubled Rogers. He was ready for the promotion. Rogers thought deeply about the game, had captained one of the top club sides in English rugby and knew what was required of the role.

He recalled: 'I know when I captained Bedford that it was easy to worry about other players and my own game was affected. But in an international side, each player is capable of doing his particular job well and that makes the captain's job easier.'

Confidence in the ability of his teammates afforded Rogers the luxury of thinking about the technical aspects of the England captain's job, despite the absence of tactical support and advice from the RFU.

He said at the time: 'We have to do all the basics properly and build from there. We have to obtain dominance in the pack at every phase. I just hope we can do all this and the other things will follow.'

Rogers was just 26 when he took over as England captain, although he may have appeared to many rugby followers as a veteran. The marauder in England's back row for five seasons could hope for a sustained spell as the national team captain. Life was certainly changing fast for the Bedford boy. In addition to his new England responsibilities, Budge had left the family pub to live and work in London as a technical salesman for his Bedford employers. He moved into a London flat with a strong rugby flavour. His flatmates were Welshman John Powell-Reece, secretary of Richmond RFC, and Ernie Reece, the Richmond No. 8. The England rugby captain designate, all 13st 8lbs of him, was sleeping on a camp bed for two weeks prior to his baptism of fire against the Welsh. It wasn't ideal preparation but Rogers was no ordinary rugby player.

Barry Newcombe pointed out: 'The facet of Rogers I most admire is his dedication, a force that drives him right against the odds, a force that has kept him on top for so long. If Rogers can transmit that into this new England side, he will be the best captain since Jeeps.'

Rogers was overjoyed at the news. 'Every time I am selected for England, I think it's marvellous,' he said. 'To be captain was beyond my dreams.' Those in the game knew Rogers would be fine because he had demonstrated the required leadership skills with Bedford. Despite his modest demeanour, he possessed a streak of ruthlessness and determination that made him such a difficult opponent. He was helped by having a team that contained six new caps who were determined to change England's fortunes. They had suffered four defeats in six matches leading up to Budge's debut as England skipper. Changes were needed in leadership, tactics and personnel. England's performances had been laboured and their scrummaging was suspect. Rogers was clear about his new responsibilities. A few days prior to the match, every player selected received a letter from their new captain designed to build team spirit ahead of the match against Wales. Rogers was an astute thinker and would have learned from the men he had played under: Dickie Jeeps, Richard Sharp, John Willcox, Ron Jacobs and Perry himself. He would have absorbed the ideas of his predecessors but was mature and experienced enough to be his own man. However, he was going into unknown territory and knew, despite the support and advice of his teammates, that when the players crossed the line he would be on his own.

As an independent-minded individual, Rogers didn't take long to upset the rugby authorities. In those days, the international rule stated that players should not assemble more than 48 hours before a match. The England team traditionally gathered on Thursday afternoon prior to the game, when the captain would run the practices and organise the match preparations for the following day. Budge wanted the team to meet on Wednesday night, with the players paying their own hotel bill for the extra night. Bob Weighall, secretary of the RFU, soon got to hear of the transgression and wrote Budge a stiff note containing the polite message: 'Please allow me to assure the president that the Wednesday practice will not take place.'

Safe to say the additional day was cancelled, leaving Rogers frustrated and slightly angry. There were no coaches at this time, no tactical plan and no guidance from the selectors about how the new captain should set up his team. During this period, Don Rutherford had a coaching post with the RFU with responsibilities for the whole game rather than the national side. It is unclear exactly what his role was or what impact it had at international level. Looking back, Budge believes this should have come as no surprise – that was the way it was, it was the same for everybody and it would be some years before change was to sweep the old rules away forever.

One thing the new captain could do was try to inspire some kind of spirit in his team. He was aware that the Southern Hemisphere countries could turn a game with a few minutes of play, inspired more by collective will than by a change of tactics. Passion and fervour can win matches. Rogers hinted that Wales might have more of this than England: 'The Welsh had an advantage in set moves because their players live close to each other, while the England players were thinly spread. Their players are drawn from a relatively small group of clubs. We will have to do all our work when we train on Friday, but I'm hoping my letters to the players will help.'

Wales also had a new captain at Twickenham in Alan Pask. The opposing skippers differed in their approaches to the game. Pask said before the match that as long as his team won he was not overly concerned about gracing Twickenham with free-flowing rugby. Rogers, on the other hand, took a slightly different view, which provides a revealing insight into his philosophy of rugby: 'I agree that winning is of paramount importance, but hope that the game is played in a way which is enjoyable for all players and spectators.'

England's main chance of victory lay in keeping it tight up front and winning the loose ball. The cunning of Rogers and Perry at the breakdown, and the ball-playing skills of Taylor and John Spencer, should have ensured that the white shirts had the advantage in the loose. Rogers was keen to keep the traditional roles of open- and blind-sides, despite rule changes and the All Blacks's experiment with playing left and right. Taylor, a natural open-side, was Budge's teammate in the East Midlands side and knew he could play on the other side of the scrum. If both players seem much of a type, Rogers was clear about their specific roles: 'Basically, I am the tackler, the man who gets there first, and Bob is then at hand to try to use the loose ball. He is a more skilful player, but not the hardest worker.'

If Rogers was clear about his team's approach to the Welsh game, his opponents were brimming with confidence after their triple crown success the previous season. They had a powerful pack that was well equipped to deal with the revitalised England team. The Welsh had no discernible weaknesses. As captaincy debuts go, this was as tough as it gets.

Somebody once said that if you play sport you had better get used to losing. Unfortunately, the match against Wales at Twickenham proved an anticlimax. Despite the change in leadership and a handful of new caps, England lost the first match of Rogers's captaincy 11-6 in a particularly dull encounter on a cold winter's day. Budge's new team ended the season with the wooden spoon, failing to win a game, with only a draw against Ireland preventing a complete disaster. Reflecting on that season, Rogers believes England's poor performances contributed to his being ignored by the Lions for the trip to New Zealand that year. This is probably why Budge failed to include his first game as England captain as one of his favourite matches – because of the disappointment in defeat and England's inglorious season. A hard-nosed belief that, given the circumstances, this was nothing to celebrate may have left him feeling this was a match best forgotten.

It also didn't help England's cause that Rutherford missed three consecutive penalties in the match. Watched by millions of TV viewers, Rogers had a quiet word with the hapless England kicker before his fourth attempt late in the game. 'I just asked him if he was happy about taking it. I knew there were only 20 seconds left to play, so it made little difference.' Rutherford's final kick went over the posts as the referee blew the whistle. Rogers was exasperated, not with his own game but with his team's failure to get the ball from their own set pieces, the Welsh strength and dominance of the line-out, and the fact that neither back-row was able to influence the result. Rogers's memory of the match against Wales may have been clouded by the effects of a head injury that required several stitches after the game. We can guess that Alan Pask was the happier of the two new captains. The following season failed to see the expected turnaround in England's fortunes and we must skip a couple of years for Budge's next memorable match – England against France at Twickenham in 1969, when the outcome was more favourable for the home team.

Rogers captained England in all the Five Nations matches in 1966 but, dogged by persistent injuries, played just two in 1967, those against Scotland and Wales. France won the Five Nations in both years, although England twice had the consolation of the Calcutta Cup. Up until 1967, Rogers had enjoyed an injury-free career, quickly climbing up through the rugby ranks before reaching the high point of the England captaincy. Team captains at international level vary in their approach and effectiveness, from the astute and nuanced direction of Mike Brearley to the tub-thumping leadership of Bill Beaumont. Bobby Moore made over 90 appearances as England captain and led quietly and by example. There is no definitive captaincy model and the player in charge needs to fit the role to his particular personality. Rogers was not a shouter and simply expected players to give their very best at all times.

David Perry, Bedford's other England captain in the 1960s, believed that neither he nor Budge were brilliant captains: 'Budge was an incredible player, but not a great captain. He led from the front and by example – players would follow him everywhere.' Perry had interesting ideas on the England captaincy at this time: 'I was told by the selectors that the reason I had been picked as captain was that I was the most likely player to hold my place for that season – I suspect it was much the same for Budge and others.'

Perry was not the 'reluctant captain' the press often insinuated. In fact, on hearing the news, he told journalist John Reed: 'I was astonished. I'm tickled pink. It's a tremendous honour.'

To captain one's country is the highest honour in sport and one that Rogers relished. The extra hours he had put in on the training field had paid off as he moved from a promising young No. 7 to one of the best players on the international stage. Budge's dedication to fitness was legendary and helped to extend his career. It was also a contributory factor in his being made England captain in 1966. He had come a long way from that debut match in Dublin in 1961 and spent seven uninterrupted years in the England side – two as captain – before losing his place for the 1968 Five Nations Championship.

Rogers's punishing fitness regime, often training hard on his own, was eventually to take its toll. It is rare for an athlete to go through a 20-year career at the highest level and not be subject to either injury or loss of form. It happened most famously to Tiger Woods, Bobby Moore for a time, the young Ian Botham and many others. It also happened to Budge Rogers, much to the intense frustration of the man whose dad once said 'lived for rugby'. The time at the top for all elite athletes comes with a health warning. Career high points are often tainted by the prospect of inescapable decline in performance as the years take their toll. International rugby players are no exception. In a sport that places more stress on the body than most, rugby players are only too painfully aware when they can no longer compete at the highest level.

Rogers was one of the most honest players of his era and, with his enthusiasm and peerless fitness levels, no other athlete could have done more to prolong what was already a lengthy career. Rogers's game was based on speed of thought, swiftness of reaction and courage, sporting virtues that carried him to the very top. Once those magnificent powers began to wane even a fraction, or were dulled by his failing body, the great flanker was no longer able to play at the levels he had set himself, and that others expected of him. Budge knew he had years left playing for Bedford but to continue to perform to his own exacting standards at international level was another question entirely. For once, his place in the England side was no longer assured.

For England's first two matches of the 1967 Five Nations, Bob Taylor was brought in for Rogers, slowed by injury and sacrificed following the heavy defeat to Australia in the first week of January. England beat Ireland narrowly in the first match but fared less well against France in Stade de Colombes, where they lost 16-12. The former England captain did not enjoy the indignity of being selected as reserve against Ireland and France. 'There is no doubt, it hurt and I was disappointed,' Budge said. 'After my injuries, I was fighting fit again.' After the defeat in Paris, changes were demanded for the tough game against Scotland. Taylor was retained as flanker but in a role reversal Rogers was recalled at No. 6 for his 28th cap. In truth, the Midlands Counties duo were asked to play left and right of the scrum rather than the more traditional open- and blind-sides. The combination appeared to work as England won 27-14 and Rogers and Taylor kept their places for the final match against Wales in Cardiff. A comprehensive 34-21 defeat at the hands of a youthful Welsh side brought the England players down to earth with a crash.

This extraordinary encounter became known as the 'Jarrett' match after the 18-year-old ran up 19 points on his debut, which included one of the most thrilling tries seen at the Arms Park for many years. Bill McLaren of the BBC was as excited as any in the stadium. 'Jarrett is treating this like a seven-a-side,' he told viewers. The *Playfair Annual* for that year was even more excitable. 'The most remarkable match of all time,' pronounced their correspondent. England were just four points behind with less than 15 minutes left but found themselves 19 points down with only eight minutes to go, only to get six points back in the dying minutes. England had played their part in a tremendous match and finished the series runners-up to the eventual champions France.

Despite the defeat against Wales, Rogers remained in the selectors' collective mind and was chosen for the England tour to Canada in the autumn of 1967 under skipper Phil Judd. The tour, arranged to mark the Canada RFU's centenary year, was managed by Micky Steele-Bodger and included one 'Test' against the host nation on 30 September at the Empire Stadium, Vancouver, which the tourists won 29-0. The extensive tour included visits to Victoria, Ottawa, Montreal, Vancouver, Banff and Alberta. The Canadians were generous hosts and laid on barbecues, logging shows and a pre-dinner 4,000ft lift in a gondola. The RFU's official itinerary for the tour refers to the tourists as the 'England rugby touring side'. The Canadians were much bolder and described their visitors as 'England' in all match programmes.

The match programme notes for the international describe the England No. 7 as 'a great player who has given yeoman service to his country'. Rogers, along with the rest of the England team that day, was hoping a cap would be awarded after the match against Canada. Unfortunately, despite media pressure, the RFU decided the match did not constitute a full Test, so the 'England internationals', as the team were called, were denied their extra full cap and the 'special cap' awarded for the match was not a full one. The trip to Canada was a pleasant diversion for the England squad. Under skipper Judd, the experience was good fun and lacked the pressure of the far more demanding schedules of Southern Hemisphere tours. With an eye on the following season, Rogers was back in the senior squad and the selectors' thoughts.

By teaming up Taylor with Rogers in a back row partnership, the selectors were able to include two of the best footballers in the country. Taylor was exceptionally talented –'a better player than me,' declared Rogers – but there is no question that the Northampton flanker with the sparkling feet lacked the Bedford man's extraordinary workrate. Writing in September 1967, the influential rugby journalist John Reed called for the Rogers and Taylor duo to continue. 'The selectors would,' argued Reed, 'be wise to retain the East Midlands pair on the flanks of the pack this season.' Reed had no doubts that Rogers's return was long overdue, remarking that 'his tigerish tackling, voracious covering and anticipation, and non-stop running is still good enough for Rogers to achieve one of his few remaining ambitions, to play against the All Blacks.'

Under such media pressure, the selectors could hardly ignore Rogers's claims. He was back in the fold and desperate to play against New Zealand. The tourists began their trip with three provincial fixtures before facing England at Twickenham in early November. Brian Lochore's side included Meads, Laidlaw, Nathan and Going and could be regarded as the greatest All Blacks team ever. It was with nervous trepidation that the England team, including Rogers, took the field at Twickenham in front of 70,000 expectant fans. Brutally honest with himself, Rogers admitted that he did not play well that day and could do nothing to stop the rampaging New Zealanders, who completed a routine victory 23-11. Unfortunately, Rogers was left out of the side for the entire 1968 Five Nations series. The soaring upward trajectory of one of the greatest ever rugby union careers seemed suddenly to have run out of steam.

The effects of serious injury brought what looked like a premature end to Budge's England career. But the injuries and subsequent loss of form failed to discourage this most determined of players as he worked tirelessly to regain his place in the national side.

An indication of the extent of his problems was that Rogers made just 21 appearances for Bedford in 1967/68 and 19 in 1968/69, when he would normally have played 30-plus, even with his international commitments. But rugby people knew not to underestimate the recovery powers of the Bedford legend as he fought to prolong his career through sheer bloody-mindedness. Rogers took time to recover from a severe pelvic strain. The injury was serious and some mornings Budge found it difficult to get out of bed. His surgeon believed the injury was more common in professional footballers and was caused by over-training. Budge's commitment to fitness was, to say the least, unusual among rugby footballers of his day. Not many would have trained alone after lunch on Christmas Day, but for Rogers it was second nature. But his exceptional dedication to fitness began to wear down his body. Rogers was not to play for his country again until he was recalled for the Ireland match in February 1969.

In truth, injury was not the only reasons for Rogers's two years in the international wilderness, as he is the first to admit. A law change introduced in 1964 restricted the 'destroy the fly-half' mentality of the traditional flanker role, allowing more freedom for the No. 10. The new law relating to offside read: 'A player is offside in a loose scrummage if he advances in front of the hindmost foot of his own players. He is offside at a set scrummage if he fails to retire behind or advances in front of the line through the hindmost foot of his own team.'

Bad news for the flanker, good news for fly-halves everywhere. The revision meant that the flanker was now required to stay behind the ball from the scrum and the line-out, while the old rule was at the very heart of Rogers's all-action game. The new offside law meant that the flanker had to stay back, preventing quick No.7s like Rogers from getting to the man or ball fast enough. The changes forced the flanker to think more constructively. Budge was the first to admit that he struggled to adapt his game to the changes: 'In the first year of the changes, I was not playing quite right. It took a season to adjust.' Eventually Rogers welcomed the changes. 'I'm more and more sold on the idea than I was,' said Budge. Indeed, both Budge and Bob Taylor worked effectively together as right and left for England on a number of occasions.

In the late 1960s, England needed all their best players at the peak of their powers, and an on-form Rogers had been sorely missed. After finishing runners-up in 1967, without their former captain England managed to win just one game the following season, ending the tournament in third place behind champions France. Rogers's place in the side was taken by the young Northampton flanker Bryan West, who gained eight caps over a two-year period in Budge's absence. Although a good young player, West lacked Rogers's experience and, finding themselves backed into a corner, the selectors turned once again to the most reliable England player of the past seven years. Budge was back.

In December 1968, an England trial was arranged in Falmouth down on the Cornwall coast. In those days, a committee of six picked the England team and it looked like a committee decision to send 30 of the country's finest on a 600-mile return trip to the South West for a trial. Perhaps the selectors thought that the bracing sea air might clear their muddled heads. In the previous season's five matches, the England selectors tried 28 players – an indication of the inconsistency and short-term thinking of those who picked the national team. However, despite the remote location, the trial was a success. An 11-11 draw between the whites and the blues gave the selectors much to think about. With Bill Redwood and Bob Hiller both injured, Rogers captained the whites from his usual position as flanker. Reporter Peter Laker, one of the most perceptive rugby writers of his day, understood the importance of the occasion: 'A player of Rogers's class and determination needs no sharper spur. He is one match away from Lord Wakefield's record ... and hopes to show the selectors that his consistency with East Midlands, the county semi-finalists, is that of the "in" player.'

Laker explained to his readers that Rogers was discarded the previous winter following England's collapse against the All Blacks. Budge felt he was playing some of his best rugby at this time: 'I wasn't simply going for the record but if you think you are playing well and being considered then you want to play. However, I did feel a bit old-mannish in the trials, looking around and asking: "who's that?"'

In an era that demanded fresh positional and tactical thinking, the astute Rogers had the ability to adapt more than most. The 'discarded' Bedford flanker was determined to seize his opportunity. The Sunday after the Falmouth trial, the legendary Cliff Morgan reported that Budge 'had a rousing game and his play was of the highest order'. Rare praise indeed.

Budge missed the second trial due to injury but was back for the final trial in January 1969, this time under the guise of England v The Rest, with Rogers as the Rest captain up against his rival flanker West. In Rogers's team that day were Bob Taylor and David Rollitt, familiar faces in the England back row. The Rest ran out 16-8 winners, giving the selectors more problems than solutions as they met to pick the team for the first match of the Five Nations series. Their settled plans following the first trial were blown to pieces. Budge followed up his excellent game in the first trial with another outstanding performance, leading John Reed of the *Sunday Express* to write: 'It was the Rest back row of Rogers, Taylor and Rollitt who set the fuse to the bomb ... they were outstanding figures in a Rest pack which swamped the England forwards with their drive and vitality.'

Along with Rogers, Rollitt was unstoppable – 'his grey head charging through the "England" ranks with the ferocity of a bull,' wrote Reed. The Rest skipper had made up the selectors' minds for them. It was now impossible to leave Rogers out. When the 27-man 'Club England' squad for the Ireland match was announced, Budge was in despite needing stitches in a head wound suffered during the final trial. With the exception of Rogers, Micky Steele-Bodger and his fellow selectors had picked a young team. New caps Keith Fielding, Keith Fairbrother, David Duckham, John Spencer, Roger Shackleton and Nigel Horton all lined up alongside the 30-cap Rogers. Bedford's other triallist Pat Briggs did not make the side, nor did Budge's former back-row partner Bob Taylor. The Ireland match was Budge's 31st England appearance, equalling Lord Wakefield's long-standing record. He had won his long fight to regain the England place he lost in late 1967. The previous November, Budge was recovering from a persistent pelvic injury, had a leg in plaster, while a damaged ligament kept him out of the second trial, leading Victor Head of *The Telegraph* to write: 'At 29, a less dedicated player might have given up hope … It is a tribute to Rogers's single-mindedness that he has overcome all these obstacles and, on sheer playing merit, has won a place in a back row for which competition has seldom been keener.

Thrilled by his recall to the colours, Rogers returned to Bedford for the match against Oxford University the following Saturday and the week after travelled to Redruth with the East Midland side in the county championship semi-final with Cornwall. These two games were ideal preparation for his return against Ireland in Dublin.

Budge is back

Budge chose England's matches against France and Wales in 1969 as two of his most memorable and for wildly different reasons, as we shall see. As I have got to know Rogers, I have become aware of his self-deprecatory manner, an impressive quality in someone who has achieved so much in life and his chosen sport. So it is typical of the man that when it came to choosing his most memorable matches, he would leave out one of the most important to him as an individual, simply because England didn't win: his first game as England captain and his 'comeback' match against Ireland in 1969, in which he equalled Lord Wakefield's record of 31 caps.

Walking out at Lansdowne Road on that winter's afternoon was an extremely emotional moment for this undemonstrative character. Much as the East Midlands game against South Africa at Leicester in 1960 defined the rest of Budge's career, the game against Ireland nine years later was equally as meaningful, but for a very different reason. When asked at the time if equalling Wakefield's

42-year record would worry the England No. 7, his response to his recall was characteristic: 'Strangely enough, no. The game is enough. If you are around, you would rather play for Bedford than the Wanderers second XV. Similarly, if you can make the trials you want to make the international side. It is playing for England and not a record which drives me on.'

Lord Wakefield was in Dublin to witness the Bedford man equal his record number of England caps. Wakefield told journalist Vivian Jenkins: 'I can assure you I hope to split a bottle of champagne with Budge sometime.' Even the teetotal Rogers may have weakened on this auspicious occasion, for this was truly a time to celebrate. The tributes came thick and fast as the Kempston postman was pressed into service once more. Larry Lamb at the RAF wrote warmly: 'To gain this number of England caps places you amongst the immortals of rugby football. To your great playing skills, you have brought a personal modesty and a bearing on the field which not only does you credit but makes us all feel proud.'

Budge's former headteacher William Brown wrote on Bedford School notepaper: 'My wife and I congratulate you on achieving so much.' Mike Weston's message simply read: 'Congratulations and good luck.' Old school friend Roger Dalzell added his own humorous and personal tribute: 'You have brought great honour to our school, club and, of course, yourself, big brother is watching you – good luck.' The East Midlands county secretary addressed his tribute to 'care of: the scrimmage, Twickenham'. Tributes from old school friends, former teammates at Bedford, the Lions, the Barbarians and England found their way to the King Billy. Glyn Hughes at the Barbarians sent Budge a handwritten note that read: 'Congratulations and thank you for your personal contribution to the success of our team. I appreciate all you have put into every game you played.'

There were many more tributes expressing similar sentiments that bordered at times on adoration and love – feelings you would not normally associate with the game of rugby, such was the respect in which Rogers was held by the game's wider community. One such tribute came in the form of a beautifully written letter from Mr Squibbs, Budge's teacher and rugby coach at Bedford School: 'I think the Lower School may be permitted to share in the delight and pride in your 32nd cap and the pleasure it has given to all Bedfordians, past and present.'

Writing from his home in Goldington Road, Squibbs asks his former pupil if he could supply some dates for his research into a 'notebook' he is writing on the sporting achievements of Old Bedfordians. I suspect this letter gave Budge more pleasure than most.

The next memorable match chosen by Budge is his 33rd international – the 1969 Five Nations match against France at Twickenham, which put him one ahead of Lord Wakefield's record. The teams appeared evenly matched for the occasion, which promised an open and hard-fought contest.

England 22 France 8
Twickenham, 22 February 1969

The result of this match was unlikely to determine the outcome of the championship, but France at Twickenham will always set the rugby pulses racing. In the team with Rogers that day were Bob Hiller, David Duckham, Nigel Horton and interestingly named 'Piggy' Powell. Rogers's teammates had amassed just 54 caps between them and none had reached double figures. But England did have Rogers, Taylor and Rollitt to win the loose ball and release the striking power in the backs.

Writing in the *Daily Telegraph* on the eve of the match against France, the old traditionalist UA Titley was lavish in his praise of the England captain: 'If all players were to play with the simple, straightforward outlook of Budge Rogers there would be no excuse for lack of enthusiasm at club level. Rogers is the epitome of the amateur – it would be hard to find a less priggish man anywhere – honest enthusiasm, but tempered by maturity by playing for England more than anyone else, as he will do after the match against France tomorrow.'

Titley wrote with real authority having been commissioned by the RFU to write the official history of England rugby. His article would have raised Rogers's spirit before the game. The ground was in surprisingly good shape following heavy snow and 70,000 expectant fans arrived at Twickenham to see England produce one of their most thrilling displays for years.

Rogers, promoted to captain the previous evening in place of the indisposed Dick Greenwood, led his men to a resounding victory. Rogers and Dick Greenwood were good friends and Budge would not have enjoyed the circumstances in which he regained the captaincy for the match against France. Greenwood, who appeared just five times for his country, succeeded Bristolian Bill Redwood as England captain. Greenwood, whose better-known son Will enjoyed a more successful career than his father, was dropped along with Rogers and the rest of the back and second row following the unexpected hammering by the Wallabies at Twickenham in 1967. After excelling in the trials, Greenwood was brought back by the selectors in 1969 to replace the injured Redwood as captain for the match against Ireland. Re-appointed as skipper for the next match with France, Greenwood incurred an injury playing squash against an England reserve, Tim Dalton.

On the Friday before the match, his glasses were smashed, seriously injuring his left eye. There is a wonderful photograph of Rogers and Greenwood together prior to the France game, with the latter's head swathed in protective bandages. Greenwood thought deeply about rugby and can be considered one of the game's early innovators. The former Waterloo back-row later turned some of the RFU's outdated rules on their head. Greenwood later captained Lancashire before seeing out his playing days in Italy. Like Rogers, Greenwood was a deep thinker about the game and predictably turned to club coaching, at which he excelled, before being appointed coach of the national side.

Greenwood once said: 'England teams never achieve more than 60 per cent of their potential.' His innovations, later championed by Rogers himself, led the IRB to abandon its rules outlawing squad training sessions for international teams. Greenwood's misfortune that evening gave Budge his opportunity. Journalist Pat Marshall's report of the match against France appeared under the banner headline: 'Quiet Man Budge crushes France'.

England ran up their highest score against France since the First World War in the most thrilling manner. There was no doubting the quality of the win. Tries from wingers Fielding and Webb and a third by Larter completed a wonderful afternoon for the Red Rose team. At full-back, Bob Hiller was his usual immaculate self but the French were not to be completely outdone and produced some of the most entertaining moments of the afternoon with their dazzling rugby. But moments of brilliance could not disguise the fact that the defeat against England was the tenth in succession for Les Blues. For England, Rollitt was outstanding at No. 8 while a solid contribution from Taylor rounded off the most thrilling performance by an England team for many years. The blue shirts came under intense pressure from the England pack and committed mistake after mistake resorting to stiff-arm tackling as the game wore on.

Marshall was unequivocal in his choice of man of the match. He wrote: 'Not those masterly wings Rod Webb and Keith Fielding, nor Bob Hiller and not even hooker Pullin, who won ten strikes against the head. The man of the match in my book was Derek 'Budge' Rogers.'

Marshall had seen every one of Rogers's record-breaking 32 England appearances but had never seen him play better or with more purpose and expertise than in the match against France. After the game, the hero of the hour said simply: 'Things worked out, and the boys were just great.'

There is no question that the inspiration for England's performance came from Rogers. Leading by example, he drove the pack to levels of physical and mental pressure they didn't know they possessed. Topping up an attack here, sealing a gap in defence there, Budge's endless running and telling tackles left the French reeling.

France managed a late try from Jean-Marie Bonal and a drop goal from Claude Lacaze, but it was too little too late for the French. As the England supporters made their way excitedly out of the great stadium, their talk was of the terrific display by the England forwards, supported by superb wing play. It was as good a performance by an England pack in many years. As for the England captain, Vivian Jenkins in *The Times* wrote simply: 'Budge Rogers will be able to look back on it all with justifiable pleasure in the years to come – what a comeback.'

After the match, the question on everybody's lips was: 'Will the selectors recall captain Greenwood for the Calcutta Cup match against Scotland, or stay with Rogers?' Paul Marshall's answer was clear: 'Bob Taylor had a magnificent game and Rogers made a real success of the leadership. Leave well alone. I say.' Budge had brilliantly justified his choice as captain and the whole team deserved to play against Scotland. But selectors are fickle creatures and Greenwood, now recovered from his unfortunate squash injury, was ready for a recall. But in the end, the selectors stayed faithful to the players who had performed so well against France. Greenwood was left out of the team to play Scotland and never played for his country again. But the Waterloo back-row had achieved his ambition of captaining his country and turned his ambitions to coaching, a decision that was to define a new and exciting era in both club and international rugby. The 1969 Five Nations was a triumph for Rogers. He was once again the England captain, had broken the previous record number of England caps and had a wonderful game as his team outplayed France. Budge was back.

The teams that day were:

England: Hiller, Fielding, Spencer, Duckham, Webb, Finlan, Wintle, Powell, Pullin, Fairbrother, Horton, Larter, Taylor, Rogers (c), Rollitt

France: Villepreux, Moraitis, Lux, Trillo, Bonal, Lacaze, Puget (c), Lassere, Swierczinski, Esponda, Plantefol, Cester, Biemouret, Hauser, Dauga

Wales 30 England 9
Cardiff, 12 April 1969

In 1969, England travelled to Cardiff following a closely-fought match with Ireland, a rousing win against France and a comfortable victory over Scotland. Rogers could now forget about beating Lord Wakefield's record and concentrate all his formidable energies on leading his team out against the Welsh. Rogers's final choice of his most memorable England matches is the 1969 championship decider at the National Stadium in Cardiff. Victory for England would mean a share of the title with Ireland, while a win for the Welsh would land them the championship and the triple crown. That season, Wales had soundly beaten Scotland, thrashed the Irish in Cardiff and scraped a draw with France in Paris. The match in Cardiff looked set to be a real cliffhanger, with Wales the narrow favourites. The match was also notable for another, much more poignant reason – it was to be Rogers's last in the England jersey he had worn with such distinction for eight seasons. In the modern game, the retirement of famous sports figures is carefully managed and generally announced in advance, rather than left to the whim of selectors. There is little doubt that Budge would have liked to continue his England career, but more of that later.

Apart from the championship of 1968, when Budge missed all four Five Nations matches due to injury and poor form, the Bedford flanker had played for his country almost continuously since his debut in Dublin in 1961. In his comeback season of 1969, he played in all three championship matches in the lead-up to Cardiff, retaining the captaincy for the game against Wales. He could be forgiven for wishing he had announced his international retirement after England's previous match against Scotland at Twickenham – to say England were thrashed by Wales is an understatement. The press turned ugly. England, they screamed, had been 'humiliated', 'annihilated' and 'utterly outplayed' by a Welsh team who in contrast were 'solid and professional' and 'the best drilled team in years'.

For Wales, skipper Brian Price was a late withdrawal through injury and was replaced by John Dawes. Keith Jarrett had recovered from 'grass burns' and took his place in the Welsh side. Before the match, team coach Clive Rowlands said he regarded the opposition as a real threat, claiming somewhat generously as it turned out that 'England are very good and an improving side'. There is little doubt that Rowlands's players were extremely well prepared going into the match and were ready to face anything England might throw at them. It turned out to be very little. The wind blew close to gale force in Cardiff Bay that Saturday afternoon. England chose to have the wind at their backs in the first half and knew they had to build a big enough lead to hold off the Welsh after the break. But the most England could manage with the wind advantage was just three points despite the best efforts of full-back Bob Hiller. 3-3 at half time.

In the second half, Wales were unstoppable. JPR Williams handled the wind far better than his opposite number, placing his kicks accurately and with great effect. Reporter John Reason used a graphic sporting metaphor to describe Wales's second-half performance: 'Edwards and John left their drivers in the bag and went with the wedge, chipping behind the centres and in front of Hiller, much to the satisfaction of their forwards.'

Reason might have used 'delight' rather than 'satisfaction', but the vivid picture he painted summed up England's second-half troubles. Despite Hiller standing up well under the wind, he never had a moment to set his team on the counter-attack. In the last 15 minutes, Wales burst through the shattered England defence time and time again as JPR Williams joined his three-quarters. Everywhere you looked on the pitch, Wales were in complete control. Denzil Williams gave Powell a pounding in the scrum and with the Welsh dominating the line-out England were stretched beyond recovery as Wales ran up 18 points in the last 15 minutes, including three tries and the sweetest of drop goals by Barry John. Winger Maurice Richards was the Welsh hero of the day, scoring all five of his team's tries as he repeatedly carved his way through the English defence. Jarrett joined in the scoring fest with two penalties and three conversions as the Welsh forwards ran riot. The whole

Welsh team played their part in a comprehensive and humiliating England defeat. It was the Red Dragons's highest margin of victory since 1922 and at the end of this scintillating display Rowlands's team were crowned champions and winners of the triple crown.

For England, David Duckham made one sparkling run through the centre but that was about it. In *The Times*, Vivian Jenkins exonerated two players from any blame for the dire England performance: 'Taylor and Rogers played themselves out – the rest will want to forget.' This would have been of little compensation for Rogers in what was to be his final performance of a lengthy and distinguished England career. He would have chosen to leave in more agreeable circumstances. As one reporter observed: '*The* Welsh should have used a more humane killer – with their other weapons fully employed it was a mercy when the end came.' The *Telegraph* was merciless: 'Never before have I seen an England team fold up as this one did. England had nothing: no ideas, no initiative, no scrummaging, no defence, no pride. England were totally and utterly outplayed by the best drilled team I have seen in years.'

In a year of monumental forward battles, the Five Nations remained nicely poised to the end and in Cardiff all things were possible. But it turned out that England had no answer to the Welsh power, line-out supremacy and dazzling running. The best team were champions and fully deserved their title. At the end of the match, Rogers took leave of the international scene he had graced for so long.

If the mid-1960s were difficult years for Rogers and the England team, this should not in any way demean his achievements. Budge made his England debut in 1961 at the age of 21. He was a fixture in the side for seven years, missing only two England matches between 1961 and 1967. Rogers was dropped for the Five Nations in 1968, but regained his place and the captaincy in 1969. With the win against Scotland at Twickenham in 1962, Rogers's international career blossomed and, apart from 1968, he was virtually irreplaceable as the England open-side. There is no question that through the 1960s the Bedford man became the lynchpin of English rugby.

He captained his country with considerable distinction through a difficult time and proved a calm and reassuring presence at the top of the English game. As Vivien Jenkins wrote at the time: 'Budge Rogers will be able to look back on it all with justifiable pleasure in the years to come.'

In his *Times* column, Barry Newcombe was full of praise for the Bedford man: 'If every England player had the dedication to training and persistency which Rogers possesses, England's fortunes over the past year or two might have been considerably better.'

Over the course of his England career, Rogers continued to play in most of Bedford's club matches but appeared less and less for the East Midlands as his work commitments began to take precedence. Budge's international debut at the age of 21 was followed by regular appearances for the Barbarians and the British Lions. Club, international and touring commitments were now a regular part of the life of this young amateur sportsman. Of course, Budge loved every moment and if captaining his country was the pinnacle of his career, he has fond memories of great matches for Bedford, the Baa-Baas and the Lions, to which we now turn.

Chapter 4

County, Blues and Barbarians

P LAYING for England was always the highlight of Rogers's career. But he was keen to include two for the Midland Counties among his favourite matches: one versus South Africa and the other against the ever-formidable All Blacks. Budge was awarded his East Midlands cap in 1958 but once his England career began in 1961 he played less often for East Midlands and Midland Counties, although he hardly missed a Bedford game during this time. The county records are at best patchy but we do know that Rogers was selected to represent his county in his first season at Bedford, playing in all six of their matches.

If later in his career he missed a few county games, Rogers was the complete one-club man, missing just a handful of matches in 20 years. He speaks very proudly of his club career. Mark Howe, who sadly died at the age of 54 after a long battle with cancer, was also a true Bedford man.

Like Rogers, Howe was Bedford to his boots. The hooker made 478 appearances for the club over a 20-year period, falling just short of Rogers's record number of 485. In a moment of real humility, Howe recognised the achievements of his clubmate: 'It would be a shame to beat Budge's record. He is a legend and is Mr Bedford.'

Rogers enjoyed an unblemished time at Goldington Road, leading the club into a golden era when they stood proudly at the very pinnacle of English rugby. In addition to the demands of club, county and the national side, Rogers also managed to fit in 25 appearances for the Barbarians between 1961 and 1971, placing him joint second with Ron Jacobs and Andy Ripley on the all-time appearance list. Only Tony O'Reilly with 30 made more. The Bedford flanker also captained the Baa-Baas on five occasions, including a match in Natal on the 1969 tour of South Africa. By any standards, Rogers's senior playing career was a remarkable feat of endurance and a testament to his breathtaking commitment to the sport and to the intensity with which he played his rugby. Arguably, the key match in such a long and illustrious career was not one of his record-breaking England performances, or Bedford's triumphant club knockout final at Twickenham in 1975, but at Welford Road, Leicester for the Midland Counties against the touring South Africans in 1960, which we referred to in a previous chapter. We can now look at the match in more detail.

Midland Counties 3 South Africa 3
Leicester, 5 November 1960

Rogers regards this match as one of the best he ever played – he was just 20 years old. On a shivering cold November day, 20,000 excited and noisy fans looked forward to seeing their local heroes do battle against the famous Springboks. The tourists had a 100 per cent record on the tour, but by their own admission were not prepared for the challenge mounted by a fiercely determined Midland side. Before kick-off, the atmosphere inside the ground was expectant. The county side included skipper Don White, Jeff Butterfield and Bedford's Barry Williams. Among the spectators were RFU president AT Voyce and, interestingly, three England selectors. The scene was set for a classic encounter and so it proved. At the heart of an exhilarating display by White's men was the brilliant young prospect from Bedford. As one newspaper reported: 'Rogers had the game of his life.' His ferocious tackling kept his team in with a chance after they conceded an early try by 'Stompie' van de Merwe. A crunching tackle near the end of the game, when Rogers took out winger PJ van Zyl at the knees, lifted the crowd and Budge's teammates.

Inspired, Don White scored the late try that secured the 3-3 draw, making amends for his earlier mistake when the skipper gifted the Boks their solitary try. Young Rogers was fully involved in the move for the divisional side, punching a gaping in hole in the tourists' defence and allowing White to level the score. Vivian Jenkins of *The Telegraph* described the scene: 'Had the Springboks gained possession, they might have scored. Instead it was the 20-year-old Midlander Rogers who managed to grab the ball. He had the wit to do the right thing. He opened the game up to White on his right, who made ground .... As the movement raced on, every voice in the crowd rose to a roar.'

White somehow found the energy late in the game to run half the length of the pitch and make it over in the corner following an exchange of passes with Chilton and Butterfield. It was White's moment but the selectors will have made a mental note of the bracing presence of the young Bedford No. 7 and the contribution he made to White's try. Jenkins wrote generously of the youngster's performance: 'He played a storming game throughout.' The careers of Budge and White overlapped by two years and we know that the younger man was hugely fond of the Northampton Saints veteran. Later, in the early 1970s, Rogers joined White on the East Midlands coaching committeee, which worked on the first rugby union coaching manual. In essence, the project turned out to be a development of the Midland Counties coaching programme, so influential were the senior Midland clubs at that time.

Budge had a magnificent game at Welford Road on that November afternoon in 1960. The qualities he showed throughout his career were all in evidence. His carries were decisive and his turnovers heroic. Like the best open-sides, he was brilliant at the breakdown, winning ball after ball. Budge was a quick learner and would have been eager to see how the Springboks developed attacking moves from loose scrums. As much as he would have admired the opposition, he knew it was his job to protect his scrum-half and keep an eye out for the opposing fly-half. In the Springboks game, he was simply everywhere. As his teammates have said repeatedly, once Rogers was over the ball he was almost impossible to shift. It was as good an individual performance as anyone at the ground had seen. Before the match, a friend sent him a card that said simply: 'Don't budge Budge.' He needn't have worried.

The following day, the press were effusive in their praise for Rogers. The *Daily Telegraph* columnist wrote: 'The Bedford flanker brainily modified his play to cope with the tourists' breakaways.' The *Bedfordshire Times* hailed the Blues's new hero: 'Rogers has game of his life against the Springboks.' The young flanker had seized his opportunity and to this day believes the game at Leicester was the most decisive in his career. Such an eye-catching display under the watchful eye of the selectors meant that his full England cap could not be long delayed. In 1960, Budge had played well in England trials, but saved his best game for the biggest occasion – a tough encounter with the formidable Springboks. In one, Budge moved from being a promising young club flanker to one of the most exciting prospects seen in English rugby for some years. The match at Welford Road announced Budge's arrival on the international stage.

Midland Counties 3 New Zealand 15
Leicester, 28 October 1967

New Zealand's tour of Britain and France in 1967 was a hastily arranged affair. The All Blacks had a trip to South Africa scheduled that year but pulled out at the last minute because of the South African government's objections to the inclusion of two Maoris in the Kiwis' party. Tests against England, Scotland, Wales, France and Ireland were arranged, although the Ireland leg of the trip was cancelled due to a foot and mouth outbreak. The rampaging All

Blacks won all four Tests, including a 23-11 drubbing of England at Twickenham. They won 14 of their 15 matches on the tour. Only East Wales, with an immensely impressive 3-3 draw, prevented the All Blacks winning 15 out of 15. The match against England was notable for more than a superlative display by the tourists – it was also the first rugby international to be televised in colour. England fans would have been excited to see All Blacks stars like Lochore, Meads, Kirton, Laidlaw and Going in the comfort of their own homes, even if defeat might have taken the edge off the novel experience.

In addition to their triumphant displays in the Tests, the All Blacks enjoyed success in their club matches. The New Zealanders have taken a liking to Leicester's Welford Road ground over the years. They were unbeaten in their previous five visits up to 1967, scoring a combined total of 88 points while conceding a miserly nine. The sixth All Blacks were looking forward to another routine victory this time, although some of the older players might have remembered that on the previous occasion the two sides met only a late All Blacks score secured a win for the tourists. Perhaps this time it was the county side's turn to win.

Rogers always enjoyed playing county rugby and his breakthrough at senior level came against the Springboks in 1960. In the 1960s, county rugby was the step between club and country and being selected to play against an international touring side offered an opportunity for the top players to impress the England selectors. But by the mid-1960s, Rogers's career was fully established and he was an automatic choice for his country. He had already made 29 of his 34 England appearances, and toured South Africa with the British Lions and New Zealand with England. Budge had captained his country and built a reputation as one of the finest flankers in the history of the English game, and always relished the challenge of playing against the best sides in the world.

The 1967 All Blacks were arguably the greatest ever. They successfully combined unrelenting power up front with backs possessing great flair and imagination. We do not normally speak about the All Blacks in terms of creativity but they had learned from the recent success of the Welsh. To be successful in the modern game, there was an increasing need to combine brute force with quick-thinking artistry. For the older generation of New Zealanders, Barry John may have come from another rugby planet but in 1967 they embraced the Welshman's football skills. Despite their late conversion to attacking rugby, an All Blacks team containing beasts like Colin Meads would be unlikely to compromise their traditional values of psychological toughness and unquenchable spirit. On the 1967 tour, the New Zealanders underlined their undoubted superiority in all departments of the game and showed just what set them apart from the rest of the world. Warren Gatland, who understudied the indestructible Sean Fitzpatrick, knows a thing or two about what makes the All Blacks special: 'I've been in the changing room and I know the forces at work in there. When a player pulls on that jersey, there's such an emotional charge ... the All Black jersey is among the most iconic and recognisable. That's something, isn't it?'

In a remark that should send a sharp reminder to any player that pulls on an England jersey, Gatland continued: 'There's not a coach in modern All Black history that has needed to motivate a player.' Lochore's 1967 tourists included flankers Kel Tremain and Waka Nathan and half-backs Chris Laidlaw and Earle Kirton. With the 'Godfather' Colin Meads terrifying the opposition up front, the balance in the team could hardly have been better. They came to Leicester for the match against the Midland Counties at the end of October full of confidence in their invincibility. Perhaps it is the sheer awesome presence of the New Zealanders that leads Rogers to choose this difficult fixture as one of the stand-out matches of his career. The Midlands fielded a strong team that day which included seven full England internationals in full-back Bob Hiller, Bob Taylor, Oxford Blue Danny Hearn, Peter Larter, prop-forwards Tony Horton, Bob Lloyd and Phil Judd, and captain Budge Rogers. The match was televised, adding to the sense of anticipation around the ground. History may have favoured Brian Lochore's side but the tourists knew they would be in for a tough game at Leicester, and so it proved. The players took to the field greeted by the band of the Royal Leicestershire Regiment. Welford Road was tense with excitement as the kick-off approached.

For Rogers, the match has stayed in the memory not for the thrilling rugby or the sheer excitement of playing the All Blacks, but for two incidents during a fractious first half. The first involved Budge and Waka Nathan. The second, much more serious, left a teammate paralysed from the waist down.

Waka Nathan had a habit of obstructing opponents by any means possible. This frustrated Rogers, who decided to take the matter into his own hands. Following a line-out and completely out of character, Budge swung round and punched Nathan hard in the face, breaking his jaw. After the match, the England flanker was keen to apologise to the New Zealander but was persuaded against doing so by RFU secretary Bob Weighall, who said simply: 'Budge, let it lie.' What possessed Rogers to swing a punch so early in the game? In the encounter between England and New Zealand in 1964, Budge came off the pitch at the end of the match to be greeted by Micky Steele-Bodger: 'Budge, why didn't you hit Graham? He's been obstructing you the whole game?' So, at the first line-out in the 1967 Midlands match, it was Waka Nathan who did the obstructing. On this occasion, Budge wasted no time and took his opponent out of the game. He clearly hadn't forgotten Steele-Bodger's strong words.

The 'Black Panther', as Nathan was known, was a great ambassador for his country and did much to restore pride to the whole idea of Maori rugby. The All Black flanker's finest moment of his playing career came in a Test match against the British Lions when he terrorised David Watkins, driving him back with tackle after tackle. Shortly after the match, Watkins switched allegiance to rugby league. Perhaps Waka's relentless assault helped the Welshman to make up his mind. The Maori's whole-hearted approach to the game took its toll – two broken jaws, two ruptured Achilles tendons, broken fingers and torn ligaments in both knees are just some of the injuries suffered by Nathan in his renowned playing career. The 'Black Panther' later became an accomplished Maori coach and respected administrator. The All Black lynchpin knew how to enjoy life and enjoyed a beer – he worked for a brewery company and eventually owned his own pub. Nathan was Maori player of the year on two occasions during the 1960s and saved his best rugby for the Tests against the Lions, scoring two tries in the All Blacks's 26-17 victory in the third Test at Christchurch in 1966. He made 37 appearances for the All Blacks and scored 23 tries. He never lost a single Test match in the whole of his playing career. Later, the famous All Black became managing director of the Lions brewery in New Zealand. Budge's great friend Roger Bass, who lived and worked in the country for many years, remembers Waka telling his teammates in the run-up to a match against the British Lions: 'Boys, we drink Lions and we eat Lions.'

The second of the two first-half incidents that stand out for Budge on that day at Welford Road was the appalling injury suffered by England international and Bedford teammate Danny Hearn. The centre broke his neck following a mistimed tackle on his opposite number Ian McRae. Hearn's head thudded against McRae's thighbone and the stricken 27-year-old was rushed to Stoke Mandeville Hospital, where he eventually recovered, although tragically he was never able to walk again. Oxford rugby Blue Hearn trained as a teacher and taught economics for a time at Bedford School, later coaching rugby at Haileybury. Following his accident, Hearn continued to teach the school's first XV, in which one of his pupils was Budge's son Guy. The fact that he taught and coached from a wheelchair after the accident says much for the great courage of a wonderful rugby player.

Budge remembers being first to Hearn following the tragic incident but had the presence of mind not to pull him to his feet. He visited his friend at Stoke Mandeville on several occasions while Hearn was undergoing treatment. At the end of one visit, Budge asked the patient why the nurses were so hard on him. 'They have to be,' replied Hearn. 'I can't afford self-pity if I am going to get over this.' Of course, it was heartening for Budge and his teammates to witness Hearn's slow recovery and to see their friend return to the classroom and the rugby field, but there remained a great sadness at the fate of a close friend and teammate.

Hearn's accident challenged the way the sport treated its players. For his injuries, Hearn received the modest sum of £3,500 in compensation, an unusually high amount at the time thanks to the 'generosity' of the RFU, which paid Hearn an additional *ex-gratia* payment. Hearn received tremendous support from the rugby community and from his friends in education. Paul Smith, a Cambridge Blue and later a headteacher at Truro School, was a sixth-form student at Aylesbury Grammar School at the time of the accident. Smith visited Hearn in Stoke Mandeville with the members of his school team, much to the delight of the England centre.

The courageous Hearn showed no bitterness regarding his injury and became great friends with McRae. He continues to love the game that cruelly changed his life. Unable to play, the deeply religious Hearn turned his attention to helping other players with similar injuries. In 1996, he gave evidence on behalf of Ben Smolden, a 21-year-old hooker who was left tetraplegic when a scrum collapsed during an under-19 Colts game between Sutton Coldfield and Burton-on-Trent. In his testimony, Hearn criticised the standard of control exercised by the referee. Before the accident there had been 25 collapsed scrums, which never should have been allowed to happen. Hearn insisted the standard of refereeing was 'not of the highest competence', which wasn't a personal attack on a particular referee but a criticism of the standard of officiating in general.

In 2016, both schools and rugby clubs discussed the option of stopping the tackle in all forms of junior rugby. A report from 70 doctors and health professionals concluded: 'Children are being put at risk of potentially fatal head and spinal injuries and we call on the government to remove all harmful forms of contact from school rugby.'

A study in the *British Journal of Sports Medicine* (2015) found that a child playing rugby over a season of 15 games faces a 28 per cent risk of injury, and up to two players in every school or youth team will suffer concussion from collision incidents. These findings are alarming and a real concern for the sport but the introduction of head injury protocols will help. The Department for Education's robust defence of team games, which reads like a 19th century report, cites the virtues of 'teamwork', 'bouncing back from defeat' and 'resilience'. Rugby is an extremely physical game and it is unlikely that new laws will prevent further serious injuries, although the new concussion protocols will help.

This match against the All Blacks in 1967 was not one Rogers was ever likely to forget. The attack on Nathan and the terrible injury to his friend have lingered long in the memory. The match was hard fought and closer than the scoreline suggests despite the home team playing with 14 men for 65 minutes. 'We played well,' recalls the Bedford man. 'The match didn't seem like 15-3.' Following the match at Leicester, the selectors picked most of the Midland Counties players for the England team to face the All Blacks a week later. Sadly, the policy misfired and England performed badly on the day.

Rogers, along with several of his teammates, was dropped for the next international and had to wait until February 1969 for a recall. Perhaps the tragic fate of Danny Hearn played too heavily on the collective mind of the England team at Twickenham that day.

Teams:

Midlands, London and Home Counties:
Hiller, Cox, Hearn, Lloyd, Webb, James, Gittings, Sheriff, Rogers, Taylor, Owen, Larter, Horton, Godwin, Judd

New Zealand:
McCormick, Clarke, Thorne, McRae, Dick, Herewini, Laidlaw, Lochore, Nathan, Jennings, Meads, Tremain, Hopkinson, Major, Hazlett

Barbarians 3 New Zealand 36
15 February 1964, Cardiff Arms Park

The match against the Springboks in 1960 and the fixture against the New Zealand tourists at Leicester in 1967 were key matches in Rogers's career. Yet another important milestone was his first Barbarians Easter tour in 1961. Many more tours were to follow and Budge played some of his best rugby in the Baa-Baas black and white jersey. Budge made three more appearances for the Baa-Baas following the tour to South Africa in 1969 – the first against Oxford University at the end of 1969 and two games against Leicester Tigers, one in 1970 and his 25th and farewell appearance the following year. Rogers's Baa-Baas playing days finished in 1971 and he showed his loyalty and affection for the club by serving on the committee in two spells between 1972 and 1981.

In recent years, some have questioned the role of the Barbarians in the modern game – although not Roger Uttley. Watching the 125-year anniversary match against Argentina in 2015, the former England man was reminded what the Baa-Baas stood for in the game: 'The Baa-Baas showed an abundance of all the positive qualities needed in the modern game and it was brilliant to watch the match with JPR Williams on one side of me and Budge Rogers on the other – we enjoyed the whole day.'

With no ground, no clubhouse and no home matches, the Barbarians as a club have been an anachronism in modern sport but one whose proud traditions have contributed more than most to the enduring popularity of rugby union. Rogers made 25 appearances for the Baa-Baas between 1961 and 1971, including the trip to South Africa, which brought back fond memories of the Lions tour in 1962. Budge is proud of his Barbarians record and, like many, remains a great supporter. Despite the horrific-looking scoreline, the Barbarians match he lists as one of his favourites is against the fifth All Blacks at Cardiff in 1964. The match against the Barbarians was the All Blacks' final fixture in Europe before they left for a short trip to Canada on their way home – it had been a long and thoroughly exhausting tour. But skipper Whineray and his players were determined to sign off with another victory.

Two of the three defeats suffered by the Baa-Baas that season were in Wales, against the Cardiff club on the Easter tour and this devastating loss in February, the tourists' easiest win of their visit. The All Blacks fielded a strong side determined to end their trip with a flourish. The Baa-Baas team for Cardiff was designed to take on the New Zealanders at their own game. Their team consisted of 13 capped players, including Watkins, Sharp, Pask, Dawson and the man who that year's *Playfair* described as 'the brilliant Rogers'. It was a formidable group of players and one that would have relished the challenge of facing a great All Blacks team. It promised to be a thrilling encounter. The Barbarians have always set out with the intention of playing open rugby, while the fifth All Blacks had gained a reputation for what the *Playfair* described as 'a lack of enterprise' once they had gained the lead. After this particular match, the editor was made to eat his words.

Any match against the All Blacks is memorable for an international rugby player and this one was no exception. Cardiff Arms Park in February 1964 was the setting for the 36th match of the tour. Wilson Whineray's team included Chris Laidlaw, Don Clarke, Earle Kirton, Brian Lochore and Colin Meads. This was arguably the greatest All Blacks team ever to visit these shores. Whineray's team won 34 of the 36 matches, losing one and drawing one. They won four of their five international matches, with Scotland holding on to a hard-fought 0-0 draw at Murrayfield. The tourists began their trip with thumping wins over Oxford University and Southern Counties before travelling to Wales, where they faced an extremely powerful Newport side. The game, played out in filthy conditions in late October, was decided by a single drop goal from the boot of Penarth's Uzzell. The home side achieved a famous victory largely by denying legendary full-back Don Clarke the opportunity to exercise his famous shooting boots. Newport's fly-half on the day, David Watkins, who Rogers considers one of the best players he ever played against with his pace and wonderful sidestep, has clear memories of the match: 'It was a momentous day, to defeat the best rugby nation in the world. All the schools were given holidays and there were over 25,000 people in Rodney Parade.'

The Black and Amber hero Uzzell has equally fond memories of that day in South Wales: 'A 3-0 score didn't do us justice. I shouldn't even have been at the game. I was at St Lukes College and bunked off lectures to play. Fortunately, the principal turned out to be a rugby fan.'

Beware the wounded tiger! Newport skipper Brian Price faced the All Blacks machine twice more on the tour – for Wales and in Budge's match for the Barbarians. Price knew that the New Zealand defeat at Rodney Parade would have been a shock to the tourists, who would keep asking themselves the question: 'What happened at Newport?' In February, they had fully recovered their form having narrowly beaten Ireland, won in Cardiff, triumphed over France in Paris and soundly defeated England at Twickenham. Only Scotland managed to stem the All Black tide with the draw at Murrayfield.

This fifth All Blacks were superbly led by their captain Whineray. There is little doubt that the New Zealander was one of the outstanding captains of his era. He led his country in all but two of the 32 internationals he played in and his record includes series victories over South Africa, Australia and the British Isles. We know from Rogers that the tourists' captain was a 'lovely man', a true gentleman of the game – some would say unusual for a prop-forward. Awarded an OBE by the Queen, Whineray later received the ultimate honour of a knighthood from his own country. His already-illustrious career reached its peak in the 1964 match at Cardiff, a year before he finally retired. The Barbarians historian Alan Evans wrote: 'The match is remembered for the coruscating exhibition of 15-man rugby by the men in black.' Eight tries without reply in a 36-3 drubbing was the Barbarians's heaviest defeat against the All Blacks and a real source of embarrassment for everyone involved. But rather than focus on the plight of the losers, we should salute the manner of the All Blacks's brilliant victory, as the home crowd generously agreed at the end of the match.

The result at Cardiff was a shock. As Evans said, nobody saw it coming. The Barbarians had selected a strong team. Skipper and prop Ronnie Dawson, lock Brian Price and Gerry Culliton at blind-side all played in the famous victory against the Springboks three years earlier. Rogers was in his usual position of open-side, Alan Pask was at No. 8, while Alan Clarke, continuing the old Barbarian tradition of including a member of the tourists in their team, also featured in the pack that day. Going into the match, the Baa-Baas had every reason to feel optimistic. The Cardiff crowd were boisterous in support of the 'home' team and the noise levels in the stadium increased when the Baa-Baas went ahead in the first half in the most unexpected fashion. Guest player Clark caught the ball from a drop-out by his more famous brother Don, called for a mark and dropped a goal in great style from 40 yards. It was to be the Baa-Baas only score of the game. Buoyed by their lead, the men in the black and white shirts held their own for 30 minutes as the All Blacks eased their way back into the game.

The tourists went ahead just before the interval when they snatched the ball away from Sharp and Meads sent Tremain over for their first try of the match to take his team into a 6-3 half-time lead. Early in the second period, Budge's old adversary Waka Nathan stole the ball from Clarke and released Laidlaw, who sent Meads over for the second try. Not a soul in the noisy crowd, who were beginning to switch their allegiance at the prospect of seeing the All Blacks at their scintillating best, could have predicted what was to come. Sharp, a late replacement for Mike Gibson, was returning from a long lay-off and looked unfit, while his scrum partner Clarke struggled to cope with the All Blacks onslaught that came early in the second half. Tries from Graham and Dick followed. The latter score was the try of the match as the ball went through seven pairs of All Black hands before Dick touched down. The rout continued, with Nathan and Caulton both going over before Whineray completed the try scoring, much to the delight of the crowd. Full-back Don Clarke added to the Baa-Baas's humiliation by kicking six conversions in succession. The All Blacks were merciless.

Whineray's try on the stroke of 80 minutes is worthy of a special mention. In his book *The Barbarians*, Evans repeats Terry McLean's eye-witness account of the moment: 'There was Whineray, going hell for leather, Meads alongside him and Flynn flashing across to make the tackle. The Tower of Babel was a quiet country pub compared to the Arms Park. Amid the fantastic noise, Whineray passed to Meads, or so it seemed ... he sidestepped the other way. It was the dummy pass to end dummy passes. Hook, line and sinker Flynn bought it. Whineray slackened to a trot as he carried the few more yards to the posts.'

At the final whistle, Whineray was carried from the field to the tune of 'for he's a jolly good fellow'. As onlookers at the feast, the Barbarians players could only admire what they had witnessed in the second half. In *The Times* the following day, Uel Titley attempted to put some perspective on the match: 'The club has fostered all that is best in the amateur game. The idea of these matches is to end a tour on a happy note and to send the touring team away in friendship.'

This does rather sound like a quote from *Tom Brown's Schooldays* and would have been little consolation to the vanquished Barbarians. Both sides went into the match expecting to win a closely fought encounter, not a rout. *Playfair* was brutal in its frank appraisal of the Cardiff second-half massacre: 'Even those who were fearful of certain weaknesses behind the scrummage were totally unprepared for the appalling defensive failures revealed in all their nakedness, especially after the change of ends.'

Alan Evans gave a more considered response to the All Blacks's second-half display: 'It was as if Whineray's men suddenly realised that they were in the final moments of their long tour and they should leave an unforgettable calling card.'

They certainly did that. It was as if the two teams had switched shirts and it was the All Blacks who played the type of fast-flowing open rugby usually associated with their opponents in the black and white jerseys. In fairness to the Barbarians, this All Blacks side possessed some of the finest forwards seen anywhere in the world at that or any other time. Whineray, Young, Meads, Nathan and

Tremaine were all world class. Gray at prop, Stewart alongside Meads and Graham in the back row would walk into any British test team. For many, Chris Laidlaw was the perfect scrum-half and dominated that incredible last 40 minutes in Cardiff. As an indicator of the strength of their team, one of the All Blacks's reserves that day was none other than Brian Lochore, who was just setting out on his own brilliant career.

Like many of the Baa-Baas that day, Rogers was a frustrated second-half bystander. Despite the assertions by friends and family that he played everything to win, Budge has said that he often enjoyed matches despite being on the losing side. Of course, his tenacious concentration and drive made him a winner and prolonged his career long after others of his generation had fallen by the wayside.

However, Budge was able to admire great players and teams whatever the result, such was his love for rugby. As long as he felt he had done everything he could for his team, that was enough. The match against the All Blacks at Cardiff in 1964 was such a match, Budge would have learned from the defeat and from the All Blacks's assault. He could only admire their exhibition of flawless rugby as the tourists indulged themselves late in the game. In time, he would have reflected on the beauty and strength of the Kiwis's exhibition which, more than anything, made this one of his 'memorable matches'.

Teams:

Barbarians: Wilson (Oxford Uni), Watkins (Newport), Phillips (Fylde), Flynn (Wanderers), Simpson (Sandhurst), Sharp (Wasps), SJS Clarke (Blackheath), Rogers (Bedford), Pask (Abertillery), Culliton (Wanderers), Jones (Penarth), Price (Newport), IJ Clarke (Waikato NZ), Dawson (Wanderers) (c), Cunningham (Aberavon)

New Zealand: DB Clarke, Dick, Little, Arnold, Caulton, Watt, Laidlaw, Nathan, Tremain, Graham, Meads, Stewart, Gray, Young, Whineray (c)

If the international matches were the summit of a Barbarian's career, Rogers also recognises that some of the most intriguing matches for the Baa-Baas in his time as a player were against the major clubs and counties: the fixture against Leicester early in the year, the Mobbs Memorial match at Northampton against the East Midlands in the spring and, of course, the famous Easter tour of Wales. The Mobbs Memorial game occupies a special place in the Barbarians's calendar and is one the Bedford club have enjoyed a close connection with down the years. Edgar Mobbs was a pupil at Bedford Modern School and many of the town's best players, including Rogers, have featured for East Midlands in the match. Initiated in 1921, the match has developed from an event to mark the death of a distinguished soldier who died in the First World War to a means of raising funds to support youth rugby. In 2008, *The Telegraph* ran a headline on its sports page that read: 'Mobbs match falls to the modern era'. In recent years, due to the pressure of professional rugby, the Barbarians had been forced to select mostly uncapped players for the match, which was against the club's traditions. The fixture continued but, with Northampton and Bedford playing the British Army RFU in alternate years, Goldington Road hosted the Baa-Baas's final appearance in the Mobbs in 2008. However, Franklin's Gardens in Northampton remains the spiritual home of this very special rugby occasion and with good reason.

Lieutenant-Colonel Edgar Mobbs of the Northamptonshire Regiment (Sportsmen's Battalion) was shot in the neck in an attack on a German machine gun post at Ypres in 1917. He was just 35 years old. Mobbs was a soldier of immense courage, a quality he also displayed in his sporting career. He made 250 appearances for the Saints, played ten games for the Barbarians and seven for England, including one as captain against France in 1910. East Midlands rugby historian Peter Eads wrote of the Saints hero: 'Edgar Mobbs was a wing three-quarter of genius. He was 6ft 1in, weighed 14 stone and was nearly an even timer in the 100 yards sprint.'

Eads continued: 'For Mobbs, a match was never lost until the final whistle was blown and he was at his superb best when his side was ten points down at half time. Then he played with his full genius and drew from his team more than they knew how to give.'

It is not widely known that on the first Thursday in March, prior to the Mobbs match, officials from opposing sides assemble at Abingdon Square in the centre of Northampton for a wreath-laying ceremony in front of a statue of Edgar Mobbs, erected in his honour in 1921. It is a remarkable story and a wonderful tribute to club rugby that the game continues to be staged almost 100 years after Mobbs was tragically killed. The Barbarians club, the East Midlands county RFU, the Army and both Bedford and Northampton are to be congratulated for supporting the contest for almost a century. The most recent Mobbs match between Northampton and the Army at Franklin's Gardens on 13 April 2016 ended in a 22-14 victory for the Saints. The former soldier's memory also lives on in the Mobbs Memorial youth rugby competition funded from the proceeds of the senior match.

The links between the Bedford and Northampton clubs, the county side and the Barbarians have featured heavily in Rogers's career. In the 1950s, Don White, erstwhile mentor to the young Rogers, captained the East Midlands in nine Mobbs matches and was succeeded in the role by Ron Jacobs. In the 1960s, England captains Rogers and Bob Taylor continued the legacy of White and Jacobs by regularly committing themselves to the fixture. Rogers made 16 appearances in the Mobbs match between 1957 and 1972, always for the East Midlands. The Bedford man was captain of the county side for most of these games, even if his first loyalties were always to his club and country. Rogers loved playing for the Barbarians and all that meant, including the notorious Easter tours to Wales.

Baa-Baas' legendary Easter tour

Rogers was a regular Easter tourist in the black and white jersey. The Baa-Baas's tour itinerary of 1938 set the tone for all future Easter weekend jaunts down to Wales. The Easter tour consisted of four matches against strong Welsh club sides Penarth, Cardiff,

Newport and Swansea. The party usually stayed in the Esplanade Manor Hotel in Penarth, which Budge described as 'a funny little hotel conveniently situated across the road from the town's nightclub'. The hotel closed in 1971 and some say its closure marked the beginning of the end of the tour itself. Over the years, the programme hardly varied:

Thursday: Settle into hotel
Friday: Penarth match
Saturday: Cardiff match
Sunday: Golf day
Monday: Swansea match
Tuesday: Final match against Newport

Micky Steel-Bodger, a prominent figure for the Baa-Baas after the war, became very fond of the Easter tour: 'I am terribly attached to the whole concept and experience of the Bank Holiday weekend in Wales, and to the starting point at Penarth in particular.'

There were few rules but players were 'asked to be in bed by 11pm on the night prior to playing and not to play more than nine holes of golf on the morning of a match'. It is not at all clear that the players universally accepted this sensible advice and the stories of the Baa-Baas's Easter tour have entered rugby folklore, as Alan Evans writes in his book *The Barbarians:* 'The tone was set on the Thursday evening. Anything might happen – I recall returning in the early hours to find four or five sheep in the foyer to be told: "That's nothing, there's a horse in the Brigadier's [Glyn Hughes] bedroom!"'

As Evans writes: 'Micky-Steele Bodger's veterinary skills were obviously called on from time to time.' Ties, scarves and blazer badges were distributed at the Thursday evening dinner to the new 'caps' as a signal to the start of the festivities and some very tough rugby matches. Rogers has particular happy memories of the weekend. At the team talk before the match in Swansea, captain for the day John Willcox reminded the party that the opposition full-back Blyth had a habit of coming into the line. To combat Blyth's excursions, the players were asked, not unreasonably, to adjust their positions and who they marked. The players considered the suggestion for a few seconds before Tony O'Reilly broke the silence: 'Thank you for the suggestion but I prefer to stay with my own man.' Of course, the tactic was dropped. Rogers loved listening to O'Reilly talking and the Irishman was always keen to oblige. 'Tony was a wonderful orator and I could, and often did, listen to him all night.'

Of course, the Barbarians Easter tour cannot be compared with playing for your country or touring with the British Lions, but the whole 'concept' enables great players of their period to play alongside rather than against their contemporaries. For example, we see Rogers, JPR Williams and Barry John in the same side, which would have been a real treat for players and spectators alike. Neither is selection exclusive to players from Great Britain, as Roger Uttley remembers: 'Some of the best experiences of my career were playing for the Baa-Baas ... I played for them in Cardiff alongside Jean-Pierre Rives and Jean-Claude Skrela.'

If anyone needs convincing about the contribution of the Barbarians to the game of rugby, they should be reminded of the day in 1973 at Cardiff Arms Park when what has been dubbed the 'greatest try of all time' was scored by the Baa-Baas against the touring All Blacks.

Let the excited commentator Cliff Morgan pick up the story:

'Kirkpatrick to Williams. This is great stuff! Phil Bennett covering chased by Scown. Brilliant, oh, that's brilliant! John Williams, Bryan Williams, John Pullin, John Dawes, great dummy. To Tom David, the half-way line. Brilliant by Quinnell. This is Gareth Edwards! [A dramatic start!] What a score.'

It was a special moment and nothing could better represent the Barbarian spirit than 'that try' at Cardiff. Such was Rogers's affection for the club that he chose a heavy Baa-Baas defeat as one of his most memorable matches. He was just 25 years old in 1964 and already well into his international career. There were many victorious moments in the years to come that would compensate for the heavy defeat in Cardiff, including one that will live long in the memory. On one Baa-Baas Easter tour, David Perry remembered playing in the back-row with Budge against Llanelli. At the last moment, the Welsh club's fly-half dropped out and was replaced by a 17-year-old schoolboy. The former Bedford man remembers the match well: 'Budge never nailed the youngster during the whole match, but neither did the lad make a break. Budge said after the game: "Who was that kid?" It turned out to be a very young Barry John.'

In the early 1970s, the Barbarian club held a lunch, hosted by Micky Steele-Bodger, in honour of Rogers and the Bristol and England hooker John Pullin. Like his teammate, Pullin is a former England skipper and British Lion. He captained England to victories over South Africa, Australia and New Zealand and made 42 appearances for his country.

The Bristol man was also in the Lions and Baa-Baas teams that defeated the All Blacks in the early 1970s. But despite this distinguished record, Pullin is unfortunately best remembered in England rugby circles as the skipper who took England to Ireland at the height of the troubles, when both Wales and Scotland refused the opportunity. England lost that particular match 18-9 to the Irish.

The lunch in honour of the two Englishmen was held at the RAC club and those present were treated to an after-lunch speech by Gerald Davies. Among the specially invited guests were rugby enthusiasts Denis Thatcher and Bill Deedes. It was an appropriate tribute to these two outstanding Barbarians. If the Easter tours were great fun with some outstanding rugby thrown in, Budge's next memorable match was a serious affair and one of the most exciting of his career.

Bedford Blues 28 Rosslyn Park 12
RFU Club Final, Twickenham
26 April 1975

The time you won the town your race
We chaired you threw the market-place;
Man and boy stood cheering by,
And home we brought you shoulder-high.

AE Houseman

Rogers's final choice in his list of favourite club, county and Barbarians matches is the greatest in Bedford's 130-year history. There is no question that the RFU club competition final of 1975 stands out as the Blues's finest hour. This was the day when their greatest ever player lifted the most coveted club trophy in the land. The victory over Rosslyn Park at Twickenham was the historic culmination of a series of matches at a time Neil Roy has labelled 'the magnificent seventies'. For indeed, the 1970s were years of fabulous success at Goldington Road. Such was the playing strength of Bedford at this time that the second XV would have been a match for most of England's top clubs.

The key to Bedford's success in this period can be traced to the relationship between Goldington Road, Bedford School and the Blues's greatest ever player, Budge Rogers. In 1975, the rugby stars were truly aligned over the lovely old market town. Such was Rogers's reputation that top internationals would happily travel down to Bedford School to play in the annual fixture against the school first XV. Some of these players later took up residency in Bedford so they could play for the Blues and were attracted by coaching jobs at the local school alongside teachers like Murray Fletcher and George Cullen. The combination of expert coaching at the school and the high esteem in which Rogers was held in the game meant success was pretty much guaranteed – and so it proved.

If Bedford's success was founded on its links with the town's schools, the connection with Cambridge University boosted the club's playing strength. Roger Dalzell, Mike Lord – later Deputy

Speaker of the House of Commons – Fred Inglis, Frank Booth and Geoff Frankcom were all Cambridge graduates, while Oxford provided Roger Bass and Danny Hearn, who both did their teaching practice at Bedford School before taking up posts at Haileybury. It is said that Bedford's colours of light blue and dark blue were chosen because of the club's close proximity to Oxford and Cambridge, but there is little doubt that the links were much stronger with Cambridge than with its rival to the west.

At the height of their success, Bedford were able to attract top-class players from throughout the region. Hertfordshire lad Larry Webb proved a magnet for players from Hertfordshire, including Jack Smith, who played 340 times for Bedford and also captained the county at cricket. Tony Jordan, Derek Wyatt and Jeremy Janion all came to Bedford from the Eastern Counties. Roy and Beard wrote later: 'With some hard men in the front five and two men in the back row who were to captain England, the Blues were a great attraction to top-class backs in particular.'

For all of the above reasons, in the 1970s Bedford became the centre of rugby in the South Midlands. The club had been building for success since their inception in 1886. In 1975, the Blues were about to fulfil their destiny.

The Blues won the *Sunday Telegraph* English-Welsh pennant in 1970, an early forerunner of today's professional rugby Premier League. The Blues narrowly missed a second honour in 1975, when Pat Briggs's side finished second in the English section of the *Daily Telegraph* competition behind Northampton. The season was marred only by the sad death of Blues president Eric King, who suffered a heart attack at Northampton's Franklin's Gardens ground. King would have enjoyed seeing *The Telegraph* trophy being presented to the club by Jack Bailey, former master at Bedford School and later secretary of the MCC.

The first four winners of the RFU club competition were Gloucester, Coventry (twice) and Bedford. The new competition was introduced in 1971 to meet a desire by the clubs for an official national club trophy. Based loosely on soccer's historic FA Cup, the

RFU club competition had a knockout format with 32 clubs entered in the first round. The use of replacements, which had already been introduced in international matches, was extended to the new competition. Originally sceptical about playing for trophies, Rogers grew to accept it and appreciate the benefits it could bring to smaller clubs: 'Until this season, I felt the competition had not achieved its objectives. However, things have changed this season. We have seen at Bedford how it can create interest. It draws players and supporters together and, of course, it gives the Morpeths and Orrells a chance of glory.'

In the 1974/75 season, Bedford drew Bournemouth in the first round. The players went down to the south coast the day before the match and on a sunny November day crossed their opponents' line 11 times in a 66-6 victory. It was a record score in the competition, with Derek Wyatt scoring a club-record six tries. Wyatt had a phenomenal try-scoring record at club level. 'He was one of Bedford's most exciting players in an exciting era,' wrote the authors of the *125 History of the Blues*. Wyatt joined the club from Ipswich, making his debut in 1973. That season, he scored 33 tries in 29 appearances and continued in the same vein for the next five seasons. With Bob Demming (73 tries in 147 matches), Bedford were often unstoppable at this time. Essex-born Wyatt, an international long jumper in his teenage years, scored more tries than anyone in the Blues's 125-year history, something the England selectors could not ignore. The winger was chosen for the Calcutta Cup match at Murrayfield in 1976 and came on late in the game as replacement for David Duckham in what was to be his one and only England appearance. Wyatt later joined Bath, where he continued his epic try-scoring exploits. Wyatt was an interesting character. He studied at Oxford as a mature student and gained his Blue in the Centenary Varsity match. When his playing days were over, this try-scoring phenomenon went into publishing and in 1997 became the Labour MP for Sittingbourne and Sheppey. A good constituency MP, Wyatt was pilloried by the tabloids for claiming 75p for two scotch eggs and £1.79 for five mini pork pies in his MP expense claim. Wyatt stood down in 2010 to concentrate on his considerable interests in internet technology. In 1975, the 25-year-old Wyatt was a key figure in Bedford's great run in the RFU club competition as his tries at Bournemouth got Bedford off to a great start.

The second round draw gave the Blues a tough-looking home tie against Sale. They had faced the Cheshire club a few weeks earlier in a dress rehearsal, winning 19-4, so they knew what to expect from the northerners. In front of a noisy full house at Goldington Road, the Blues won a hard-fought match 23-3 but the final score did not tell the whole story. Key to the victory was the manner in which Alun Lewis subdued Sale's Steve Smith. The England scrum-half hardly got into the game.

In the third round, the Blues welcomed Gosforth to Goldington Road. Before the match, the home crowd were nervous and with good reason. Bedford had been beaten 32-0 by their opponents the previous season, the Blues's heaviest defeat at home since the First World War. In appalling playing conditions the match was a bruising, muscular encounter, with Gosforth determined to exert their physical superiority. One or two visiting players were a little too physical, leading to the referee sending off one of their three-quarters. This proved crucial. A superb running try by Wyatt gave his team a 6-3 half time advantage. Blues fans began to relax in the second half as their heroes increased their lead, running out 12-6 winners. The tie was notable for Bedford's first-ever use of a replacement and for record match takings of £1,000 – tremendous support from the Goldington Road faithful given the awful weather.

For the semi-final, the Blues were again rewarded with a home draw – this time against old friends and rivals Coventry. Packed with internationals, the Warwickshire side had narrowly beaten Bedford at Goldington Road earlier in the season and again the home fans faced a nervy afternoon. Once again, the conditions were dreadful following a snowstorm on the Thursday before the match, but on the day the Goldington Road stand was packed to capacity. A crowd of over 3,000 paid a record £2,000 in matchday receipts to see their team face a strong Coventry side led by the legendary David Duckham. The supporters were full of expectation at the prospect of these two great clubs going head to head, with a final at Twickenham awaiting the winners. With the slope in their favour in the first half, the Blues went ahead after eight minutes when a John Howard try was converted by Neil Bennett. The home team went in at half time with a six-point lead, which was quickly reduced to three when Coventry kicked a penalty goal straight after the interval.

The tension inside the ground was almost unbearable as the home side defended desperately for most of the second half. With the crowd urging their team forward, the match took an unexpected turn. Andy Hollins charged down a defensive kick from the opposition scrum-half and went over in the corner. The try proved the defining moment in the match as the Blues took their place in the final. Coventry had been magnificent. But a stubborn and well-organised defence saw the home side through against a team who had never been beaten in the competition. Bedford took their chances in a magnificent match and the home fans could look forward to a day out at Twickenham three weeks later.

Bedford coach Pat Briggs has clear memories of the semi-final: 'They had nine English caps in the back line, so I knew we would be up against it. Unlike the blitz defence of today, we tried the drift defence and it worked. We were the first club to try this. We decided to drive Coventry inside, with Budge always prepared ready to tackle. I knew if we had 40 per cent of the ball, we would win.'

Their opponents in the final were the form team of the season. In 1975, Rosslyn Park were top of the *Daily Telegraph* table for clubs in England, with Bedford in eighth place. The London club had also beaten the Blues 20-16 at Goldington Road earlier in the season, making them firm favourites in most people's eyes. Rugby fans could look forward to a friendly, if fiercely fought contest. Relations between the two clubs had always been cordial, leading *The Telegraph's* John Reason to write in his column: 'The way is now clear for what should be the best-tempered final in the brief history of the competition ... it looks like all the referee will have to do is blow his whistle at the start of the game and blow it again at the finish.'

How Budge relished the prospect of another appearance at the ground he had graced for so long. He was as excited for the club as he was for himself: 'The final is a great thing for me and for the club. It is the highest spot in my career for a long time. Having played only for Bedford throughout my years, this is in many ways a culmination for me ... the great thing about this final is that so many people are involved at the club. It is wonderful to see everyone so excited about it.'

Budge's philosophy of playing rugby meant that he was desperate to be match fit for the final. The Bedford skipper set out each season fully aware that his team would not win all of their matches. Budge insisted that his players enjoy the game whatever the result by moving the ball quickly rather than resorting to the all-too-familiar tactic of endless kicking common at all levels of the game. The 1975 final should be played in that same spirit. The Bedford team, which included six internationals in Rogers, Neil Bennett, Tony Jordan, Bob Wilkinson, Brian Keen and Derek Wyatt, together with British Lion Alun Lewis, all signed up to their captain's ethos – after all, it had brought them success and got them to the national club final.

The night before the match, the Bedford party stayed in the comfortable surroundings of the Richmond Hill Hotel. On the Saturday morning, Rogers gave a brief team talk. It was nothing too tactical or complicated. He simply said: 'Relax everybody and try not to get too worked up. We can't play a cup final at Twickenham if we are too tight and tense. Above all, let's enjoy the occasion – let's play the way rugby should be played.'

The players left the hotel in good spirits and excited about the challenge that lay ahead. They knew they were about to face a formidable Rosslyn Park side that included two England internationals in the wonderful Andy Ripley and Lionel Weston, a product of Bedford Modern School. The previous season, under the inspirational leadership of former Cambridge University captain Phil Keith-Roach, the young Park side showed outstanding form in winning 28 of their 35 matches. Former England captain WJA Davies wrote the following tribute to Rosslyn Park in his programme notes: 'Rosslyn Park may not consistently compare with the Harlequins, Blackheath or Richmond, but for constancy of purpose in providing games for the greatest number they will yield second place to none. Which club has done more to encourage the youth of this country or foster this enthusiasm than Rosslyn Park?'

As with the FA Cup finals at Wembley, one set of supporters quickly gained the upper hand on a warm and sunny April afternoon. The Blues fans among the 15,000 present were passionate, organised and easily drowned out the Park fans on the far side of the ground. Given their excellent form that season, Park were clear favourites to win, with the strength and power of their forwards likely to prove the deciding factor. Could Bedford control Park's two giants, Ripley and the junior All Black flanker Anderson? Could Bedford win enough of the ball to get their backs playing their trademark free-flowing rugby? The answer came late in the first half when Keith-Roach took the first of his five strikes against the head. Ripley found McKay with a lengthy pass and the winger swept around Bob Demming with ease before going over in the corner.

The smaller Bedford team gritted their teeth, held firm and even began to gain the upper hand in the line-outs and around the breakdown. Rogers, Edwards and Hollins began to take charge as Jordan was tackled inches from the line. The Blues's backs, growing in confidence, mounted attack after attack against their retreating opponents. Just before the interval, they got the breakthrough as Wyatt sprinted over for a try after some delightful handling from the Bedford backs. It was 6-4 to the Blues at half time.

The second half began in dramatic style with what the *Daily Telegraph* described the following Monday as a 'wonder try'. The authors of *125 Years of the Blues* described the moment which changed the game for Bedford: 'Bob Wilkinson, under pressure, made a clean catch and sent our back row forwards with a splendidly timed pass. From then on, the ball was moved swiftly and purposefully from man to man and back again, until finally Chris Bailward was given it with the Park's posts ahead, A few paces, and he plunged over for a try in an exultant leap.'

Bailwards's triumphant leap for the line was greeted with a crescendo of noise from the Blues supporters. Neil Bennett converted the try and Bedford led 12-4. The Blues went hard at their rivals. They used their ball-carriers to create chaos in Park's defensive line and rather than play cautiously for the remainder of the match, they ran their opponents ragged. Bedford had far too much pace and accuracy in their attacking game and two further tries by winger Demming and another by Brian Keen increased Bedford's lead to 28-4. Rogers stamped his authority at every breakdown and the blue shirts were running everywhere. The Londoners were stunned by the onslaught but inspired by Ripley they rallied in the last quarter to score two tries of their own, with the final score reading 28-12 to the Blues. Every Bedford player had played their part in the victory but there were some real stars that day, none of them more impressive than Bob Demming. The Blues winger was an interesting character, a schoolteacher in London's East End. The West Indian was the Blues's hero that day with his non-stop running, capped off by two tries. If Demming grabbed the headlines, there were other heroes too. Nineteen-year-old Cambridge medical student Alun Lewis had made just 18 first-team appearances before the final but was hugely impressive throughout the 80 minutes. The Welshman later toured with the British Lions but was never selected to play for his country. Tony Jordan was a wonderful sportsman. Eastern Counties captain, Barbarian, Cambridge double Blue, the 28-year-old played seven times for England. Not content with his rugby-playing activities, Jordan played first-class cricket for Essex in the summer months. At 6ft and just over 13st, Jordan was not huge for a full-back but he had pace and natural athleticism and made a major contribution to his team's performance against Rosslyn Park.

But it was Blues's skipper Budge Rogers who led his team to victory in what was the greatest day of his remarkable club career. Amid joyous scenes, Rogers was chaired off the pitch as the Bedford fans cheered their team to the echo. The Bedford skipper was

Budge pictured in the back row of the Bedford School under-11 cricket team (1950)

Budge on the right of his form tutor at Bedford School (1952)

The young Rogers waiting to receive a pass from team-mate Roger Dalzell in a school match on a misty day at Bedford School (1957)

Captain of the school boxing team (1957)

Bedford School rugby first XV. Budge is pictured on the right of the middle row

During a visit to Goldington Road in 2016

A nostalgic visit to his former school in 2016

The old pavilion at Goldington Road in 2016

Victory shield marking Bedford's cup triumph hanging proudly in the old Scrum Hall bar at Goldington Road

Statue of Bishop Trevor Huddleston situated in Bedford town centre. Huddleston spoke to the British Lions party prior to their controversial tour to South Africa in 1962

The British Lions 1962 party to South Africa. Budge is pictured in the centre of the back row

Attempting a charge-down during a match on the 1962 Lions tour to South Africa

Budge in support against the All Blacks in the second Test at Lancaster on England's ground-breaking tour of New Zealand in 1963

The Barbarians squad for the 1963 Easter tour of Wales

The 1963 England Five Nations team. Back row: K. Kelleher (referee), J. Roberts, L. Rimmer, R. French, F. Wright, W. Morgan, V. Harding, J. Horrocks-Taylor, W. Patterson, L. Boundy (touch judge). Middle row: P. Jackson, C. Jacobs, R. Jeeps, R. Robinson, J. Willcox. Front row: M. Weston, D. Rogers

A Bedford cricket club dinner in 1963

A proud England No. 7 shaking hands with Prime Minister Harold Macmillan before the 1963 Five Nations match against Scotland

The England team in the 1966 Five Nations at Twickenham, with Budge as captain

Ted Rudd, ably assisted by Budge Rogers, tackling Welsh winger Davies at Twickenham in 1966

1968 England tour to Canada with Phil Judd as captain

Receiving the award for the record number of England caps from previous holder, Lord Wakefield

England team to play Ireland at Dublin in 1969, Rogers's comeback season.

Budge and Greenwood at the England training headquarters before the match against France in 1969. Rogers replaced Greenwood as skipper for the match when the latter sustained an eye injury playing squash in the week prior to the game

Rogers showing his OBE with proud parents at the gates of Buckingham Palace in 1969

Presentation dinner

Budge practising his public speaking skills

Budge at the BBC with Cliff Morgan and Jimmy Hill

England and Japan teams on the 1971 tour to the Far East

A very happy Budge and Nanette with their families at their wedding in 1971

Budge as captain of the triumphant Bedford cup-winning team of 1975

1976 England selection panel with Sandy Saunders as chairman

Budge at a friend's house. In the background is Rogers's cherished Jowett Javelin

Two England greats at the launch of Budge's new company

Two old friends in Australia for the 2003 World Cup. On the right is Phil Harry, former president of the Australian RFU

everywhere: a tackling machine, a strong ball carrier and a menace at the breakdown. Budge's never-say-die running and chasing was an inspiration to the rest of his team.

The day belonged to Bedford. The club's belief in open, running rugby had been joyously vindicated. If Bedford's success that day in 1975 was the culmination of a 130-year rugby journey and the efforts of generations of the Blues's members, one person deserves special mention. Pat Briggs, a teacher at Bedford School for 22 years and the Blues's coach on that famous day, made his club debut in 1963/64. A Cambridge double Blue, the No. 10 scored 387 points in 238 matches during his time at Goldington Road and captained the side in 1969/70, when Bedford won the *Sunday Telegraph* English-Welsh pennant. A Barbarian, the fly-half was an England triallist alongside club colleagues John Frankcom and Danny Hearn, and was extremely unlucky not to receive a full cap. Briggs remembers playing for the Possibles, captained by Budge Rogers, against the Probables, captained by Dick Greenwood, in a final England trial. Briggs was asked to move to the Probables at half time to replace the injured Roger Shackleton. Budge was furious. 'We're winning,' he told his friend. 'Come on, you stay where you are.' So John Finlan was promoted as the Probables's fly-half, had a terrific 40 minutes and was picked for the next England game ahead of Briggs. His chance had gone.

Briggs and Rogers first met in the 1962/63 season, when Christs College played their annual lent term fixture against a Bedford XV at Goldington Road. After the match, Budge introduced Briggs to his headmaster Bill Brown. When the head asked the young Cambridge undergraduate what he intended to do after university, Briggs replied: 'I am seriously thinking about teaching, sir.' Brown replied: 'Would you like to teach at my school?' Briggs, somewhat surprised by the offer, answered: 'Yes, of course.' 'OK, good,' replied Brown. 'Send me a letter.' Briggs began his teaching career at Bedford in 1964 and stayed for 22 years. Briggs was one of a generation of Oxbridge sporting undergraduates who turned to teaching for a career. He recalls the Cambridge cricket Blue, former

Bedford School cricket coach and later *Daily Telegraph* columnist MH Stephenson who, when asked to give two reasons why he took up teaching, declared: 'July and August'.

In the summer months, Cheshire-born Briggs played Minor Counties cricket for Bedfordshire, scoring first-class 50s against Essex and the MCC. At Cambridge, his first XI captain was none other than the great Mike Brearley, with whom he opened the batting. Briggs has clear memories of facing Wes Hall at Fenners, just a short walk from his current home opposite Parker's Piece. Briggs learned his cricket under the guidance of Essex skipper Brian Taylor and the great umpire Dusty Rhodes, both of whom coached at Cambridge. This was the perfect grounding for a young man about to embark on a teaching and coaching career. Briggs later returned to the north of England after accepting the headship at William Hulme's Grammar School in Manchester, where he stayed for ten years, before moving to Malaysia as principal of a college in Negeri Sembilan.

The former Bedford coach said of the match against Rosslyn Park: 'We had been a strong side for a few years, with a back row that included Budge, David Perry and David Coley, who often scored more tries between them than the rest of the team put together.'

As Bedford coach in 1975, Briggs left nothing to chance. In this respect he was ahead of his time. He prepared a rundown on the strengths and weaknesses of every player in the side as a tape-recording and printed hard copies for the whole team. His argument was that if every player accepted the strengths and weaknesses of the rest of the team, this would help in team-building – and it worked. The video of the 1975 final is still used as a model for 15-man rugby, something for which Briggs can take credit. As he remarked: 'It was real 15-man rugby. After all, two of our props scored tries.'

If the multi-talented Briggs was the inspiration behind the scenes at Twickenham in 1975, Rogers was his man on the pitch. In his third period of captaincy, Budge led his beloved Blues to glory 19 years after his Goldington Road debut. His fitness, strength, skill and determination shone through on that spring day in what was a culmination of a wonderful club career for Bedford Blues's most famous player. Peter West, an old-school rugby enthusiast writing in *The Times*, was fulsome in his praise for the two teams: 'Bedford and Rosslyn Park produced a final at Twickenham on Saturday that did the game and the knockout competition proud.'

In the following Monday's *Guardian*, under the banner headline 'Twickenham enjoys return to chivalry', David Frost wrote: 'Bedford and Rosslyn Park brought Twickenham and the national knockout cup competition to life on Saturday with a captivating display of non-stop, aggressive, creative rugby much to the liking of the happy, short-sleeved crowd.'

The Bedford club produced a glossy souvenir booklet to mark the 1975 triumph in which Budge reflects on the final: 'Winning the KO Cup was, I think, my most thrilling and satisfying day in rugby. It was different to other high spots in my career because there had been a progressive build-up to the final ... the whole squad had put so much into the previous rounds and then in the final produced a truly magnificent game ... the win was special.'

In his book *Writing in the Field*, Victor Head described Budge as that 'tireless fox' who steered Bedford to an emphatic victory at the scene of so many of his memorable moments. Rogers may have harboured sceptical thoughts about the cup competition in the early days, but surely after this match he would now embrace the highs and lows of cup rugby and the pleasure it brought to thousands of fans across the country. Budge has spoken out against any form of league rugby and continues to express his belief that players should enjoy a hard-fought game of rugby even if they find themselves on the losing side – winning isn't everything. But the national cup belonged to Bedford and how he would have relished the occasion. The Blues fans down the years had enjoyed some wonderful moments: a win against the Barbarians, welcoming the All Blacks to Goldington Road, winning the English-Welsh Pennant and now they had the biggest club rugby prize of all. The final against Rosslyn Park even surpassed the heady days of 1939. Ex-Bedford player Rick Chadwick has a clear memory of Budge's performance in Bedford's historic cup run: 'Budge was a warrior, the Martin Johnson of his day. He had the ability to keep us in the game against top clubs like Rosslyn Park. Compromise was not in his vocabulary.'

Chadwick, who made over 100 appearances for Bedford, is clearly still full of admiration for Rogers. He continued: 'We took a battering in the first half but only conceded one try ... the job Budge did on Andy Ripley was phenomenal. His half-time team talk was basically, "We've got 'em – play rugby and hit them hard now."'

Gareth Davies, president of the club for the past 12 years, recalls his friend's exploits on that glorious day at Twickenham: 'That day, he led by fearless example and demanded that everyone followed – and they did. Budge had the ability to sniff blood and sensed when we had opponents on the ropes. We saw this so many times and the cup final was a perfect example.'

Despite this strong winning mentality, Rogers was always a great champion of fair play and was as gracious in victory as he was in defeat. His friends remember he had no time for cheats or thugs in sport. Rogers displayed all these great sporting qualities that day at Twickenham in April 1975.

While the fans made their happy return to Bedford, the team began their own post-match celebrations. The Blues's skipper had booked Franks restaurant in Jermyn Street, where the players had a joyous evening paid for out of their own pockets – this was 1975, after all. Later that year Bedford, as champions of England, travelled down to play the Welsh champions Llanelli. The match was also the occasion for the switching on of the Llanelli club's new floodlights by the great Phil Bennett. Gareth Davies drove down to South Wales for the match while Rick Chadwick travelled with the rest of the team by train, which involved a complicated journey via Paddington Station. A match between these two clubs on a Saturday afternoon was bound to involve a degree of drinking, which was fine for those travelling back on the train. For drivers like Gareth Davies, a late-night dash back to Bedford after a modest couple of pints seemed like a good plan. The local traffic police thought otherwise, although after hearing the players had played in the match against Llanelli and met Phil Bennett the day before, the officer simply said: 'Fair enough boys. Be on your way now – but be careful, mind.'

In 2014, the club organised a reunion at the House of Commons for the victorious cup-winning team. There were 90 people packed into the room to greet the winning captain. Budge graced the occasion with a wonderful speech, showing all the ambassadorial qualities that were to serve him so well in the years to come.

Rick Chadwick recalls: 'He could always find the right words for any occasion and always articulated his thoughts with great dignity, as befits a great man.'

Pat Briggs remembers another occasion when Budge's forgetfulness got him into hot water: 'After Budge retired, he loved to entertain his friends in the West car park at Twickenham before England matches. On one occasion, he had forgotten his pass and an officious car park attendant refused to let him in. "I don't care who you are – you haven't got a pass." Budge being Budge, he was eventually allowed in.'

This would never happen in Wales, where Budge was adored by the rugby-loving and highly knowledgeable Welsh fans. 'Hiya Budgie, come on in boyo, we'll take care of you,' was the usual response to the Englishman's appearance at the Arms Park.

The cup final of 1975 marked the beginning of the end of Rogers's career. A couple of years later, when his playing days were over, he was not short of interesting things to occupy his time. In September 1976, Budge was invited to open Malvern Rugby Club's splendid new clubhouse and took the Public School Wanderers to Malvern to mark the occasion. Three years later, Budge was invited to the centenary celebrations of the Worcestershire club.

In 1978, an interesting offer came from the BBC inviting Budge to compete in their *Past Masters* TV programme. This was not an exhibition of priceless paintings but a competition in which recently retired figures from a variety of sports were invited to compete against each other for the title of 'Past Master of Sport'. After some thought, Budge accepted the offer and joined a distinguished group that included World Cup winner Bobby Charlton, diver Brian Phelps, legendary footballer John Charles, England cricketer Brian Close and Olympic gold medallist Lynn Davies. Budge had always been an outstanding athlete and was confident of at least holding his own in such formidable company. True to his competitive nature Budge came third in the event, a testimony to his enduring fitness. The BBC event was an enjoyable diversion after his career in top-class rugby and a world away from that tense, but ultimately glorious day at Twickenham in 1975.

The teams for the unforgettable game at Twickenham were:

Bedford: Jordan, Demming, Howard, Chadwick, Wyatt, Bennett, Lewis, Keen, Barker, Bailward, Hooker, Wilkinson, Edwards, Hollins, Rogers (c)

Rosslyn Park: Codd, Fisher, Saville, Bazalgette, McKay, Treseder, Weston, Barlow, Keith-Roach (c), Hinton, Rogers, Mantell, Anderson, Ripley, Link

Chapter 5

The perfect 7

AT this stage, it is worth examining the position Rogers played in throughout his rugby career. In recent years the open-side flanker has worn the No. 7 shirt, but it was not always the case. Match programme notes from Rogers's school and club matches show him wearing No. 15, but he definitely operated like a modern No. 7. Similarly, the full-back has not always worn the No. 15 shirt, but today we can safely say that the possessor of the No. 7 shirt is the open-side flanker. With that little piece of rugby pedantry out of the way, what are we to make of the job, whatever the number?

Stephen Jones, the *Sunday Times* rugby correspondent, likened the role of the open-side flanker to 'one who gets his nose over the ball like a truffle pig'. Others have described flankers as scavengers feasting on any scraps they can find. Open-side flankers should be quick and first to the ball at the breakdown, ready to clear up any loose play by the backs.

Budge Rogers is generally regarded as one of the greatest open-sides the English game has ever produced and a model for his position. Before we look further at the role of the No. 7, it might be helpful to identify the essential qualities necessary for an effective open-side.

In an article in *The Independent*, England rugby coach Eddie Jones expressed very clear views on what he expects of his open-side flanker: 'If you look at rugby around the world, and particularly Test rugby, you need to have someone who is consistently good at slowing down opposition ball. A No. 7's primary job is to ensure that when you're in possession, you get quick ball from the first ruck.'

Warming to his theme, the Australian continued: 'When the opposition have it, you make it slow. Then the really good 7s – David Pocock and Richie McCaw, George Smith and Sam Cane – see other opportunities to slow it. We have to pick a bloke who, at the moment, can do that primary first-phase job.'

There is little doubt that Budge Rogers was such a 'bloke'. Outstanding flankers, we might argue, have the fewest responsibilities of any player on the pitch, but should have the skills and qualities of every position. In the modern game, it is a position that demands quick and accurate decisions because bad ones can lead to penalties and even yellow cards. Since most of the back play is usually on the open side, where there is more space, it is the No. 7's job to be the first to any breakdown or loose ball. The essential attributes for the position are courage, speed, strength, fitness, tackling ability and handling skills, all of which Rogers had in abundance. Like the best flankers, he was always involved in the game, winning the ball in open play and joining in attack. Rogers would often linger just behind the backs, ready to provide support and pick up any loose ball to begin a new phase of play. The very best teams in the modern game prefer a quick open-side with the ability to get off the scrum quickly and get to the ball.

Writing in *The Times* in November 2015, under the banner headline 'Great English No. 7s', rugby correspondent Owen Slot asked the question: 'Does the perfect No. 7 exist in England?' Slot's article was written after the 2015 Rugby World Cup and we can guess the answer to his question. It is never a very productive exercise trying to compare players from different generations, but given Rogers's record we can assume the former England captain would have excelled in today's professional game. He may have been one of the last players in English rugby to possess the qualities of the perfect open-side, alongside Neary, Winterbottom and Neil Back. Slot does find his ideal No.7 in an unlikely place. He rates Wasps's George Smith as one of the greats of the 21st century, perhaps the greatest in the professional period, up there with McCaw and Pocock.

It is no coincidence that all these great No. 7s learned their rugby in the Southern Hemisphere, where there is much more emphasis on quick ball and running rugby. In his article, Slot gives us George Smith's assessment of what makes an ideal open-side: '[He must be] dynamic, a nuisance around the breakdown ... good timing [and] correct body position are all important features of what makes an ideal No. 7.'

In the 2016 World Cup, Australia's specialist No. 7s Pocock and Michael Hooper had a decisive impact on the tournament and blew England out of the water at the breakdown. Smith cannot pinpoint a reason for the dearth of Northern Hemisphere flankers possessing the qualities demonstrated by Pocock and Hooper. Is it the European weather? The great Australian accepts that conditions do have an influence on a team's style of play and should be factored into a team's style of play. He says: 'With the rain and wet conditions, possession is really important, not forcing the pass. We have a game trying to play expansive, but sometimes that doesn't work.'

This pragmatic view on tactical thinking is persuasive, given mid-winter conditions in northern Europe. But if Smith believes weather conditions should influence tactics, he does not believe that a bitterly cold, muddy and windy playing environment have a significant influence on developing the skills of an open-side flanker: 'I wouldn't say that one country produces certain types of players. I'd say it comes down to the individual in harnessing their skills. When I was growing up, I had that natural ability to try and steal the ball and try and be quick to a breakdown. That was just ingrained in me from a young age ... it was instinctive what I turned out doing.'

So for one of the greatest open-sides in modern rugby, what makes an ideal No. 7 is 'natural ability' and an instinctive understanding of the role. The peerless Wallaby clearly has little time for over-coaching or complex technical advice, although he does rather give it away when he says things were 'instilled in him from an early age'. For Smith, the secret was to watch better players and learn from them. This very much sits with Budge Rogers's assertion that he received no formal coaching or technical help in his younger days – players were encouraged to think for themselves. There was simply no coaching available when his game was developing, either at club or international level. But given that most international sides today are overwhelmed with tracksuited, laptop-toting back-up staff, George Smith's view on how players should develop their game is illuminating.

The views of Rogers and Smith on the qualities needed to become a first-rate flanker are of little help to the aspiring young No. 7 if it all comes down to natural ability and instinct. Both Eddie Jones and George Smith are being a little disingenuous here. Just before the England squad assembled for the 2016 Six Nations championship, Jones invited Smith to join his camp to work with James Haskell and Chris Robshaw on the defensive breakdown. Smith worked through some drills but more importantly advised the loose forwards to 'rip up the textbook'. For Smith, England needed to change their whole approach. Paul Gustard, the England defensive coach, remarked on Smith's thinking: 'He wasn't thinking like an Anglo-Saxon, where you try to build a process around making the tackle, getting to your feet and getting over the ball.'

Haskell and Robshaw were told to 'get the ball', with the tackle only a part of the process. The Aussie was keen to break down the regimented mindset of 'tackle-feet-compete' outlined by Gustard. Smith's brief was to make English loose forwards as effective and efficient as possible at the breakdown. In an illuminating article in the *The Times* in March 2016, Alex Lowe quotes Smith as saying he is not trying to turn Haskell into David Pocock overnight: 'Not every player will be the same body type or body composition ... it is all about working and improving things within their strength.'

Rogers knew his job inside out and thought about every aspect of his role as England's open-side. Eddie Jones and George Smith may say that you can't teach people to be great players, but they can be helped to think about their role more clearly and consider how things like body position and body shape help them to win the ball, just as they can in soccer, with players being encouraged to 'get on the half-turn'.

What made Rogers and Smith great open-sides was their passion for the role, a strong desire to be at the heart of every facet of play, quickness of thought and speed of reaction. Fitness and energy are essentials. While Rogers was playing, he was as fit as anyone in the game. Natural ability and instinct are givens. These are highly exceptional, once-in-a-decade elite performers who have the ability at the highest level to make a significant difference to their team's results, time after time. The distinguished rugby journalist Stephen Jones said George Smith 'seemed to know where every ball would pitch ... he knows where every breakdown is likely to occur ... he is an arrow, with a magnet on its tip.'

Jones's description fits Rogers perfectly. In addition to Smith, Richie McCaw and Rogers, Jones picks out the great England flanker of the 1980s, Tony Neary, as an outstanding No. 7. In the opinion of most judges, the Liverpool University graduate was one of the best post-war wing-forwards. Neary toured with the British Lions on two occasions but never had the kind of success on tour he had with England. Arguably the greatest moment in the career of Rogers's successor was the match against Scotland at Murrayfield, where Bill Beaumont's England won the grand slam. It was a fitting end to a great career.

There were many similarities between Rogers and Neary. Both had an uncanny knack of being exactly where the ball was and both kept their place in the England side when the selectors were at their most capricious. Neary was a worthy successor to Rogers in the England open-side role and his example did much to inspire his successors Winterbottom and Back. The modern open-sides are heavier and stronger than their predecessors but perhaps lack the same level of agility and speed over the ball. As the game has changed, positional roles and responsibilities have changed with them. Budge Rogers was one of the all-time greats in this key position, feared by opponents in every rugby-playing country in the world.

What precisely made Rogers such an effective No. 7 in the 1960s and 1970s? Budge has thought about this question recently. He believes the first ingredient was his level of fitness. He trained so hard and with such commitment that his level of fitness became a model for others – for Budge, fitness simply meant being able to run hard for the whole 80 minutes of a match. The idea of fitness incorporating upper body strengthening and bodybuilding was some years away.

Budge's level of fitness enabled him to track the ball all over the field – a vital strength for a world-class No. 7. Match reports of the day would describe the Bedford man's performance as 'ubiquitous'. In other words, Rogers was all over the pitch. He would go into a tackle on a fly-half and be on his feet in the same movement. His running at speed made him a vital link when a winger needed to pass back inside, and despite being a weak handler in his early days he created many tries for his teammates at both club and international level. A vivid demonstration of Budge's fitness came when he was the one player up with Andy Hancock when the latter scored his famous try in the dying seconds of the 1965 match against Scotland. No other player could have stayed with Hancock.

Another quality that brought Rogers to the notice of the England selectors early in his career was his tackling, which was as effective sideways on as it was head on, or from behind. His tackling ability and competitiveness was developed initially in the under-13 side at Bedford School, when the rugby master awarded Rogers five stars for, among other things, tackling. Budge's teammates remember how pleased they were to hear the shout 'mine' when a centre was coming on to a crash ball. Rugby reporter Victor Head offers this delightful account of the Bedford and England No. 7: 'He possesses an uncanny prescience which enables him to move to the scene of vital activity. Yet his approach is imperceptible, phantom-like. At one moment he is battling for a line-out ball, seconds later he is in the van of a footrush, only to bob up at the other side of the field to provide an extra man in a passing movement.'

A further attribute that marked out Rogers for greatness was how he perfected the art of charging down kicks by diving at the boot about to kick the ball, rather than jumping upwards hoping to get a block. Budge scored many tries using this tactic. Bob Hiller recalls how he faced Rogers for the first time in a match for Harlequins against Bedford at Twickenham. Budge charged down Hiller's first two clearance kicks, creating a try for himself and one for a teammate, Tony Lewin. The Bedford flanker began to gain a reputation as a charge-down specialist. One of the most delightful items in one of Budge's scrapbooks is a handwritten letter from young Oxford University student, Nick Silk, asking Budge if he could explain the techniques involved. Budge was happy to reply but neither he nor Silk could have imagined at the time that within a few seasons they would be playing together in the England team.

Finally, Budge was hugely effective at the loose ball. His sheer disregard for his own safety meant that he allowed his team to secure possession time after time. Superb fitness, immense personal courage, speed of thought and action were all qualities that made Rogers the complete No. 7. He was also able to modify his game when the laws were changed. In 1965, when an ankle injury kept Rogers out of action for six weeks, his place in the side was a concern – but not simply because of injury.

Victor Head wrote at the time: 'Budge's reputation was largely that of a destroyer of opposing half-backs. Swift as a cat, with a shattering tackle, when he detached himself from the scrum a half-back had to be very quick indeed to get his pass away. The new laws were designed to revive open play and break the throttlehold that wing forwards had on the game.'

Rogers was quick to adapt his game and borrow from the All Blacks style of forward play, in which 'the big men run and handle like three-quarters'. Budge, said Head, had been one of the few home players who could emulate their example.

Chapter 6

From leather balls to laptops

I N Budge Rogers's time, rugby was forced to confront the reality of modern sport. We have seen how the game became enmeshed in politics in the case of apartheid, but in addition to external pressures the game faced its own internal problems. In the 1970s, a tension arose between those who believed in preserving the old amateur values and a younger generation whose heads were turned by the temptations available in other sports. But professionalism was just one issue facing rugby union during this time. Throughout its remarkable history, this noble sport has been beset by violent and over-aggressive play – not a convincing image for potential sponsors. We saw in Chapter 3 how laws favouring defensive play promoted endless kicking, leading to negative rugby and dull matches. Poor pitches and slippery leather balls also did their bit to diminish the sport as a spectacle. Fran Cotton emerging out of the fog covered from head to toe in mud in the old amateur days is a less appealing image to commercial sponsors than the brilliance of Maro Itoje or Owen Farrell.

If we believe the match reports and the views of commentators at the time, violent play had reached unacceptable proportions and controversy on the pitch often involved the touring All Blacks. The infamous Meads was sent off in the match against Scotland at Murrayfield in 1963 and continued to provide the rugby reporters with tasty headlines. On the 1967 tour, Meads punched Clive Rowlands in front of 80,000 fiercely patriotic Welsh supporters at Cardiff Arms Park. The unrepentant Kiwi, in defiant mood, complained after the game: 'I didn't punch the wee man. What happened was Clive was yakking and kicking the ball. Wales had bugger-all backs in those days – they kicked it all day. Our man put up an up-and-under and I had a five-yard start. Clive was under it and I got the little bastard. Ran right over the bloody top of him. He put on a good act. Eighty thousand people booed me and all I did was kneed him up the arse – god, the memories are good.'

The visit of South Africa in 1960/61 produced matches of extreme 'rough housing and thuggery' as much from the home side as the touring Springboks. In 1962, the centre and sometime test pilot Roux broke the jaw of fly-half Richard Sharp in a head-high tackle and in the 1974 Lions tour to South Africa the phrase 'get our retaliation in first' was attributed to the Springbok centre. Chris Laidlaw later described the intimidating approach of the All Blacks of 1963 and 1964: 'If an opponent begins to win too much possession at the line-out, for instance, he is thumped, sometimes by his marker, sometimes not … any member of the opposition who deliberately sets out to spoil All Blacks possession in ruck or maul, by fair or foul means, is summarily dealt with by knee, elbow or fist.'

On the issue of violent play, Rogers is typically forthright: 'There is no question that rugby was always, and is even more so since the professional era, a physical game and there has always been a tenuous link between physicality and violence. In my experience, with one or two exceptions in the games I played in, violent behaviour was the province of a very small number of people. These were predominantly from the front-five forwards, who were the players with the greatest physical contact with their opposite numbers at the scrum and line-out – these are the players who might resort to foul means.

As Rogers says, everyone knew who the guilty ones were and most were adamant that there should be no place for them in the game. Violent types were often slightly inadequate players who resorted to cheating to disguise their shortcomings. Having said that, any player can be provoked, as Budge remembers: 'Anyone can be provoked viz., my punching Waka Nathan. I regretted it the moment I realised the extent of the damage. In those days, referees often had very difficult afternoons. Today, we have yellow and red cards, touch judges, and TMOs [television match officials] to support the referee.'

Rugby, by its very nature, is a highly physical game. Muscle-bound packs need sufficient strength to batter their way across the gain line. Hulking ball-carriers have always invited heavy tackles bordering on the illegal. In this sense, rugby has nothing to apologise for. Physical force is simply part of the game and players will overstep the mark, as they do in most sports. At the elite level, players will endeavour to achieve those small gains that mean the difference between victory and defeat. The laws of the game have evolved to protect all that's good in rugby from its worst excesses. In 1968, kicking into touch outside the 25 was outlawed. In 1971, points for a try were increased to four and then five points in 1992. A goal from a mark was made invalid in 1976 and in an attempt to encourage youngsters into the game mini-rugby was introduced in the early 1970s. More recently, increasing awareness of the dangers of head injuries has led to new laws regarding tackling. Over-aggressive, violent play is slowly being legislated out of the game.

Towards the end of Rogers's playing career and during his time as chairman of selectors, arguably the most persistent issue was the inexorable march towards 'open' rugby, which dwarfed concerns about off-the-ball punches and dodgy pitches. In his foreword to the 1970/71 *Playfair Annual*, Bill Ramsey, then president of the RFU, wrote: 'The game has grown immeasurably; many countries now play it and are desperately keen to expand their horizons. TV has brought a new dimension; millions, who had never seen a game, now watch the international matches with growing enthusiasm.'

Here, Ramsey is clearly aware of the pressures building on amateur rugby, although he is quick to defend the commitment of amateur players: 'No player in any commercialised professional sport could be induced for financial gain to play any harder than does the rugby footballer for the pride of representing his country.'

Despite Ramsey's stout defence of the old values, in the 1980s the mood at the top levels of the game began to change dramatically. In the 1960s, it goes without saying that top rugby players played all their matches in their own boots. Rogers always wore a pair of handmade boots crafted by Wimbledon bootmakers GT Law. Budge has retained an invoice (dated 3 January 1962) addressed to his home at the King William for a pair of 'rugby boots', at the handsome price of £5 ten shillings. A real craftsman, Mr Law would trace the outline of the foot on a piece of brown paper, from which he would make a last for individual players. Unfortunately, the company's business suffered when Adidas and Puma, through their agent, the former international athlete Robbie Brightwell, offered the England team free branded boots. The days of the handmade boot were more or less over at that point. Rogers maintains that the Adidas boots were of inferior quality and he continued to play in his handmade pair until the firm went out of business. Later, Budge's colleague, the Devonian Mike Davis, said that he couldn't afford rugby boots so he bought a pair of much cheaper football boots and dyed them black.

Adidas and others, particularly through the insatiable demands of TV, had gained a foot in the door and nothing was ever going to be the same again. When rugby union finally became fully professional in the 1990s, Rogers believes that the authorities may have missed an opportunity from the start: 'There is little doubt that professionalism has brought about the most dramatic changes in the game that we have seen or will ever see, and was a huge challenge to the game's rulers. The RFU was slow off the mark as far as players' contracts were concerned. This allowed the clubs to quickly put the top players under contract, which in turn led to problems with the management of players, culminating in the threatened players' strike in 2000.'

There is no question that the players' strike was an embarrassment to the RFU and it is an issue covered elsewhere in the book. In any case, the crisis of 2000 was short lived and Rogers rightly prefers to focus on the more positive aspects of the advent of fully open rugby. The most important is the improvement in players' fitness and the way coaches prepare their teams for games.

Rogers's views on the issue are clear: 'Although club and international teams have employed coaches since the early 1970s, their influence was limited by players only being available in the evenings due to work commitments. Once players became full time, a wholly different regime emerged with daily training and practice led by specialist coaches for the forwards, defence and backs. More recently, kicking coaches, line-out specialists and sports psychologists have swelled the coaching staff at the elite level.

The recent obsession with physicality has been imported from American pro-football, so much so that international rugby players are on average four stone heavier than those in Budge's time. Despite this apparent 'bulking up', they are also fitter and faster than at any time in the history of the game, and playing under tremendous pressure to win. Rogers says: 'It is vital for top clubs to remain in the Premier League and few can achieve this without wealthy owners. Within the professional game, there is more time for coaches to develop tactics and a more strategic approach than Mike Davis ever enjoyed. There is a danger, though, with the stakes so high in the modern game, that coaches often resort to a 'not losing' approach, particularly with the big clubs in the hands of rich backers.

Of course, international teams have benefitted from having fitter, better-prepared players. Coaches have teams of experts at their disposal in squad sessions, complete with data analysis to monitor individual performances on the field of play. But the sheer size of the players and the physical intensity of the professional game are bringing their own problems and an increasing number of impact injuries, with concussion becoming a real problem. Rogers argues: 'Some major changes to the laws of the game are required and we need a means to differentiate between the elite echelon and the non-professional and school-age players.'

With so many years in the game as a record-breaking international and high-ranking administrator, Rogers remains passionate about rugby and concerned for its future. His thoughts on the impact of the laws on negative styles of play, rugby's problems with violence and aggression, and the advance of professionalism help us to understand more fully the development of the game over the past 50 years. Rogers's thoughts on the thorny issue of the laws are particularly interesting. He believes that the many law changes introduced since the beginning of the professional game were designed to make rugby more of a spectacle for TV, rather than in the pure interests of rugby itself.

Rogers argues: 'For all the TMR [television mobile resources] etc., the authorities turn a blind eye to definite breaches of the written law. For example, the law says that the ball shall go into the scrum midway between the front rows. In my view, if this law was refereed to the letter it would improve the scrum.'

Budge tells an interesting story that highlights the problem of the scrum. When a former president of the RFU asked two England under-20 props, who had just won the World Cup, what they saw as the purpose of the scrum, they answered quickly: 'To get a penalty.' Enough said. But the world of senior executives and charismatic coaches comes at a high price. Rogers believes that today's players and coaches are 'too frightened of making mistakes and are too conservative – European players do not play with their heads up as do the All Blacks, for example.'

Perhaps the most fundamental change in the game of rugby is not the law, or the highly paid players and wealthy owners, but the fact that it has abandoned the values promoted so strongly by Ramsey, Rogers and others in the 1960s and before. The game has progressed far beyond the ethics of *Tom Brown's Schooldays*. Today, at elite club level, there are CEOs, executive boxes, and European rugby. At international level, there are lucrative players' contracts, heavy playing schedules, top international coaches and instantly available TV replays. Over-aggressive and blatantly violent play will be picked up by TV and off-field judges supporting pressurised referees. In the 1980s and 1990s, rugby was forced to respond to the brave new world of professional sport. It was a time of rapid change and at various stages of his career Budge Rogers was at the heart of the action.

From the beginning, professional rugby attracted money and lots of it – money for players, coaches, officials, clubs and the RFU. Huge amounts of cash came from commercial sponsors, wealthy individuals and through ticket sales. The extent of the change in the financial state of rugby union since the game went professional is dramatically illustrated by the following figures. In 1971, with a total of four staff, the turnover of the RFU was £100,000. By 2016, staffing levels had increased to 400, while turnover had grown to a staggering £200m. As a man driven by a deep passion for his sport, Rogers has mixed feelings about this revolution in rugby's finances: 'My hope is that the traditions and camaraderie which have been an integral part of the game for 145 years will not be subsumed under a mountain of cash. But we shouldn't forget there are thousands of young men and women who continue to play simply for fun and for the sheer love of the game.'

Chapter 7

On tour

TOURING is a central part of an international rugby player's life. Top players travel the world in comfort, stay in the best hotels and play in some of the most iconic stadiums in sport. Budge Rogers certainly did his share of touring. As a player there were trips to Australia, New Zealand, America and the Far East with England, and South Africa with the British Lions and the Barbarians. Following his retirement, Rogers toured Canada as manager for the England under-23s and Japan with the senior team.

But it is as a player that he recalls overseas excursions with most affection. If the overseas tour is the more exotic feature of an international rugby player's life, the Baa-Baas's traditional Easter tour of Wales, of which all Barbarians will have fond, if often sketchy memories, was a vital part of the rugby calendar.

Budge has selected the following two tour matches among his most memorable: the British Lions against South Africa in 1962 and England against New Zealand in 1963. But before we look at these stand-out games more closely, this section provides the opportunity to reflect on the circumstances surrounding some of the more controversial tours, apartheid in South Africa being the most obvious example. Last but not least, no section on touring in a book on rugby would be complete without the traditional stories – or at least, those fit to publish.

But we begin with one of Budge's best-remembered matches – the final Test against the Springboks on the British Lions tour to South Africa in 1962. The Lions resumed their touring programme in 1950 after a 12-year break, enjoying moderately successful tours of New Zealand, Australia and South Africa. The 1955 tour to South Africa was a relative success, with two wins and two defeats in a drawn series. Four years later, in 1959, the Lions travelled to New Zealand to face the mighty All Blacks in a four-match series. Three narrow defeats followed by a 9-6 victory in the final Test meant the party returned home in good spirits with their pride intact.

Despite his natural modesty, Rogers would have been aware that the party for the 1962 Lions tour to South Africa would be announced in March that year and that his name might be on the list. As the day approached, the locals at the King William pub and friends down at Goldington Road waited with keen anticipation. The letter from the Lions tour's committee was just as eagerly awaited as the notification of Rogers's first England cap in this rugby-loving town. Nobody was surprised when the letter from Lions secretary CW Wilton arrived at the pub on 28 March. This time the letter, marked 'Confidential', arrived before the touring party to South Africa was released to the press. The letter invited those selected to assemble in Eastbourne on 13 May for departure to South Africa. The party were due to return to the UK on 30 August. An exciting but long and arduous adventure lay ahead for the cream of British rugby. The Lions party included England teammates John Willcox, John Dee, Mike Weston, Dickie Jeeps, Richard Sharp, Herbert Godwin, Sam Hodgson and Peter Wright, all names very familiar to Rogers. Willie-John McBride, Mike Campbell-Lamerton, Syd Millar and Keith Rowlands provided the uncomplicated strength and weight the selectors believed would be needed for the challenge ahead.

Preparations for the tour kicked off in typical style with a pre-departure dinner for players, officials and staff from the South

African Embassy at the Washington Hotel in Curzon Street. Rogers shared a table with Dai Jones, Alan Pask, McBride, David Nash, David Rollo, Rowlands and Mr Clement of the Welsh Rugby Union. He would have felt at home in this company and enjoyed the Saumon Fumeé, Sole Cleopatra and Les Champignons on offer that evening. Back home in the King William, the congratulatory letters and telegrams duly arrived. One message urged Rogers to rest his troublesome shoulder prior to the tour, but perhaps the most interesting letter bore an Edinburgh postmark.

The new Lions captain Arthur Smith wrote to Budge warning him about the playing conditions and recommending he rest over the weeks leading up to the tour. Smith finished his letter with the words: 'I look forward to seeing you in Eastbourne, if not before, and in the meantime I would like to wish you all the best and hope that personally you have a very good tour.'

Smith was an interesting character. The Scotland winger broke the mould of the Irish monopoly of the Lions captaincy. An academic high-flyer with a first in mathematics from Glasgow University and a PhD from Cambridge, Smith had an ice-cool rugby brain, was familiar with playing conditions in South Africa and was an ideal choice as captain. The Lions skipper would need to call on all his impressive leadership skills in what was to become a very difficult tour. Rogers had every confidence in his captain: 'We didn't have a coach, just the manager Brian Vaughan, our captain Arthur Smith and Harry McGibbon. Arthur was a wonderful man as well as a great wing, and he and Dickie Jeeps ran the playing side.'

Budge's selection for the British Lions, one of the many highlights of his career, came when he was still in his early 20s. This exceptional young man was living at home with his parents, training and playing for Bedford, representing his country, while holding down a full-time job and college course. This was a hectic schedule even for this young, fit and enthusiastic amateur rugby player. Today's full-time, cosseted professionals would do well to study the life of one of the greatest England players of his generation. Budge illustrates the point well: 'I was training as an engineer in

Bedford and was given unpaid leave for nearly four months, but we hardly needed the £3-10-0 a week allowance we were given on tour.'

Rogers was naturally excited about the prospect of touring with the British Lions. The 1962 tour to South Africa would give him the opportunity to play with some of the best players from the Five Nations matches – something that was bound to improve his game. The Bedford boy had a further reason to be excited by his selection. Prior to the tour, Budge had never been further abroad than France.

He said: 'I hadn't been on a long-haul flight before and I was interested in planes. It was pretty amazing to be in a Comet. We had a fuel stop in Khartoum and walked into a wall of heat, and then later the pilot let me and Richard Sharp into the cockpit for the landing at Salisbury.'

When the party eventually arrived, Budge could be relied upon to be a model sportsman: intelligent, well-mannered and a good tourist. Prior to leaving, players were advised to avoid engaging in political controversy, of which there would be plenty. Rogers was less concerned about events off the field over which he had no control and was keen to focus fully on his role in the squad. He realised he would need to step up the attacking part of his game to compete with the other flankers on the trip. He was desperately keen to do this and knew full well that the traditional 'death to the fly-half' mentality might not be enough against world-class opposition. His laudable desire to improve the attacking part of his game would have impressed the tour management. All the backs were aware how difficult all the tour matches would be and of the necessity to make the most of their chances. One of the things Budge loved most about being on tour was that the players were living the life of professional sportsmen.

He recalls: 'It was the first time we could give as much time to the game as needed. So, if you loved training like I did, it was great – and I was always checking to see if I beat Haydn Morgan, my fellow flanker, in the sprints.'

The 1962 tour to South Africa presented a huge challenge for the Lions. The tour was complicated by the politics of the host country.

Clearly, this is not the place for a detailed analysis of apartheid and sport, which is well documented elsewhere, but a biography of one of the greatest rugby players of the 1960s and 1970s cannot avoid some discussion of the political quicksand of racism and South Africa. At this time, multiracial sport was forbidden by the government, which meant that visiting teams could only tour South Africa with all white players. New Zealand was the first country to boycott South Africa and other countries followed, some with extreme reluctance. Macmillan's 1968 'wind of change' speech and the D'Oliveira affair of 1968/69 led to a more unified approach to South Africa by the wider international community. The 1977 Gleneagles Agreement codified the international challenge to apartheid and served to further isolate sport in South Africa.

The relationship between apartheid and rugby was complex. There is no question that the issue divided the rugby community, producing the greatest schism in the game since the split in codes, and more recently, professionalism. Some officials, commentators and players hid their heads deeply in the sand, hoping that the whole thing might go away, while other, more outspoken individuals supported the anti-apartheid movement. It was not until after the Soweto riots in 1976 that Danie Craven finally accepted the call for change, leading the South African government to reluctantly accept that discrimination was wrong and should be ended.

One of the most outspoken opponents of segregation was former All Black and New Zealand Labour MP Chris Laidlaw, who became impatient with the sheer arrogance of the South African Rugby Union and its apologists. Laidlaw lamented the 'tragic failure of rugby to come to grips with the problem of racism in South Africa'. He added: 'The emerging reputation of the rugby player throughout the Anglo-Saxon world as an outdated, boorish oaf ... was given a new dimension by the quarrels over apartheid in sport... it has dealt rugby a vicious blow from which it may never recover.'

In 1962, most young international rugby players knew little of the links between politics and sport. David Perry, Rogers's teammate at Bedford and England, argued that the rugby authorities should have been aware of the situation in South Africa. Mistakes were made that could have been avoided. This is not to excuse the RFU but, as Perry pointed out, the RFU, like the players, were all amateurs. Most would have abhorred segregation and injustice but were keen to tour and believed politics should be kept out of their game.

Perry said: 'Players today are fully briefed on all issues related to touring. Just look at the 2016 England cricket tour to Bangladesh – the players were briefed and given a choice. That would not have happened back when we were playing.'

There was an attempt to prepare the players for the controversial trip. Rogers remembers pre-tour talks from Archbishop Trevor Huddlestone and RFU officials setting out what the players could expect. Teammate Bill Mulcahy has clear memories of these meetings: 'We had some sort of briefing from an embassy individual before we left about the situation in South Africa. I asked him about some South African fella who'd written a book about his mixed-race marriage and how he had to leave the country.'

On the 1962 tour, the players were carefully managed and chaperoned away from witnessing the more obvious and insidious effects of racism in the places they visited. It would have been difficult for a young man in his early 20s to come to terms with this complex and troubled country. Fifty years ago, international sportsmen were not subject to the constant media glare of today. Indeed the players could often count sports journalists among their friends.

When journalists travel on the same team bus, they are likely to develop friendly relationships with players and officials. 'What goes on tour stays on tour' was the unwritten rule. Whatever the outcome of matches, there was not the public exposure we have become used to today and the players were not normally asked for their opinion on matters relating to the local political situation. Reflecting on the tour to South Africa over 50 years later, Budge said recently: 'The situation in South Africa was the only time that politics became an issue.' The argument was: did sporting links with

South Africa accelerate the path to freedom or not? All Five Nations countries, not just England, backed the Lions tours during apartheid in the belief that it was good to maintain the links. History will be the judge.

As a tourist, Rogers remembers four distinct groups of people in South Africa: Afrikaans, who owned the farms; the wealthy white British, who owned and ran industry and commerce; black South Africans, who worked in the mines, in service and were the majority population; and the Indian people, who ran small businesses and shops. This is, of course, a generalisation, but it is how many people viewed South Africa at that time. The Lions tour party were wined and dined by the rich white urban elite. 'They all had black servants,' recalls Rogers. 'I felt they seemed a little cynical – I felt like we were trophy guests.' On the other hand, the Afrikaans were much more reserved.

Budge remembers: 'Some Afrikaan farmers drove us out to their farm to shoot springbok and hardly said a word on the journey. We thought, "this is going to be a long day". But once we had shot and they saw we were thoroughly enjoying ourselves, they relaxed and we found them much more genuine people.'

On one occasion, the touring party were taken out to the 'big hole' diamond mine owned by the de Beers family – a massive hole in the ground where thousands of tons of earth were dug, crushed and run through an angled bed of soft plastic. The diamonds simply stuck on the plastic while the waste material ran through. The Lions players were mesmerised by the whole process.

These were wonderful experiences for the Lions party and ones that lived long in the memory. As we will see towards the end of this book, friendships forged on tour were at the heart of what the game meant to Rogers and others like him. It is natural that he would feel this way and most players believed that changing political systems were outside a rugby player's sphere of influence. This doesn't mean they didn't have strong views on the difference between right and wrong. With all that said, the tourists had a job to do on the pitch against one of the strongest rugby teams they would ever face.

With one eye on the Barbarians's victory over the Springboks in 1961, when the tourists lost their last match of the tour, former naval commander Vaughan decided a huge pack that included Syd Millar, Keith Rowlands, Mike Campbell-Lamerton and Bill Mulcahy would provide the Lions with the best chance of victory. This was thought to be the most effective way of coping with both the strength and guile of the Springboks. The Lions, of course, built their game on the traditional virtues of the set piece – you got the impression that the Lions pack would have been happy if their backs hadn't touched the ball for the whole tour. As Rogers remembers: 'There was far more loose ball in those days and players were less skilled, and this played into the hands of the more physical teams.' Vaughan had a strong core of touring experience as the basis of his team. In addition to Millar and Mulcahy, the selectors retained three-quarters Jeeps, Niall Brophy and David Hewitt and forwards Bryn Meredith and Haydn Morgan, all of whom featured in the 1959 Lions tour to New Zealand. But would the selectors find a regular place on tour for the explosive talents of the young England flanker Rogers?

The tour started in the worst possible way. Stan Hodgson, the Durham City and England hooker, broke his leg in the first half of the opening match against Rhodesia in Bulawayo. The injury to Hodgson placed Bryn Meredith, the only other specialist hooker in the group, under severe pressure. The Welshman played in three of the next four matches before help arrived in the form of Coventry's Bert Godwin. If the party was now up to strength, there is little doubt that Hodgson's injury cast a deep shadow over the tour.

Budge's rival for a place in the Test side was Haydn Morgan. Rogers had played well in Bulawayo, settled into the tour and was given the nod ahead of the Welshman for the first Test at Ellis Park. In what was largely a war of attrition, with the two packs cancelling each other out, the match ended in a 3-3 draw. The highlights of an otherwise forgettable game were a wonderful try by Ken Jones, matched by an equally scintillating score from South Africa's John Gainsford. After the first Test, Commander Vaughan declared somewhat prematurely: 'We've got the measure of the Springboks. That, you must admit, was clear at Ellis Park. We'll play the next two Tests tight as well and then, when we're up in the series, we'll turn on the running stuff in the final Test.'

Sadly, the 'running stuff' idea was a managerial fantasy as the Springboks grew into the tour. The sustained physical assault by the men in green jerseys was relentless. The Lions lost Richard Sharp for the first two Tests after he was knocked cold by Mannetjies Roux in an early provincial game against Northern Transvaal. The incident was controversial to say the least and a tragedy for Sharp. Rogers believed the Englishman was a marked man on the tour: 'I said to Sharpy before the Transvaal game: "Just move it on for the first ten minutes – nothing too clever."' But Sharp couldn't curtail his natural instincts and within a few minutes of the start set out on a mazy run before Roux hit him hard and high. 'I don't think it was deliberate,' said Rogers generously. 'But it certainly was a bit high.' However, it wasn't the brute strength of the Springboks that caused Rogers to miss the next two Tests.

Frustratingly for the young flanker, he tore side muscles playing in an impromptu game of football after training. 'It was just after the first Test that I tore my stomach muscles, which put me out for weeks, including the second Test,' recalled Budge. 'I then got fit and played against Western Province before the third Test, but playing football at the end of a training session I went into a tackle with John Douglas and damaged my hand. I was off for another two matches before the last Test.'

As Budge remarked later: 'There is nothing more frustrating than being part of an international touring party and not being able to play – it's no great fun when you are injured. Ironically, despite the injury, I was as fit as I had ever been in my life.' There was one moment during his enforced absence that lightened Budge's mood – his 23rd birthday.

The players marked the occasion by presenting the injured flanker with a hairnet designed to protect his mop of unruly hair in the shower. Rogers was easily identifiable on the rugby field with his skull-cap protecting his ears. 'I was always cutting my ears – game after game,' he said. Before a match, he would pull the stuffing out of the cap and wear it tight against his head, which seemed to do the trick.

But moments of such light-hearted fun were rare on this particular tour. Rogers later reflected on the Lions's unfortunate injury toll: 'We had significant early injuries, losing David Nash, the Welsh No. 8, with a neck injury, Richard Sharp, our fly-half, with a broken cheekbone and Stan Hodgson, who was a bloody good hooker, with a broken leg in the first game.'

The injury to Nash was to end his playing career, one of a growing number of injuries that blighted the 1962 trip. If they didn't know before the series began, the Lions quickly realised what they were up against and for Rogers one Springbok stood out among his teammates.

'The Springboks were a great side but the one who always stands out in my mind is Frik du Preez,' Budge remembered. 'He ran 40 yards in the last Test in Bloemfontein and bumped off about six tacklers. He was not especially tall, about 6ft 2in, but was very thickset, quite similar in build to Colin Meads. However, he was hugely athletic, more so than Meads.'

The stomach injury meant that Budge couldn't be considered for the second Test in Durban. The match was memorable for all the wrong reasons. The referee refused to award an apparent pushover try by Rowlands, denying the Lions a victory for which they had worked so hard. But a 3-0 defeat was no disgrace. The Lions were heartened by these performances as they approached the third Test. But with the series still in the balance, an 8-3 defeat in Cape Town, involving an uncharacteristic error by a recovered Richard Sharp, meant the Lions were left playing for their pride in the final Test. Match by match, the South African pack gradually gained the upper hand as the Lions's backline failed to make the most of the possession won by their forwards. Fortunately, Rogers recovered from injury in time to take his place at No. 7 in the fourth Test, one of the two most memorable of his many trips abroad.

British Lions 14 South Africa 34
Bloemfontein, 25 August 1962

The tour trundled on until late August but, in the days leading up to the final Test, the players relaxed at the Kruger National Park. Crossing and re-crossing the Crocodile River, the party travelled through mountain passes, catching sight of elephants, giraffes, leopards and lions, while enjoying the local passion fruit, paw paw and bananas. A few nights camping under the stars away from the pressures of international rugby would have lifted the players' spirits. Following a 500-mile journey, the much-depleted group arrived in Bloemfontein ready for the final Test.

Dickie Jeeps was handed the captaincy for the match in recognition of his record-breaking 13th appearance on what was his third successive Lions tour. Jeeps had been carrying an injury but recovered quickly in time for the match. Sharp was included in spite of his recent disappointing form. Despite the narrow defeats in the previous three Tests, it became increasingly clear that the South Africans were far superior in most aspects of the game – they were also improving as a unit match by match. By the fourth Test, this very good Springbok team were firing on all cylinders. Before the game, the Lions's management decided they had nothing to lose and went for all-out attack, accepting the risk that their midfield might be exposed. This brave, perhaps foolhardy, effort failed miserably and the Springboks took full advantage.

The frustrated Rogers, who impressed the manager early in the tour with his knack of charging down kicks, had sat out most of the trip but wouldn't have worried that the Springboks had found their form in the final Test – he would have relished the thought of being back in the action. The flanker had impressed the selectors in a warm-up game against Western Province, a performance that inspired the *Durban Daily News* reporter to write: 'Budge Rogers must have clinched his place in the Test side with an outstanding display at open-side wing-forward.'

The match at Bloemfontein, in front of 60,000 fans, was notable as the last in the distinguished career of the Springbok skipper

Claassen. Stand-off Oxlee maintained his series scoring spree, running up half his team's points, and his superb kicking proved to be the difference between the two sides. In the final Test, the Springboks were quicker to the ball throughout and their forwards were in devastating form. Claassen's men were more effective in the loose and the back row, keeping the Lions defence constantly on their guard. The tourists held their own in the line-out but were generally outplayed all over the pitch. The Lions knew full well that by putting all their emphasis on attack, they were leaving themselves wide open – and so it proved. The Springboks sensed weakness and went in for the kill, scoring 13 points in five minutes. The defeat was hard to take. The Lions forwards had almost won the first Test at Ellis Park, but by the time they reached Bloemfontein injuries had taken their toll and the Springboks pulverised them in the second half. *The Times* rugby correspondent was damning in his match report: 'To be frank, some of the British tackling was barely above preparatory school level and nobody can expect to win matches in such circumstances.'

In the face of the South African onslaught one Lion stood out, as *The Times* reported: 'Among the forwards the comparative freshness of Rogers, who has played only four times in the past two months because of injury, stuck out like a sore thumb amid his rather jaded and surprisingly immobile colleagues.'

'Rogers played a blinder,' wrote *The Times* correspondent. How the Lions had missed their open-side and his unquenchable spirit and speed at the breakdown. His bone-shuddering tackle, which led to Rowlands's try, was an example of just what the Lions had needed in the previous Tests. One can only speculate what might have happened if Budge had played in all four Tests. In addition to the No. 7, Jeeps was his usual reliable self, although Sharp had not fully recovered from his injuries and looked low on confidence. As Budge said later: 'In the last Test, we were four players short of our best team.'

The Lions showed promise early in the game, with Mulcahy providing an effective link between Sharp and Rogers. But a late try by the 17-stone Campbell-Lamerton was too little, too late as the forlorn Lions trooped off the pitch at the end of a long and chastening tour. What had looked so promising early in the South African adventure ended in heavy defeat for the tourists. The hard pitches and the altitude in the high veld contributed to a long injury list as the tourists failed to sustain their early potential. Amid the disappointment of Bloemfontein, at least one tourist enhanced his growing reputation. In case the reader might sense some favouritism in this report, let others make the case. The *Playfair Rugby Football Annual* for that year reads: 'Du Preez and van Zyl mercilessly exposed the weakness of a defence with only one man, in this case Rogers, quick enough for the task.'

Injuries and a heavy touring schedule took their toll on the Lions's performances, but as Budge remembers things were different in the rugby world of 1962: 'We lost the series but we weren't hammered … winning and losing was not quite as dramatic as it is today because there was not the same media coverage, and if you lost, you lost. It wasn't a great success in terms of results but it didn't ruin the tour.'

Rogers enjoyed the opportunity to see some great players at first hand, the best of whom, he believed, was Dickie Jeeps: 'Arthur Smith was a great wing and Pask and Sharp could be brilliant, but for me, Jeeps stood out. He was a fantastic player. Not that quick, didn't have a long pass, but always gave his fly-half good ball and took a hammering if he needed to. I remember his tigerishness and ebullience.'

Rogers admired Jeeps's courage and resilience and remembered hearing him yelling 'tackle, tackle, tackle' throughout Budge's England debut in Dublin. 'He was still doing it years later when we were watching England play from the stands at Twickenham,' Budge said.

The 1962 Lions tour was not without its controversy, as the young Rogers was to discover. If the Lions party was welcomed everywhere they travelled in South Africa, on the pitch the welcome not so hospitable. In all contact sports, there is a line between physical aggression and violence that should not be crossed. At times on this tour, the illegal became the acceptable. Golden boy Richard Sharp was targeted for special attention and had his jaw broken. The Lions were incensed. Syd Millar spoke for many of them when he said: 'Roux was a madman. You don't tackle like that. You'd be off the field now.'

Bill Mulcahy recalls the match between the tourists and the Combined Services in what became known as the 'Battle of Potchefstroom'. According to Mulcahy, everybody in the ground seemed to be wearing uniforms and 'there were fists flying' and the crowd were 'baying for blood'. Rowlands, the Lions's biggest forward, was another target for special treatment and the referee let the home side get away with 'murder'. There was digging, raking and late tackling. 'It was horrendous,' said Mulcahy. 'My opposite number pulled me down in the scrum, so I smacked him. I had to look after myself but rugby football is a game, not organised warfare.' With the referees leaning towards the home side, close calls went with the Springboks, which made the difference in the first three Tests. With such treatment, the Lions began to run out of key players as the series slipped away.

Never at a loss for words, Willie-John McBride was brutally honest about the differences between the two sides, despite the closeness of the early matches: 'I discovered very quickly, as we all did, that rugby in South Africa was superior to ours in just about every way. They were fitter, better organised and more committed; they had a pride and will to win that totally outstripped us.'

A win-at-all-costs mentality against the Corinthian ideal was only ever going to produce one winner – and so it proved as the Lions returned home to reflect and lick their wounds. From the comfort of the stands, Greg Thomas and Clem Thomas argue in their book *125 Years of the British and Irish Lions* that errors by the selectors contributed to the Lions's defeats: 'They obviously had little idea of the difference between a tight-head and loose-head prop, or an open-side and blind-side flanker.'

This failure to provide specialist blind-side flankers for the tour of 1962 was, according to the authors, a fatal error: 'They seemed totally unaware of the propensity of the Southern Hemisphere countries to drive the blind side for long periods. Their first instinct, when in any sort of trouble, is to close it up and go down the narrow side.'

Playing non-specialists can unbalance a team and make the difference between winning and losing in a tough playing environment like South Africa. The 1962 Lions were unable to impose themselves in the breakdown and lacked flair in attack as a result. It didn't help the Lions's cause that some very good players declined the invitation to travel. The 1959 tourists Phil Horrrocks-Taylor and Ken Scotland made themselves unavailable for business reasons and the Pontypool centre Malcolm Price turned to rugby league, signing professional forms for Oldham. Schoolteachers Alan Pask and David Nash nearly missed the trip when their local authority announced it was only prepared to offer them unpaid leave for the duration of the trip. The Welsh local education authorities had strong views about the political situation in South Africa. The South African Sports Association offered to fund Pask and Nash's tour, but their generous offer was politely declined because of the danger of infringing their amateur status.

But despite everything – refereeing 'inconsistencies', losing the series, aggression bordering on violence, rock-hard pitches and the length of the tour – most of the tourists cherished the experience. Rogers remembers flying over the Kariba Dam and Victoria Falls in Dakota and golf at the delightful Durban Country Club, where he chased a monkey that ran off with his ball. Staying at the luxurious Arthur's Seat Hotel in Cape Town was a delight and a privilege.

Lasting friendships were formed, as Budge recalls: 'A wonderful friendship developed between "Wigs" Mulcahy, our Irish lock, and Dave Rollo, our Scottish prop. After a few drinks Rollo, who never wore a jockstrap when he played, and Mulcahy would both be talking simultaneously in their broad accents, with neither able to understand each other.'

These are fond memories that last a lifetime. Dickie Jeeps remembers meeting his hero Sir Don Bradman in South Africa and saw the experience as one of the highpoints of his career. Inevitably on such a long tour, some players became homesick and for very good reasons. Syd Millar's wife gave birth to their son while her husband was away on tour – it was four or five days before he heard the wonderful news. Millar's son was three months old when he eventually arrived home. Today, with instant communication, the proud father would have probably flown home for the birth and returned to the tour a few days later. Despite their reservations about selection, rugby writers Thomas and Thomas were generous in their assessment of the Lions's performance in South Africa: 'History should not judge the 1962 Lions harshly for they could quite easily have won the series with better selection, a bit more luck and different tactics. They headed home via Nairobi, where they rounded off their trip with an 11-try 50-0 victory over East Africa.'

Despite playing in only two Tests, the 1962 Lions tour was a key milestone in Rogers's career and further established his reputation as one of the most exciting talents in world rugby. Rogers, now fully recovered from his injuries, returned to England with his confidence high and could look forward to the new season with real optimism. Budge thoroughly enjoyed his first Lions tour, which made the disappointment of 1966 even harder to take. But at least he was one of the few Lions players to come out of the tour with his reputation enhanced. He spoke for British Lions down the years in expressing the special experience of a Lions tour: 'It was something I would not have missed out on for anything. To play alongside players you have only ever played against was something really special, in particular to see the friendships coming together with people from different backgrounds and countries.'

The teams for the match in Bloemfontein were:

British Lions: Willcox, Cowan, Hewitt, Weston, Brophy, Sharp, Jeeps (c), Millar, Meredith, Jones, Rowlands, McBride, Mulcahy, Rogers, Campbell-Lamerton

South Africa: Wilson, Engelbrecht, Gainsford, Wyness, Roux, Oxlee, Uys, Kuhn, Hill, Bezuidenhour, du Preez, Claassen (c), van Zyl, Hopwood, Botha

Dickie Jeeps died on 7 October 2016, aged 84. Rogers and Jeeps played together for England and the British Lions, and remained good friends for many years. The Cambridge-born scrum-half attended Bedford Modern School, where he excelled at rugby and cricket. But rather than play for Bedford, he preferred to return to his home club Cambridge City, where he stayed for a few years before moving to Northampton Saints. The scrum-half made 24 appearances for England, including 13 as captain. He toured with the Lions on three occasions, including the 1962 trip to South Africa. In addition to his glorious rugby career, Jeeps played Minor Counties cricket for Cambridgeshire and was later appointed chairman of the Sports Council at the age of 44. At his funeral, the pallbearers were his former teammates Bob Taylor, Derek Morgan, Malcolm Phillips and Budge himself, all now well into their 70s and 80s.

New Zealand 9 England 6
Christchurch, 1 June 1963

Rogers's first tour with the British Lions proved to be a mixture of frustration, long periods of inactivity and a handful of matches in which he played really well. It was all the more frustrating because he never played for the Lions again after the 1962 tour to South Africa. Being selected for the Lions and having the opportunity to play with the best players in Britain meant a great deal, and to be left out in 1966 was the greatest disappointment of Rogers's career.

So the next on his list of favourite matches abroad is against the All Blacks in 1963, not for the British Lions but for England on their first-ever tour to New Zealand – the first by any of the four home nations. The importance of the tour in building relations between England, New Zealand and Australia cannot be underestimated and was the beginning of a rugby relationship that was to endure, with a few bumps along the way, for over 50 years.

After finishing the 1963 season as Five Nations champions, England embarked on what was to prove a challenging tour of Australasia in May. The tour programme was severe, with five matches in New Zealand and one against Australia squeezed in at the end of the trip. Three Test matches and three provincial games in 18 days with a small party would stretch any side, even the Five Nations champions. It was a daunting but exciting prospect.

The party, managed by Tom Berry and Micky Steele-Bodger, and captained by Mike Weston, was largely inexperienced. Most of the group had four caps or less and only Weston, Jacobs and Rogers had more than ten. There was no Willcox, Sharp, Jeeps (now retired) or Peter Jackson, but Budge would have enjoyed having the familiar face of Bedford colleague David Perry as companion and teammate. With a relatively small party, injuries further reduced England's playing strength, with Horrocks-Taylor and John Ranson all missing matches. To balance the usual crop of injuries, it would have been heartening for the tour management and senior players to see some of the debutants excel. Hosen replaced full-back Willcox for the tour and scored two dropped goals and six penalty goals. He also converted three of his team's seven tries. In all, Hosen contributed 30 of his side's 54 tour points. The Northampton and Cornwall full-back was one of the real successes of this tour, even if he wasn't quite in the class of the All Blacks's legendary kicker Don Clarke. Skipper Weston, Malcolm Phillips, Mike Davis, Perry and Rogers all came home with their reputations enhanced.

Like the rest of the players headed for New Zealand, Budge received a charming letter from the president of the RFU congratulating him on his selection. The president, Cyril Gadney, was clearly excited by the prospect of the visit, telling the players they were going to have a 'stupendous tour' and that 'we come first to play rugger ... and to play well'. Warning that the journey down to Australasia would be 'long, tiring and tedious', Gadney advised the players to keep 'extremely fit'. He insisted: 'We cannot afford to take anyone on this tour whose fitness is in doubt.' The terse note was not without encouragement. It added: 'We are fortunate to have a great team spirit and a grand bunch of chaps.' The party met for a pre-tour get-together in Bristol a few weeks before assembling in London on 9 May.

Mr Gadney was right about the journey out being 'long and tedious'. Following a two-day break in London, which included a night out at the London Palladium to see Sammy Davis Jnr, the party flew to Amsterdam on 11 May before taking a flight to Vancouver. From there, there would be an overnight stop at the Waikikian Hotel in Honolulu. The players were pleased to be able to stretch their legs and enjoy the sunshine. For hooker John 'Bomber' Thorne, the stopover proved a painful experience. Such was the extent of his sunburn that he became ill and missed both Test matches. From Hawaii, the party flew to Nadi in Fiji before arriving at Wellington. What sounds like an exciting and exotic adventure would have been in reality extremely tiring. After days on economy class flights, the players had just a few days to recover from their ordeal before facing their first provincial opponents Wellington on 18 May. Rogers remembers: 'It was a completely ludicrous schedule but great fun, and an extraordinary mix of old-style touring and some high-quality rugby from us in the two New Zealand Tests.'

With three Test matches and three provincial games in 18 days with a small squad, the party were kept busy throughout the tour. The trip began well with victory against Wellington, although Rogers recalls he didn't have a particularly good game. *The Times* rugby correspondent agreed: 'Rogers is a great forward and he had an excellent first half, but marred the second by impetuous play which put him offside. I feel he could cure this and be of even greater value to the team.'

A 14-9 defeat at the hands of Otago brought the party down to earth and was a reminder of how tough the international matches would be. England faced the All Blacks in the first Test in Auckland on 25 May, their third match of the tour. That day, Rogers was introduced to some of the players he was to encounter on so many occasions over the next eight or nine years: Meads, Clarke, Lochore and the fiercest opponent of all, Waka Nathan. Given the team's lack of preparation, a 21-11 loss was not disastrous. In the first Test, Rogers's performance was again hampered by offside problems and there is little doubt that the All Blacks had sought to neutralise Rogers's work in the breakdown. Under the headline 'Budge was a marked man', AA Mulligan of the *Bedfordshire Times* wrote: 'Budge's fame Down Under had preceded him and he was a marked man from the outset – marked, it would seem, also by referees.'

Concerned about Rogers's treatment by the opposition and the referees, Budge's good friend Roger Bass took time to write to the England flanker after the tour: 'I was up in Auckland for the first Test. I thought you played particularly well and my New Zealand friends said you were the best England forward they had seen for years. By the way, you were never offside, and to be quite honest … nor were you nearly offside. You made a great effort to stem the tide when the dice was loaded in the first half hour.'

Despite the close attention of the referee, Rogers played a decisive part in a wonderful English try in the second half. In typical style, the flanker broke away on the blind side of a maul 35 yards from the All Blacks goal line, with Ranson in close support. Ranson went over for the try to put his team back in the game. But Clarke kicked his team to victory, finding time to score a try of his own late in the game. The scores might have been closer had the England kicker Hosen not received a painful blow to the face in the second half. But overall, the tour management would have been encouraged by their team's performance. Rogers felt he played well at Eden Park and looked forward to Christchurch with renewed anticipation.

With games coming thick and fast, Rogers and his teammates had little time to reflect on their performances in the first Test. In comparison with their opponents, England were a little underprepared. The team never even took a physiotherapist with them – inconceivable today. Coventry sponge-man Harry Walker did his best and was kept busy with his small group of players, five of whom, including Budge, played every match in New Zealand and Australia. This may sound amateurish, even complacent on a tour of such importance, but the players were genuine *amateurs*. Some may have given up their jobs or interrupted their careers to go out on tour. Every single one of the England players put rugby before their careers for the length of the trip. Ten shillings a day pocket money for the duration of the trip is an indication of the financial sacrifice by these touring pioneers.

The team's preparations for the next Test were marred by another defeat, this time at the hands of a young side at Hawke's Bay in front of 18,000 rowdy home supporters. One win from five games, including a lost international, was painful, although the tourists were encouraged by their performances, even in defeat. But with tough matches against the home side and Australia to come in quick succession, the party needed to re-group and revise their tactics in the short time they had before the second Test. On Saturday, 1 June, in front of a full house of 40,000, the All Blacks, led by Wilson Whineray, and including the infamous Meads, were confident of a second win. But on the day, they faced a far more determined England team, who were coming to terms with the physicality of Meads and his teammates. The All Black was a tricky opponent, as Rogers remembers: 'Micky Steele-Bodger ran the touch line and I have this everlasting image of him jumping up and down screaming blue murder in one of the New Zealand Tests when I dropped on a ball and got a boot in the back from Colin Meads for my trouble. Meads was a hell of a player, but he could be a bit naughty.'

The England selectors – the captain and tour manager – made changes for the second Test. Sykes and Wightman came in for Dee and Pargetter respectively, with Perry moving to No. 4. The programme notes were generous to the tourists, recognising England's good work on the tour to date despite some poor results: 'They have shown at Auckland that they are a foe to be reckoned with, and their fine sporting spirit and style of play have left a lasting impression.'

The match had all the ingredients for a thrilling encounter – and so it proved. New Zealand led by two tries to a penalty goal at half time. In the second half, England drew level through a fine try from Phillips. Hosen did well to catch a high ball under pressure, threw it inside and Rogers picked it up off his toes, chipped the ball over Clarke, and Phillips won the race to the line, going over in the corner in the classic manner. Sensing victory, the England pack gained in strength and began to drive their opponents back to their own line.

Weston and Horrocks-Taylor joined in the fun with sidestepping runs that almost brought their team a second try. With the tourists gaining in belief, Don 'The Boot' Clarke intervened, breaking English hearts with a 60-yard kick that sailed over the posts. The deciding penalty from Clarke and the sequence leading up to it were almost bizarre, as Budge explains: 'We had a scrum on their line and Juddy, who could swivel his hips to get a strike against the head, said to Vic Marriott, "stop f*****g pushing Vic". We won the line-out as Horrocks kicked to our right, which Clarke marked. He then went to kick at goal from 50 yards but one of us charged too early so Clarke, who had missed his kick, now had a penalty attempt. He replaced the ball ten yards into his own half and the outrageously long kick sailed between the posts.'

Rogers is convinced that England scored two pushover tries in the match – both of which the referee denied. It was an exceptionally tough way to lose a game they could easily have won.

After the match, the tourists were applauded by the local press for their excellent try and the manner in which they sliced through the All Blacks defence on several occasions. It was England's first tour and the schedule was punishing. For some, the workload would prove costly. Mike Davis joined the injured list when he badly damaged his shoulder in the second Test but, with no replacements and his team in with a chance of winning, he stayed on the pitch. So near, yet so far.

England's first-ever overseas tour was a ground-breaking initiative. The visit was also highly successful for the home nation. Takings from the Test matches amounted to £85,000, which made the tour more profitable than the previous visits of the French and British teams put together. The visit generated huge interest in a nation with a consuming passion for the game of rugby and the tourists received a warm welcome wherever they went. The tour also raised an interesting debate about styles of play. The All

Blacks have always believed they play their best when they use their most effective weapon – the pack as a unified, driving force. Forget running and passing footballers. Possession at all costs is the backbone of the All Blacks's game plan – from scrums, line-outs and rucks. Their approach may have discouraged the emergence of flair players, but this would not have troubled them too much. If the New Zealanders worked hard on their physicality, as Rogers remembers they were also highly skilled, especially in the forwards, who usually won the matches for them. 'They always kicked the ball behind our forwards to turn us,' Budge recalls. The speed of the scrum-halves combined with the strength of the forwards was a combination that proved almost unbeatable. Rogers said recently that the All Blacks were the benchmark team for the whole of his career: 'They rucked the ball like no other team and if you went on the deck, then god help you.'

Six serious matches against tough opponents with a small squad of players, and without the influential Richard Sharp, was surely a mission bordering on recklessness. But there was a belief that such a valuable rugby experience would galvanise England performances over the following seasons. Rogers believes the experience was good for team morale: 'We had a long, difficult journey but it was enjoyable. Things went wrong on tour but this brought us all together.' In every match, the England players certainly knew they had been in a game. Did they learn from their experience? Unfortunately, the tour precipitated a steady decline in England's fortunes as fierce rivals Wales began to stamp their authority on the Five Nations Championship. The tour front row of Judd, Goldwin and Jacobs had never played together as a unit before the tour and never did after it. The rest of the pack, which included Owen, Davis, Wightman and Perry, became strangers in the seasons following the tour. Inconsistency of selection is a recurring theme at this time and Rogers remembers playing with a whole succession of No. 6s throughout his career.

Budge's contribution to England's cause in New Zealand was exceptional and his reputation was further enhanced. As one commentator wrote: 'Rogers was superb.' Club colleague David Perry also excelled in this powerhouse of rugby, particularly in the line-out, where he was outstanding. Perry believed Rogers learned from playing against the All Blacks, particularly tremendous players like Kevin Tremaine, who had the same qualities as Budge. He also loved playing against the All Blacks heroes, like skipper Whineray, who he described as 'a lovely man', although Colin Meads could never be described that way. The great Don Clarke made a terrific impression on Rogers, not just in his superlative kicking but in his all-round play and general demeanour. There were lessons to be learned from the tour, which was too physically demanding for such a small party. But the visit to New Zealand took rugby into a new phase in its development and generated a huge appetite for the international game.

With the New Zealand schedule completed the exhausted party left for Sydney, but not before Rogers was stopped in the street by a small boy, who presented the England flanker with a scrapbook containing a pictorial diary of the tour. The party were welcomed in Australia. In the words of *Rugby News* on 4 June 1963: 'This is the first purely England rugby team to visit Australia – it is an historic occasion.' The short stopover in Australia was not helped by the standard of the party's accommodation, a rather rundown hotel in Coogee Bay. It is little wonder that England were beaten 18-9 in a match played in pouring rain in front of a disappointingly low attendance of 7,800 at the Sydney Cricket Ground. But *Rugby News* spoke for most Australian rugby supporters when it said: 'We hope, and beg, that next time a longer stay will be made here, though Australians are grateful and delighted to have this fleeting glance of England's champions in action.'

But it was one match too many for a tired group of Englishmen. The return flight from Sydney via Singapore, Calcutta, Karachi and Cairo, followed by a day in Athens and a stopover in Rome, appears exotic but must have been exhausting for the whole party.

While in New Zealand, Budge remembers seeing the following advert in a local paper: '30-year-old farmer with 40,000 sheep would like to meet lady of similar age and interests for a long relationship and who has two tickets for the New Zealand v England Test match. Please send photographs of the tickets.'

Teams for the Christchurch Test on England's historic tour to New Zealand were as follows:

England: Hosen, Sykes, Phillips, Weston (c), Ranson, Horrocks-Taylor, Clarke, Perry, Rogers, Wightman, Owen, Davis, Judd, Jacobs, Godwin

New Zealand: Clarke, Caulton, McKay, Uttley, Walsh, Watt, Connor, Graham, Tremain, Nathan, Meads, Stewart, Clarke, Whineray (c), Young

Having toured South Africa with the British Lions and New Zealand and Canada with England, Rogers's next major tour, having been omitted from the Lions's 1966 tour to New Zealand, was with the Barbarians in 1969. It was the club's second visit to South Africa and their first for 11 years. The 1969 tour coincided with Wales's tour to New Zealand and Australia, depriving the Baa-Baas of the likes of JPR Williams, Gerald Davies and Gareth Edwards. However, despite missing these great names, the club had so many top players to call on that they were still able to select a strong group. England provided emerging stars like David Duckham and Rodney Webb among the backs, and John Pullin, Bob Taylor and Rogers among the forwards. Among the Scottish contingent were Frank Laidlaw and Alistair Biggar, while the Irish names included Alan Duggan and Barry McGann.

All things considered it was an expectant party, led by Brigadier Glyn Hughes, that left for Johannesburg in May of that year. The tour schedule consisted of six matches, five in South Africa and one in Rhodesia. Rogers was one of the eight players left out of the first match at Ellis Park against a Quaggas side containing five Springboks, including the captain Piet Visagie. A 29-3 victory in front of a crowd of 30,000 was a huge confidence boost for the tourists. The Baa-Baas' backs were outstanding, as Reg Sweet from the *The Star* reported the following day: 'Duckham carved numerous openings through a defence which crumbled badly ... Webb is a superlative runner of tremendous power ... the most thrustful winger we have seen since the days of O'Reilly.'

For the next match against Natal at King's Park, the Brigadier brought in all eight of the players who missed out on the first match. In were Chris Saville, Colin Telfer, Nigel Starmer-Smith, Keith Fairbrother, John Pullin, Geoff Bayles, John Jeffrey and Budge Rogers as captain. In difficult playing conditions, the Barbarians lost the match 16-14 despite being ahead at the interval. The tourists had failed to use the strong wind to their advantage in the first half and although they battled hard in the second period, with Rogers scoring two tries late in the game, it was a question of too little, too late for the Baa-Baas. The visitors had played their part in what was a tremendous game of rugby, as Percy Owen, writing for *Associated Newspapers,* confirmed: 'More than 15,000 people in Durban have sore throats today. It's nothing serious but that's what you get from watching the Barbarians in action.'

An unfortunate consequence of the match in Durban was a hamstring injury to Rodney Webb that would keep the winger out of the rest of the tour. The third match was against the fledging South African Barbarians – the first-ever match between the two clubs. Many felt this game would be the highlight of the tour, but the match was ruined by dubious refereeing that manager Hughes later described as 'incomprehensible'. The South African press were clearly embarrassed by the performance of Jannie van Wyk. 'The persistent shrill of the whistle was like a mother-in-law with all the grouses in the world,' wrote Reg Sweet. The South African officials were equally shocked. Boet Erasmus, after whom the stadium in Port Elizabeth is named, was unforgiving. 'This was a case of forgetting the game and getting on with the whistle,' he said.

The sole British journalist on the tour was *The Telegraph's* John Reason, for whom Rogers and most in rugby had the greatest respect. Reason went one step further with his criticism: 'This was another saga in the sad, sad story of one-sided refereeing in South Africa.'

These comments annoyed Glyn Hughes, who said that Reason's view was an 'exception'. The row over the referee rumbled on. Billy Hullin revealed some years later: 'I was being whistled up at every third scrum and if I asked the referee what it was for, he would take us back ten yards. There was never any attempt to offer an explanation.'

Fortunately for the tourists, the South Africans missed ten kicks at goal and tries by O'Shea and Gallacher limited the score to 23-11. But the Barbarian players and most of the 25,000 people in the crowd came away feeling frustrated at the standard of rugby on show – frankly, they deserved better. The tourists had two games to salvage something from the tour. Club historian Alan Evans spoke for the Barbarians supporters when he said: 'There was every chance that reputations would be restored and appetites satisfied.'

The fifth game of the tour was at Newlands against a strong South Universities side. The students team included four current Springboks while, in the continued absence of Webb, Duckham was switched to the wing. The 25,000 in attendance that afternoon witnessed a much better game than at Port Elizabeth. The Barbarians were ten points down at half time but couldn't quite get back into the game and the universities side held on to win 18-16.

Three consecutive defeats must have been a huge disappointment to the players as the injuries began to mount, as they do on most long overseas tours. In addition to Webb and Duckham, Biggar was also carrying an injury. The tour management considered sending for replacements but eventually decided to switch the fit players around for the final match in South Africa against the formidable South African Country Districts. The Baa-Baas's opponents included some names familiar to Rogers – Mannetjies Roux, that infamous tackler, half-backs Visagie and Dawie de Villiers, with Hannes Marais and Jan Ellis in the pack. A good crowd of 16,000 turned up at Olen Park expecting their side to win comfortably.

Instead, the Barbarians rose to the occasion and played some of their best rugby since the early days of the tour. The *Playfair Annual* of that year described the Baa-Baas's victory as an 'outstanding triumph'.

The visitors' pack dominated possession and the backs played some delightful rugby, which the home supporters thought they might never witness on this tour. The Baa-Baas led 14-6 at half time, but had to do without their open-side, who was led from the field with concussion at the end of the first period. Budge was rushed to hospital but recovered to rejoin his teammates after the match.

Further scores in the second period by Laidlaw, Telfer, Biggar, McGann and Saville left the home side shell-shocked as the Barbarians finished the South African leg of the tour in style. The local press were also delighted to see the much-vaunted Baa-Baas at last produce a display worthy of their name. Sweet wrote: 'Gone were those muffed passes of earlier matches; gone the costly failures to make the tackle. In their place was the old black-and-white Barbarian magic and it was a joy to see.'

Glyn Hughes expressed relief at his team's magnificent exhibition of running rugby: 'This must have been the strongest side we met during our tour in South Africa and we can be said to have ended it in a blaze of glory.'

Having regained their form and their pride, the party left for the potentially controversial trip to Rhodesia. Initially, the tour was to be five matches in South Africa, but the match against Rhodesia was added at a late stage. The party left a country that continued to imprison Nelson Mandela while sticking rigidly to its racist rule, and headed to another up to its neck in corruption and misrule.

In the late 1960s, sponsored by their neighbours, Rhodesia was effectively ostracised from the rest of the world. Diplomatic links between Rhodesia and the UK were severed from 1965 to 1970, when Ted Heath reopened negotiations. Denis Howells, Minister of Sport at the time, sat on the political fence regarding the tour: 'I leave the decisions to those concerned. Sportsmen have British passports like everyone else and have the right to visit Rhodesia. The government regret the decision to tour but will take no action to stop it.'

Realising the controversial nature of the decision to go, Geoffrey Windsor-Lewis, secretary of the Barbarians, felt the need to explain the club's position: 'We are going as guests of the South African Rugby Union, to whom Rhodesia is affiliated – they arranged the trip and paid for everything.'

The British Lions had played in Rhodesia in 1968, which gave the Barbarians officials some comfort. Cricket authorities in England had been more decisive, even if their hand was forced by the D'Oliveira affair, and dropped Rhodesia from their list of opponents. This was the backdrop to the Barbarians's match in Salisbury in 1969. The club justified their decision to play by re-emphasising their position that sport should be kept out of politics and playing the match could only improve relations between the two countries.

The party were warmly welcomed by the Salisbury government and the visit proceeded without incident. The match itself was a huge success. Despite struggling with injuries, Barry O'Driscoll and Alan Duggan were both in the team. John O'Shea was captain for the day but failed to score the try achieved by previous captains on the tour, Bob Taylor, Frank Laidlaw and Rogers. The visitors led 16-11 after 40 minutes, which left the home team still in with a chance of victory. But the Baa-Baas finished the game more strongly and ran out 24-21 winners.

Glyn Hughes proclaimed the tour a great success: 'Every match should have been won. Two were lost by the smallest margins, a conversion. Our losses could have been attributed to our efforts to play completely open Barbarian football and being guilty of poor handling on occasions.'

On the field, Budge enjoyed a good tour, captained the side in one match, scored some tries and thoroughly enjoyed the South African experience. At this late stage of his career, he was fit, playing well and could look forward to more top-class rugby in the years ahead. Budge's trademark thunderous tackles at the breakdown were as effective in 1969 as they were when he made his England debut in 1961. These tackles often set the tone for his team's performance, whether in the blue of Bedford, the white of England or touring with the Lions and the Baa-Baas. Budge's work at the breakdown slowed the opposition down or kept the ball away from their fly-half. Although only one of Budge's most memorable matches was on tour – England v New Zealand in Christchurch in 1963 – touring, as we have seen, played a major part in his rugby career.

An exotic excursion to the Far East

In spite of his good form for the Barbarians in 1969, the England recall never came. In 1971, the British Lions toured New Zealand with a party captained by John Dawes and coached by Carwyn James. The Welsh influence was balanced by the tour manager Dr Doug Smith from Scotland. If Rogers suffered the biggest disappointment of his career when left out of the 1966 Lions touring party, his omission this time was expected. Budge was out of the England side so had no expectations about being selected for the Lions in 1971. How the England man would have loved the opportunity to play with some of the finest backs in the history of the game against the great All Blacks. Dawes, Barry John, Gareth Edwards, John Bevan, Gerald Davies and JPR Williams were the great Welsh players in the Lions party, backed up by England's David Duckham and Mike Gibson. This group of players formed the core of one of the greatest Lions teams of all time, leading Thomas and Thomas to write in their history of the British Lions: 'It was my opinion that the 1971 Lions had backs that were without equal in my experience. Never did I see such consummate play from backs, with such unparalleled mastery of the basic skills. The 1974 team may have enjoyed a slightly better record, for they never lost a game and had the best pack of forwards ever put on the field by the British & Irish Lions. If you had the 1971 backs combined with the 1974 forwards, you would be close to creating the perfect team.'

Praise indeed. But Rogers missed all the fun in New Zealand and had to be content with an England tour to the Far East. None of the six international matches on the trip were given official Test status, with the team playing as an 'England XV'. Albert Agar telephoned Budge towards the end of the 1970/71 season and invited him to captain the tourists on their visit to Japan, Singapore and Sri Lanka as part of the RFU centenary celebrations. The first international match was against Japan at the Kintetsu Hanazona Rugby Stadium in Osaka in front of a crowd of over 13,000. England ran out 27-19 winners but they had to fight hard for their victory. The match was level with three minutes left before tries from winger Peter Glover and Jeremy Janion gave England the match. The touring party left Osaka and headed for the Japanese capital Tokyo, where they played the second 'Test' under the lights of the Chichibunomiya Stadium. England began well and led at half time thanks to two penalty goals from Peter Rossborough. The second half saw the local side pull back three points before the tourists prevailed 6-3. Further internationals followed in Hong Kong, Singapore and Sri Lanka and the tour was completed with a match in Singapore, which the tourists won 39-9. Two 'Tests' against Sri Lanka in Colombo followed, both of which England won comfortably.

The tour matches drew large crowds and were a great success in terms of promoting rugby in the Far East, but were ruined for the England captain by, of all things, a pair of crimplene shorts. The shorts were handed out to the team ahead of the tour and were designed to help the players stay cool in extreme heat. Crimplene was a synthetic material but failed to soften and was extremely uncomfortable. Fortunately, only one or two players chose to wear the shorts on the tour, one of them being the England captain. The tour opener against All Waseda University was played in pelting rain which, combined with the extreme heat, took the skin off Budge's upper thigh, causing him extreme pain.

He recalls: 'I have never known pain like it. I had second degree burns and it was impossible for me to play. The doctors put strips of polythene held by bandages to try to protect the infected area. I've got the scars to this day.'

Despite the painful 'shorts' incident and missing virtually the whole tour, the trip was not without its humorous moments. When the England skipper went up for the toss before the first match, he expected the usual coin-tossing from the referee, only to be met by the opposing skipper, who challenged the England captain to a game of 'paper, stone, scissors' to decide who had the choice of ends. Safely home in Bedford, Rogers could reflect on the fact that he had toured Australia, New Zealand, South Africa, Rhodesia and now the Far East. Somehow, rugby players in the 1960s and 1970s were supposed to fit into this hectic schedule the responsibilities of work and family.

Rogers enjoyed a wonderfully fulfilling sporting life. An outstanding exponent of his art in the amateur era, he made the most of his considerable abilities and talent. However, there were two major disappointments in an otherwise unblemished career, neither of which were under his control. Firstly, we know he was 'hugely, hugely disappointed' to miss the British Lions trip to New Zealand in 1966, the year in which he was appointed England captain. Secondly, Budge regrets never being part of a really successful England side.

The Lions trip to New Zealand is one of the great events on the sporting calendar. Taking on the world's best team in a three-match series with a scratch side made up of the best British and Irish players available is, arguably, the biggest challenge in rugby. Playing for the Lions in New Zealand is the pinnacle of any player's career and the ultimate challenge, one that only comes around every four years. No other rugby-playing nations are as passionate about the game as the Kiwis and none play with the combination of strength and flair that has been the hallmark of All Blacks teams down the years. In 1966, Rogers was denied the one tour he wanted more than any other. He would miss the get-together with old friends and foes and the challenge of facing a great New Zealand side, many of whom Budge had come to know personally.

If selected for the Lions trip, Budge may well have been made captain – the final honour of a brilliant career. Mike Campbell-Lamerton, who had played for Scotland for five years but had little captaincy experience, was appointed skipper for the tour. There was little doubt the Scot was a controversial and probably a compromise choice. Rogers and Campbell-Lamerton played for and against each other on many occasions and the Bedford man has great respect for his old teammate and adversary. The former Scotland captain made his debut for his country in 1962 and the sight of the 6ft 5in, 17-stone No. 8 is best summed up by this colourful description from Allan Massie: 'The sight of MJ Campbell-Lamerton of the Duke of Wellington's regiment surging round the tail of a line-out like an enraged hippopotamus was one of the most stirring spectacles in Scottish rugby.'

Unfortunately, the All Blacks's backing of the new Lions captain in 1966 was not shared by the British press, who were highly critical of the skipper's performance in New Zealand. One critic claimed he did not have the 'intellectual grasp for high-level captaincy'.

Massie wrote: 'He was perhaps over-conscientious and a worrier, and hardly spoke the same language as many of the team. It affected his play.'

The Lions were beaten in all four Tests in 1966, the first British side anywhere to face such humiliation. Stunned by the experience, the tourists managed to lose to British Columbia on their way home.

As we have seen, the 1960s was not a good time for British rugby in general. The Lions played 12 Tests and failed to win one. The only mitigating circumstance was that the scores in most matches were extremely close and the results could have gone either way – but they didn't. The 1966 Lions needed to get everything absolutely right to stand any chance against one of the greatest All Blacks sides of all time. As the results show, they got hardly anything right. *The Times* rugby reporter was merciless in his criticism of the players: 'It would be totally unfair to lay all the blame at the door of the top brass. At times, the players showed carelessness and ineptitude on the field that were almost unbelievable in experienced internationals, the sort of thing that would break any coach's patience if not his heart.'

Perhaps 1966 was a good tour to miss. The Lions trip to South Africa in 1968 saw a distinct improvement in performance. But again, Rogers missed out due to injury and a resultant loss of form before his spectacular comeback in 1969. The great times he had touring, playing for England, the British Lions and the Baa-Baas have lingered long in Budge's memory. In the summer of 2003, he travelled to Australia with a group of friends to see England's Jonny Wilkinson-inspired World Cup triumph. One of the highlights of the trip for Budge was meeting up again with his old adversary Waka Nathan. At the initial meeting, the former opponents shared a perfunctory handshake. But at Wellington a couple of weeks later, Budge and Waka met again and this time the atmosphere was far more cordial as the pair embraced in a gesture of reconciliation. Among Budge's small tour party was old friend Roger Dalzell, who has clear memories of the occasion: 'It was lovely to see Waka, Colin Meads and Budge – old enemies – all hugging each other and showing real mutual respect. The rest of us felt quite out of it as the three reminisced about the good old days.'

Budge's party to New Zealand was completed by Dalzell, lawyer friend and golfer Jeremy Caplan, and Aidan Creedon, a good friend of Budge's who was, conveniently, a wine expert. During the five-week trip, the group stayed in local hotels and guest houses. Caplan arranged the golf, Creedon the wine, while Dalzell did the cooking. With Budge as the nominated driver, the intrepid quartet were bound to get into the occasional tight spot. One such incident involved a clash with the local constabulary. Dalzell tells the story: 'Budge was driving and we were travelling through mountain passes and very tricky roads. For safety reasons, there were double yellow lines down the middle of the road which you weren't supposed to cross. This didn't seem to trouble Budge, who drove at his normal speed – very fast. Suddenly, a police car appeared behind us with horns blaring and lights blazing. We pulled over and the policeman approached Budge in the driver's seat: "Sir, do you realise you have crossed the double lines 12 times in 5 miles?" From the back of the car, Caplan intervened: "I am the driver's lawyer, officer, and we would like 144 other cases to be taken into consideration." The officer smiled and gave Budge a polite warning. Our driver then asked the patrolman how long it would take to reach their destination. "About one hour 30 minutes normally, but at the speed you're driving about 40 minutes!"'

During the 2003 trip, Budge enjoyed the hospitality of his close friend Phil Harry, who he had previously stayed with during the Lions tour in 2001. Harry and Budge have been great friends for many years. Harry played for Sydney RFC and the Aussie Barbarians in the 1950s before moving into administration, where he excelled, becoming president of the ARFU (Auckland Rugby Football Union) in 1994. In addition to his rugby activities, Harry became a successful businessman and sat at the head of a large family. His son Richard made 38 appearances for Australia and was a member of the World Cup-winning Wallabies in 1999.

In 2001, on his way to stay with the Harry family in Sydney, Budge drove alone from Port Douglas to Sydney – a journey of at least 1,500 miles – in a hired Ford Focus. At one point in the journey, the intrepid Rogers left the tourist route and drove 100 miles, without GPS, to catch sight of a duckbilled platypus. Mission accomplished, he returned to the orthodox route on the way to Sydney. Budge recalls travelling with Harry by bus to the Olympic Park to watch the Lions play Australia. Harry was the only Australian on the bus.

Budge loved touring with England, the Lions and the Barbarians. There is no question that touring had its ups and downs, but the experience of playing against the top rugby-playing countries in the world in their own backyard excited a player like Rogers. In many respects, tours are the highlight of an international rugby player's career, or at least they were when Budge was playing. Today's modern game, with its relentless club and country schedule, is a real threat to the future of the Barbarians and the British Lions. Rogers's feeling of devastation at being left out of the 1966 Lions tour to New Zealand was an indication of how important these tours were to him. Rogers treasured the opportunity that tours provided to develop friendships with rugby people the world over, many of which have lasted over 50 years.

Chapter 8

Work, family and friendship

None of us are as young
As we were. So what?
Friendship never ages

WH Auden

IF 1969 was a momentous year in the rugby life of Budge Rogers, 1970 was equally so but for very different reasons. One Friday evening in the summer of 1970, a pretty young girl was helped into the lounge bar of the King William by one of Budge's friends. She was hobbling on crutches after being involved in a recent horrific car accident. The girl, Nanette, immediately caught the eye of the young rugby player behind the bar, who spent an hour or so chatting with her and his friend. The next few times Nanette returned to the pub, Budge asked her out but was turned down on each occasion. Nanette was obviously unimpressed with his fame in the world of rugby. A couple of weeks later, Budge met Nanette in a Bedford nightclub when he invited her to Sunday lunch at Christ's College. To his great surprise, she said yes and their first date was an all-day affair at Cambridge University. Nanette would have been impressed when her new date arrived to collect her in his sporty MGB but would have been less impressed when, to his embarrassment, Budge slipped and fell on her doorstep. But despite Budge's clumsy accident, the couple enjoyed their day out together. It was to be the first of many.

Budge and Nanette were married in 1971 at the pretty church in the village of Ravenstone, near Olney, a short drive from Budge's home in Kempston. Nanette came from a large Northamptonshire farming family and the wedding was, in Budge's words, a 'big do'. His best man was Bedford Blues teammate Brian Arthur, who was one of 360 people to lose their lives in a plane crash in Paris two years later. England colleague Richard Sharp was an usher together with his great friend at Goldington Road, Larry Webb. Ever the character, Budge remembers Webb taking a huge bite out of his wife's straw hat. Close friend Roger Dalzell was working away in South Africa at the time, so missed Budge's big day.

Budge and Nanette bought a cottage in the pretty Bedfordshire village of Ravensden, which they gradually extended and refurbished. Their three boys were born in the house prior to the family moving to Manchester in 1980 before returning to Bedford four years later. The boys followed very different career paths. Guy was born in 1979 and after qualifying as an accountant moved into the gaming industry. Jamie followed two years later, studying art at Exeter, and is now a secondary school teacher in south London. Mark was born in 1982 and graduated at Sandhurst, later serving in Iraq and Afghanistan. On leaving the army, Mark developed a successful career in the banking industry. Budge and Nanette have a total of seven grandchildren all living within easy reach of Bedford, making family get-togethers a regular occurrence.

Rugby and the Bedford club in particular were at the heart of the Rogers family. The first match Nanette attended was an East Midlands county match at Northampton. Budge describes the moment: 'On the way to the ground, I warned Nanette about a chap in the crowd who would be making very loud comments, mostly supportive of me, and his name was the "Voice". When I joined her after the match, she said: "The 'Voice' is my cousin Hugh White!" We became good friends and he came to my stag evening and loved mixing with my teammates.'

Once the couple were married, Nanette committed herself wholeheartedly to the club and formed a group of wives and girlfriends who provided the after-match meal. Having visited the Scrum Hall bar, it is very easy to imagine the bustle and good humour of the after-match entertainment. Fortunately, it remains part of the life of this old rugby club. The time and effort Nanette and her friends gave to Bedford has been a feature of sports clubs up and down the country for generations and what makes them such welcoming places.

Away from the rugby field, Rogers left WH Allen, where he had worked since leaving school, in 1965. His eight years at the firm had given the young rugby star a solid grounding in business and the technical aspects of electrical engineering. At Allen's, Budge gained his professional qualification and valuable experience as a technical representative. The firm enthusiastically supported his rugby career and were clearly proud of having Budge on the staff. But after eight years, it was time to move on. One day in 1965, at the height of his rugby fame, Budge received a telephone call from Imperial Life Canada, which was expanding into the UK, asking him to set up training programmes for branch managers across the area. He accepted the offer and began a new chapter in his working life.

After a couple of years, Budge felt it was time for another change. Coincidently, at this time he bumped into an old friend, who suggested he might think about a job as a management consultant with PA Management. His mind made up, he said goodbye to Imperial Life and joined PA, where he stayed for seven years, gaining experience in every aspect of the business. It is indicative of Budge's character that he managed to balance the increasing demands of work, rugby and family life at this time, particularly if we take into account international matches and overseas tours. In

1971, Budge left PA and joined the Lloyds brokers, Harris. Initially, this seemed a good career move but the financial crash of the early 1970s meant that selling insurance and savings policies became extremely difficult. Budge had the unwelcome responsibility of shutting down branches and laying off staff.

This must have been a stressful time for Rogers, who could at least take his frustrations out on the training ground and against opposing fly-halves on Saturday afternoons. But in 1973, the clouds at work lifted when Budge was offered a job running the new Milton Keynes branch of the insurance firm CT Bowrings. The England man clearly enjoyed the work and tells an interesting story about one particular staff-bonding exercise the company arranged for its management staff. Budge was not impressed when he was asked to lead a team to take part in the 'Courage Trophy', an exacting exercise over two days against Territorial Army recruits. The first day was on Snowdon and the second on Scafell Pike. Running up and down mountains in difficult weather was not this international rugby player's idea of fun, despite his superior level of fitness. The event was won by a team led by Major Blandford-Snell, although Budge's team were not disgraced. Some good came of the experience when Bowrings later sponsored the Varsity match at Twickenham.

In the early 1970s, with his rugby international rugby career now over, Budge could reapply himself to the career he felt he had neglected in his playing days. The former England captain is keen to point out that none of the jobs he held either in his rugby days or after were 'cushy numbers', a practice that became common for top players prior to the game going professional. Rogers's business and management career was as a licensed broker and after gaining experience with several large firms, he started his own successful business. Incredibly, when you consider today's highly paid professionals, Budge and his generation paid subs to their clubs throughout their playing days. Seasoned internationals never questioned this state of affairs until the 1980s. Rogers says: 'Rugby gave to me – I didn't give to rugby.'

Brian Marshall is a successful businessman and a good friend of Rogers. The pair first met in the early 1980s, although Marshall had followed Budge's club and international career with considerable interest. The Marshalls' three sons were at school with the Rogers boys and the two families became friends and went on skiing trips together. According to Brian, Rogers's skiing was much like his driving – fast and fearless – and he well remembers Budge leading them up some tricky slopes. When they arrived at the top of one particularly scary slope, Budge turned to his friend and said: 'Brian – it's every man for himself from now on.' Marshall has some interesting things to say about his friend's business career: 'Budge would have doubtless built up quite a business empire but he put so much of his incredible energy into rugby and its development. He put the game first rather than business success. However, in the short time he spent on developing his own business, he was very successful.'

Rogers's 'incredible energy' and determination were put to good use, enabling him to become one of England's greatest rugby players, build a successful business and find time for charity work.

Marshall confirms: 'The Lords Taverner's (Ouse Valley) was very much Budge's creation. As chairman, he raised thousands for the charity, which provided minibuses to enable youngsters to participate in sport. I must have attended at least a dozen lunches at Woburn – they were great occasions. Budge also served as a trustee for five years.'

As remembered elsewhere, his family, close companionships developed over 20 years of playing rugby across the world, together with the enduring friendships of old pals, have been the cornerstone of Budge's life. Of the latter, no friendships were more enduring than those with old school chums Roger Bass and Roger Dalzell.

Bass, a former schoolteacher now living deep in the Devon countryside, has fond memories of his famous friend: 'Budge helped me when I came back from New Zealand. He was hugely generous. He values his friendships and you could never let him down. He was always as straight as a bullet.'

In early 1960, Budge took Bass and another friend, Johnny Dore, on holiday to the south of France for some fun and time in the sun – or that is how his friend saw it at the time. Bass has some vivid, if painful, memories of the excursion. What he wasn't anticipating was a physical bootcamp involving running up and down steep climbs in the hot Mediterranean sun. All along, Budge saw the holiday as part of a get-fit campaign. The pair had a great time in France, if not in the way one of them had expected.

Bass recalls: 'The trip to France with Budge in 1961 definitely helped me to get my rugby Blue at Oxford. I had never been so fit. We would train every day, doing sprints on the beach and running for miles across sand Dunes. One day, we decided to go out on a particularly long run and came across a nudist camp. I wanted to slow down and admire the view, but Budge would have none of it. "Come on, keep going, you'll thank me for this next season," he shouted.'

If the French 'bootcamp' was tough, there was plenty of fun to be had for the 20-year-olds in France. We know that Budge loved cars and driving fast. The pair travelled to France in Rogers's Jowett Jupiter and on one occasion Budge's love of speed didn't always match his judgement on the road. Bass picks up the story:

'Budge roared down this long, straight French road and as we approached a bend he went to overtake the car ahead, and as he did so the cars locked bumpers. The two vehicles slowed down before running into a newly harvested field and crashing into some hay bales.'

The French car rolled on to its side before the family inside clambered out unhurt. Fortunately, none of those involved suffered any injuries and Budge and Roger continued on their journey down to Monaco. Budge must have quickly forgotten the incident with the family and careered through the streets of the town as if he was driving in the Monaco Grand Prix. 'If Budge had not been a top rugby player, he could easily have been a racing car driver,' his passenger and navigator recollects.

What the France trip tells us about the young Rogers is how determined he was to set down the personal standards he maintained during the years of rugby that lay ahead. His touchstones of physical fitness, speed of movement and the desire to push himself to his physical limits were established in his late teens. This was a very singular young man who was not going to accept second best as an option – his drive was to define an exceptional sporting career.

With his scrapes in France well behind him, Roger Bass went up to Oxford that October in the condition of his life. He gained his Blue, alongside Richard Sharp among others, in between training for his teaching qualification. During the holidays, Bass played for Bedford seconds and when Rogers was away on England duty he took his place in the first XV. Later, Bass moved to New Zealand to pursue his teaching career. Living in Auckland, he played top-grade rugby and coached many aspiring young All Blacks. After 14 years, he returned to England to take up a position at Haileybury School. At his new school, one of Bass's pupils was none other than Budge's son Guy, who he taught economics. When later asked what he remembered of Bass's teaching, Guy answered: 'All I remember Mr Bass ever saying to me was: "Sit up, Rogers."'

Budge attended Roger Dalzell's wedding, while the latter took Budge's parents to watch their son play for Bedford in their knockout cup final win at Twickenham in 1975. Dalzell recently remarked of his friend: 'Budge was the most incredibly loyal friend. Fame never got to him, he never talked about it – he didn't change one scrap.'

Chapter 9

A fitting tribute

ROGERS'S performance against Scotland in 1969, when England won the Calcutta Cup for the first time since 1963, convinced the Bedford legend that he was back to his best. It was uppermost in his mind that he could continue captaining his country for one or two seasons and look forward to extending his own record number of caps. Sadly, it was not to be. In England's final game that season, Wales secured the championship, signalling the end of one the greatest careers in modern rugby. Before the match, Rogers believed his team were ready face the Welsh. 'We know the score – I think we have the confidence and teamwork to do it,' he said. But when the referee blew the whistle for the start of the game, it was the Welsh who were the more confident.

In the years ahead, England would have to do without the services of their illustrious No. 7, who in the words of Uel Titley was 'England's most conscientious and gifted player'. Journalist Pat Marshall said: 'Rogers was as great a team man as ever pulled on an England jersey.' Hard-headed sports reporters are not normally known for such generosity. Heartfelt tributes from respected journalists like Titley, Marshall, Vivian Jenkins and John Reason are rare, and Rogers would have appreciated such genuine praise. We know that the rugby press travelled with the players on England and Lions tours, and Budge became friends with many of them. On one occasion, he remembers Reason ringing his parents' pub seeking a reaction from Budge's mother on her son being made England captain. 'John got terrible nonsense from mum,' he said. Of course, none of Mrs Rogers's words were printed in Reason's *Telegraph* column. The much-respected reporter, who died peacefully at his home in 1977, wrote several books on rugby, including the highly regarded *The Lions Speak*, his account of the British Lions's infamous 1971 tour to New Zealand. Like others of his time, before blogging, pod-casting and in-depth TV coverage intruded into top-level sport, Reason gained the trust of the players. Mike Gibson, John Dawes and Barry John have all expressed their respect for the *Telegraph* man and the way he orchestrated the interviews for what became, arguably, the greatest ever book on the philosophy of rugby coaching.

Although discarded by his country, Budge still had much to offer. On Boxing Day 1970, the Barbarians arrived in Leicester for their annual fixture with the Tigers. That particular Christmas, the weather was appalling.

Titley recalls: 'Players had to mince their way from all directions across countryside dominated by snow and ice, and there was a wind to suggest that there were no hills or mountains between Welford Road and the Siberian steppes.'

Not the conditions a veteran wing-forward coming to the end of his career would relish, you might think. But Rogers threw himself into the game with his customary speed, fearlessness and physical strength. His display caught the eye of the rugby reporters, if not the England selectors. Titley confirmed: 'The most outstanding performance of the afternoon was given by the oldest player on the field. Rogers ... he showed that he is anything but a spent force.'

David Frost was similarly impressed: 'The attacks were maintained by the intelligent Rogers ... Rogers made an inexhaustible contribution to the match. They say in Bedford that Rogers has never played better than this season. I am inclined to agree with them.'

The following season, in Bedford's match against Moseley, Rogers continued his outstanding form. Terry Goodwin wrote of his performance in Town's 24-13 victory: 'Budge Rogers produced at Goldington Road the kind of form that suggests his omission from the England trials was caused by someone mislaying his address.'

But the selectors stubbornly refused the claims of the veteran, in spite of his form and the loud support of the rugby press. Rupert Cherry made a convincing case for Rogers's recall to the colours: 'It is difficult to understand how the selectors could overlook Rogers. He is still playing as well as he ever did. Are they saying he is too old? Does he not fit into their pattern? There is no sign of loss of speed or stamina . . . there is no fitter man playing rugby. He is carefully scientific in his training ... he does not leave too much on the training ground.'

Rogers's wonderful form at that stage of his career demonstrated the depth of his love for the game of rugby. Why else would he carry on at the level he had set himself? At the back of his mind, was there the thought that if he played at the very top of his game he might just have one more opportunity to play for his country? Alas, the selectors continued to ignore their great servant of the past 12 years and looked at other, younger options. There were to be no more letters from the secretary of the RFU inviting Rogers to play for his country, no more wondering in suspense if they would arrive and no more pulling on the white jersey and leading his England out in rugby matches across the world. The international career of one of the most iconic rugby figures of his age ended that day in Cardiff in 1969, when Wales took England apart in the second half. There were some great playing moments to come with Bedford, but not at international level.

A special lunch, attended by Lord Wakefield, was given by the Sportsmen's Club in recognition of Rogers's record number of England caps. The Bedford man was presented with a music centre for his extraordinary contribution to English rugby. This would have been gratefully received by the former England captain, who enjoys his music. Budge received the gift with the prior permission of the RFU, who in their absolute wisdom decreed that a gift of a music centre did not infringe Rogers's amateur status. The club lunches were originally organised for visiting international cricket teams. As far back as 1934, a lunch in honour of Sir Donald Bradman's Australian tourists at the Savoy Hotel was hosted by HDG Leveson Gower, and in 1939 a similar event was held in honour of the West Indies touring team, with a welcome speech by the Earl of Lonsdale. A short film of Bradman's 1934 acceptance speech is available to view on YouTube and reveals the surprising sense of humour of the greatest batsman the world has ever seen. At Rogers's lunch in 1975, the speaker was the Duke of Norfolk, who according to Budge was a 'truly great orator'.

Rogers was certainly not finished with rugby and returned to his beloved Bedford ready to prepare for the next season and face whatever might lay ahead for the now former England captain. A telephone call from his former captain Dickie Jeeps, inviting Budge to join a new England selection committee, opened up a new and promising opportunity for the Bedford man. Just what lay ahead for Rogers over the next few years he could never have imagined. There was one last heavy bag for the Kempston postman to struggle with before Budge hung up his boots for good. Reading through Budge's six bulky scrapbooks detailing his extraordinary career, it is impossible not to be impressed, almost overwhelmed, by the response from friends, colleagues and teammates on being awarded his record 32nd cap and regaining the England captaincy. Letters and telegrams came from old school friends, work colleagues and club secretaries from across the UK, and officials from the RFU. Going through this torrent of mail, one is immediately touched by the level of affection in which Budge is held by the world of rugby.

He would not admit it but I am sure he must have been moved by such an outpouring of admiration and respect. This man, who emerged from a humble background, became, with apologies to admirers of Richard Sharp, the player of his generation. The pair had the greatest respect for each other and Sharp said of his teammate: 'The opposing scrum-half never made a break while Budge was there.'

If 1969 was the year Rogers said farewell to international rugby, it was also the year in which he was given the highest honour ever awarded to an international rugby player. Letters and telegrams of major importance had been addressed to the King William in Kempston over the previous few years – Budge's England debut letter, notification of his England captaincy and an invitation to join the British Lions tour to South Africa, to mention but a few. The letter that arrived on 9 May 1969 was different. It was the first such letter to be received by any player in the 100-year history of rugby union. It came from No. 10 Downing Street and informed Rogers, in the strictest confidence, that the Prime Minister was 'minded' to recommend to the Queen that Budge Rogers be appointed an Officer of the Order of the British Empire (OBE). The letter requested that Budge let the Prime Minister know if this were agreeable. When the notification arrived, Budge was in Port Elizabeth with the Barbarians. He remembers receiving a garbled phone message from brother Chris saying: 'I think you have won an award or something.'

A further letter arrived from Downing Street the following month containing details of the investiture and was addressed to DP Rogers OBE. The news was released to the public and Budge was free to enjoy his great honour with friends, teammates and the wider rugby community. It had been an extraordinary year. Early in 1969, Rogers had made a successful return to the England team and regained the captaincy. Two wins and two defeats represented an average season for the England team, but for the England captain 1969 was a triumph – the international comeback after a season in the wilderness, regaining the captaincy, passing Wakefield's record number of England appearances, and now the OBE. There are few who have experienced a season so full of achievement and distinction, capped off by the investiture at Buckingham Palace. There is only space here to mention a few of the messages Budge received, some of which are in such a spidery scrawl as to make them unreadable. The Mayor of Bedford wrote inviting Budge to a civic reception in his honour to be held at the town hall. The letter included the words: 'It would give me great pleasure if you could attend with your lady.' Such chivalry!

The All England Tennis Club invited Budge to join them in the Royal Box during the Wimbledon fortnight. Rugby clubs across the UK sent their messages of congratulation, including Richmond, Wasps, Rosslyn Park, Old Merchant Taylors and local rivals Northampton Saints. His former employers at Queens Engineering, who knew Rogers better than most and had watched him grow up wrote: 'Another well-merited recognition of your great service to sport, and so early in life.' The great sports presenter Peter Dimmock wrote on behalf of the BBC: 'May I please hasten to send you our warmest congratulations on your well-deserved honour.'

Bill Ramsey wrote from the RFU, as did Air Commander and RFU secretary Bob Weighall, who offered his congratulations on the OBE: 'I am delighted . . . it is indeed a long time since my early days on the selection committee when it all started.' Glyn 'Hughie' Hughes sent a message on Barbarian Football Club headed paper which is unreadable, although I can make out the word 'delighted'.

The Rogers's great family friends the Dalzells sent their own very personal tribute, which contains the cryptic message: 'E Be an OBE, Aye, and an old OB too', in the unlikely event of their friend getting carried away with his new-found fame. The Westminster Bank, Shell-Mex, Bowrings, Imperial Life and Mackenzie Hill were among Rogers's business connections who wrote to express their congratulations. One of the most touching letters came from the City University, where Budge studied for his engineering qualifications as a teenager. The Central Council of Physical Recreation sent the following message: 'I am sure the Rugby Football Union will feel justifiable pride in this recognition of your services to rugby.' A young man wrote from Weybridge requesting Budge's 'signature' and hoped that rugby's first OBE would 'play on until you get 50 caps or more'. A friend speculated: 'What next? Viscount Rogers of the King Bill! Or Lord Budge of Goldington?'

The final tribute comes from the late Sir Peter Yarranton, chairman of the Sports Council, president of the Scarborough Cricket Festival, former skipper of the Barbarians and England international. Yarranton was an extremely well-respected figure in British sport and wrote to Budge both in a personal capacity and as secretary of Wasps Football Club. His words express the respect and admiration Rogers had gained in the world of rugby during his long career: 'Quite apart from your own personal tremendous record, which in itself is not likely to be exceeded, my club is conscious of all the work you do behind the scenes for our game ... Wasps as a club would like to add a tribute because both collectively and individually we feel we know you particularly well ... Long may you continue to add the tremendous weight of your own experience to rugby, and in conclusion we all feel it could not have happened to a nicer man.'

Such an overwhelming response to Budge's achievements shows the high regard, almost awe, in which the Bedford man was held in the sport at this time, not just for his peerless personal achievements but also the recognition he had brought to the game of rugby. It is difficult to think of another sporting figure that has done more to promote their sport in the best possible light. In England at that time, one thinks of Bobby Moore in soccer and David Hemery in athletics, both of whom wore their fame and achievements lightly and in the best interests of their sport. Budge Rogers is such a figure.

Rogers took his parents to Buckingham Palace for his investiture and the opportunity to meet the Queen. How proud Mr and Mrs Rogers must have been to witness their son's latest achievement. On such occasions, those receiving honours are given strict instructions regarding protocol and what not to do or not to say. When the big moment came and Budge approached Her Majesty, she asked the new OBE: 'What is it you do exactly?' Budge replied: 'I am a rugby player ma'am.' 'I know that,' replied the Queen, mindful of rugby's amateur status, 'but what else do you do?' Budge mumbled something about 'management consultant', bowed and walked quietly away. He spent that evening in a pub in Richmond with some mates from the local rugby club. It had been an exhausting but happy day in the life of the publican's son.

Rogers was now 35 years of age. His last England appearance was in 1969 and his record 34 caps had been overtaken by John Pullin the previous season. But, as he said at the time, he was not yet ready to hang up his handmade boots and was determined to approach the new season as he always did, with one major change – he was to relinquish the club captaincy. In a career gilded with honours, the match against Rosslyn Park could be viewed as a storybook finale. Budge, of course, had other ideas. 'I will get fit, just as I have always done, and then see how I go. I would only want to make the side on merit, which is a major reason why I did not stand for the captaincy. If I had been elected, it would have committed both myself and the club. There was a time earlier this season when I was not playing well and wondered if I should be in the side. Happily, I have since been playing pretty well.'

With the cup final celebrations of 1975 quickly becoming a memory, Rogers began to think about his future. 'I'm as fit as I've ever been,' declared the Bedford flanker. Budge's rigorous, life-long regime of hard early-season training followed by evenings working on his speed and agility made him the fittest England player since the legendary Sid Smart in the early 20th century. He could look back on his England career with tremendous pride. One of the reasons Rogers regained his England place in 1969 was his supreme physical fitness. The 1975/76 season was to be Rogers's last playing for his beloved Blues. His record at Bedford is unsurpassed. With 485 appearances in 20 years, he broke every club record in his time at Goldington Road. The former England captain played 31 times for Bedford in the glory year of 1974/75, but only 23 the following season. In the hot summer of 1976, Budge considered playing one more season but knew it was time to stop. He had achieved everything he set out to and more. The prospect of a long season in Bedford's second XV convinced this fittest of rugby players that the time was up. Budge's last game for Bedford was in the Alan Lovell Memorial match in January 1976. He had been injured in a game at Bristol early that month but was desperate to turn out for his old friend Lovell, whose death at the age of 39 in 1973 was such an awful tragedy. Lovell made 320 first-team appearances for Bedford Rovers and later became secretary of the Rovers. The son of a police officer and later a publican, Lovell contributed a great deal to the club and was highly respected in the town's sporting circles. Bedford's annual match against the county was named in Lovell's honour and all funds raised at the event went towards the education of his young daughter.

Budge did play one more game at Goldington Road. In April 1978, he led a DP Rogers XV against Bedford in a match to mark the official opening of the new changing rooms and clubhouse at the old ground. Jordan, Demming, Hollins, Wyatt and Bob Wilkinson, who all played in the 1975 cup final, were in the home team, while Budge's side included David Duckham, Paul Dodge, John Carleton and Bill Beaumont. The new facilities were a great addition to the club and a tribute to the hard work of the various committees. Traditionalists would be relieved to hear that the old Scrum Hall bar survived the upgrade.

New challenges lay ahead for Rogers but in the years following his retirement hardly a week went by without Budge missing that Saturday afternoon sense of intense anticipation – although he would not have missed the grind of training on those cold winter nights at Goldington Road. He dusted off his boots one more time when he played in the Lloyds team against the Stock Exchange, reviving old memories by scoring two tries. The following day, a reporter wrote: 'We wish he had another 20 years of running and tackling to give.' Rugby fans everywhere would have agreed.

Chapter 10

'The intelligent optimist'

T HE RFU centenary of 1971 was celebrated in style. The high point of the celebrations was the International Congress hosted by Corpus Christi College, Cambridge. Over 100 delegates from 49 countries attended the event, which included lectures on most of the main issues in the game and visits by delegates to clubs and schools around the country. The aim of the conference was to foster good relations between the different countries whose one common thread was the game of rugby. The event was a huge success. The Fijian delegates attracted large crowds wherever they went and became the star attraction. Of course, the early 1970s was a politically delicate time and the RFU demonstrated great organisational skill and sensitivity in staging an ambitious event. As the union's official history says: 'Delegates had been invited regardless of colour or creed, an absorption in the game of rugby being the only uniting bond.'

Rogers attended the RFU centenary dinner in April 1971 as a former England captain who, at the age of 32, had won the respect of all the rugby-playing nations. The Bedford man was honoured to be asked to present the centenary vase to 'Doug' Prentice and Bill Ramsey. With his England days over, Budge continued to turn out for his club, playing some of his best rugby in the early 1970s.

Of course, one of his greatest performances on the field was still to come – the knockout cup final at Twickenham in 1975. He also enjoyed captaining the 'England' team's visit to the Far East in 1971, which was part of the RFU celebrations.

The 1975 cup final victory was the highlight of Budge's club career and the greatest day in Bedford's history. He got through the following season and played a few games in 1976/77, but a torn hamstring at Cardiff in December that season called time on his playing days. Budge refused to accept the inevitable and played one more game before even this most courageous and driven of players realised his time was up. He knew in his heart it was time to stop.

At this time, Budge's business interests were expanding but he wanted to stay in the game he loved and had graced with such dignity. After all, rugby had been his life for over 20 years. The offer came at the right time – the opportunity to get England back to winning rugby matches again as a member of the selection panel. Rogers had gained some experience of committee working as a member of Sir George Mallaby's group set up in 1971 to review the organisation of English rugby, and with his knowledge and familiarity of the game at the highest level, there was no one better qualified to be a selector. The invitation in 1976 came from Sandy Sanders, the new chair of selectors, who was keen to have people on his committee who had recent playing experience. Rogers was only the second person, after Dickie Jeeps, to be a selector while still playing. The rugby press were enthusiastic about Rogers's appointment. Rupert Cherry wrote: 'Rogers is a man very much in the mould of Jeeps – a dedicated player, a deep thinker about the game, and, I believe, destined to become one of the game's great men, like Stoop, Wakefield, Ramsey and Jeeps. At the age of 37, he is well set in what I believe will be a long and successful career as an administrator.'

Mick Weston, Derek Morgan, Malcolm Phillips and John Currie, all of whom played for England in the 1960s, joined the panel at the same time as Rogers, providing the new chair with a fresh perspective on the job in hand. Bristol coach Peter Colston completed the group under Sanders, who had taken over the chairman's role from Alec Lewis.

One of the biggest disappointments for Rogers in an otherwise unblemished career was England's poor showing under his captaincy in the 1960s. As a selector, he was in a position to put this right. From February 1970 to November 1979, England played 40 matches and lost 20 of them. The 1960s and 1970s were not great years for English rugby. It wouldn't have helped the mood of the home fans that fierce rivals Wales were enjoying a golden era. When Lancastrian Eric Evans led the red rose jerseys to a clean sweep in 1957, it took another 23 years before Evans's triumph was repeated.

There were notable victories against South Africa in Johannesburg in 1972, a 20-3 win over Australia at Twickenham and a victory over the All Blacks in Auckland, both in 1973. But these were conspicuous highlights in what were years of mediocrity. At this time, there was also a marked deterioration in the relations between the home nations, as the *RFU Official History* points out: 'Another worrying development was the bad nature that began to mar encounters between England and the other home nations … As Celtic parochialism intensified, matches involving Wales, and later Scotland, were often played in a genuinely unpleasant climate.'

England were accused of arrogance, a claim that would later be laid at Wales's door in their successful years. Whoever was to blame for this unpleasantness hardly mattered – it was the game that suffered. The animosity was to reach its height in 1980, as we shall see. If the other home nations were ready to kick England when they were down, the selectors did nothing to help the situation. As an indication of the inconsistencies, not to mention the panic measures of the selectors, there were seven England captains between Bob Taylor in 1970 and the beginning of Bill Beaumont's reign in 1978. They are a very mixed bunch and included some wonderful players, such as Mike Slemen, Fran Cotton, Tony Neary, Peter Wheeler, Roger Uttley and finally Beaumont. Some consistency of leadership was an urgent priority. Something had to be done to get the England team back to winning ways and the new committee was a start. We know that at least one of the new members had very definite views on the reasons for the national team's poor performances, particularly from February 1970 to February 1973 when England lost 14 out of 17 matches. Budge was excited by the challenge to set England rugby on the road to recovery, but was fully aware that a shake-up in selection would not on its own provide the answer to England's problems.

The *Daily Telegraph* secured an interview with Rogers in 1976, a few days after the announcement that the Bedford man had joined the England selection panel. The banner headline for the article was written in capital letters: 'THE INCOMPARABLE BUDGE ROGERS'. Rupert Cherry, who wrote the piece, was a traditionalist and loved the spirit of the amateur game. The Varsity match, the County Championship, Barbarians Easter tour, the Middlesex Sevens and his personal favourite, the Hospitals Cup, were for Cherry the real heart of rugby union. World cups, premier leagues and all the trappings of professionalism were not for this doyen of Fleet Street. Cherry greatly admired the new selector as a player and his piece on Rogers provides us with a real insight into the former England captain's thinking about his new role. He had very clear ideas of what was needed, as he revealed in the article.

Rogers said: 'The reason England have not done so well is the system under which we are playing. We are not getting enough of the best players playing with and against each other often enough. I have not changed my mind from the time we made the Mallaby Report. I still think we should have a regional competition.'

The report recommended that the top players qualified for England should take part in a knockout competition between four regional sides, and from there go into the England trials. Under these arrangements the County Championship, cherished by the RFU committee, would take second place to the divisions. Rogers continued his carefully thought-through ideas about the future of England rugby: 'While I have been playing, I have been conscious of the players' frustrations. They know they are not getting enough top-class rugby. It is interesting now, almost four years after the Mallaby Committee was appointed, to find more and more people saying exactly what we recommended. Had we adopted the proposals, England would have a better side than they have now.'

Despite the forward-looking nature of the Mallaby Report, its recommendations were predictably shelved by the RFU. The new panel were charged with the daunting task of turning England's fortunes around. When asked if this were possible without root-and-branch change at the top level of the game, Rogers replied in his usual candid fashion: 'I am hopeful we can otherwise there is no point in doing the job. There are enough good players out there. Our job is not only to pick the right people but to instil some confidence into the team.'

In a thinly veiled criticism of previous selection practices, Rogers continued: 'The new committee also believes that a player cannot be allowed to learn a new position in international football. He has got to have a depth of experience in that position.'

When he finally called time on his playing career, Budge continued to train at Goldington Road and kept in touch with players' thoughts and feelings about the game. There is no question that he missed playing regularly. 'Had I not become a selector, I would probably have gone on playing,' he said at the time. But the time had come to move on and he saw the selector's job as a real honour, and a way to remain closely involved in the game. Cherry, who died in 2008 at the grand old age of 100, spoke for many at the time when he wrote: 'Of all the men I have met over many years in rugby football, I can say that Rogers is the most honest and uninhibited chap, who speaks his mind without fear or thought to favour anyone.'

Rogers gave the job of selector a great deal of thought. He, more than anyone, wanted the national team to start winning again. In the first few months, he struggled to come to terms with his new responsibilities, as he revealed in *The Telegraph* article: 'I am finding it difficult to concentrate on one player and find myself sitting back and looking at the game overall. Suppose it will come naturally in time and I know I am going to enjoy it.'

On the sort of qualities the new committee were looking for in a player, Rogers was clear: 'We are all agreed on discipline; we want individual discipline which leads to team discipline, and we want men who play the game in the right spirit, totally committed. I don't mean going around kicking people but totally committed to playing for England, and training for that purpose. We want men who will go out and give their all, whatever happens. I still think England is capable of better things in spite of the system under which rugby is played in this country. It is a system which puts the players at a disadvantage. They have to take too big a step to get to the top. We have not got the pyramid right.'

Rogers compared the route by which England players reach the top with compatriots in Wales: 'In Wales, the club rugby is so much stronger and all the top players are concentrated in a small number of clubs.'

A complete overhaul of how the England team were managed was the challenge facing those now running English rugby. Constant tinkering with selection had proved an utter failure. Rogers certainly had a point when he said Wales had an advantage over their rivals in the way the clubs were set up, but the Welsh had built on this by accepting the need for a new management style, which included devolving power to the coaching staff.

England's dismal record in the 1960s and 1970s exposed fundamental issues in how the national team was managed. Was the performance of the team the sole responsibility of the selectors? Who was responsible when things went wrong? Should a Carwyn Jones-type figure take charge of coaching and selection? Today, there is no ambiguity – all power resides in the coach. In 1978, these ideas were seen as revolutionary in the corridors and committee rooms of Twickenham. Look what happened to the Mallaby Report. Those in charge of the English game were not fools or entirely resistant to change. They wanted what was best for England as much as anyone. With the sporting world around them changing so fast and professionalism around the corner, did the RFU have the wit, foresight and desire to move with the times? This was the context for Rogers's first year as an England selector.

Success at last

When the selectors handed Bill Beaumont the poisoned chalice of the England captaincy in 1978, expectations remained low. The Fylde lock's reign did not begin well. Third and fourth places in the Five Nations in his first two seasons gave no hint of the success that lay ahead. In the face of failure in the late 1970s, the England selectors again resorted to their default position of inconsistency, with players coming and going with bewildering frequency. Something needed to be done. As the new season approached, Sandy Sanders decided he was no longer the man to take England forward and resigned as chair of selectors. Sanders suggested Rogers as his successor, a recommendation the RFU were more than happy to accept.

Following his retirement, Sanders sent a handwritten good luck message to his successor, passing on his congratulations and best wishes for the future: 'I have absolutely no doubt about your ability to do the job with outstanding success. The difference between success and failure is very slight and I firmly believe that our fortunes are looking better. Integrity is the key word.'

Sanders was certain that England would be in good hands – 'integrity' might have been Rogers's middle name. He was duly appointed chair of the England selection panel with the full authority to introduce any changes necessary to get the national team winning again. The Bedford man had been charged with leading the England team out of what the *Official RFU History* itself describes as 'the wilderness years'.

Rogers's first job was to make a couple of changes to his selection panel and bring in a new coach, the schoolteacher Mike Davis, who took over from Peter Colston. A former Torquay Athletic lock, the Devonian won 16 full caps before turning his attentions to coaching. Interestingly, Davis was the first England coach to be appointed for his record in schools rather than club rugby – it was a bold move by Rogers. At Sherborne School and with England Schoolboys, where he coached a succession of successful England under-18 sides, Davis had gained an international reputation for developing young players and building successful teams.

He developed a close relationship with Rogers and acted as a bridge between the selectors and the players. Crucially, Davis quickly earned the respect of Bill Beaumont and his team and was to become a pivotal figure in the success of the England side and a great ally to the new chair of selectors.

In those days, the England coach was a part-time and unpaid appointment. Davis joined the England team on the Thursday before a match and returned to his school on the Sunday. He became a full member of the selection panel, on which he became an influential figure. As Rogers explains, the work of the panel was extremely thorough in its attempt to get the right players in the team and to introduce some consistency of selection:

'Each member of the panel watched designated players while at the same time looking out for emerging talent. We all then produced a written report and circulated that among the rest of the panel. At the meetings, which often went on till midnight, we selected five teams in order of preference. Out of this came the final selection.'

For the Five Nations matches, there were also the trials as the final confirmation of the panel's ideas. The trials also provided the opportunity for uncapped players to force their way into the selectors' thinking. The thoroughness of the process was matched by the commitment to consistency of selection.

Budge continues: 'We decided that if a player misses a game through injury, he will be reinstated. That's tough on the player who is left out and may have played well. But we were determined that players could drop out injured and not be worried about losing their place.'

This new rule was fair to the players, who at least knew where they stood. Bill Beaumont was impressed by the commitment of the new panel, remarking: 'The revamped selection committee brought to their deliberations a level of common-sense, realism and consistency which had been tragically lacking hitherto.'

Beaumont did not spare his criticism of the previous selectors, admitting: 'I witnessed a series of mind-boggling acts of folly that left England beaten before they started. Our team were eight over par on the first tee [sic] and there was no way we could claw back that sort of deficit.'

The Fylde man reeled off numerous examples of players who had been treated appallingly by the selection process: Andy Ripley, Tony Neary, Alan Old and Peter Dixon to name a few. Beaumont believed the new panel under Sandy Sanders was more in tune with the players' thoughts and different demands of the modern game – they all had played in the 1970s.

The new panel's first task was an interesting one – to select a squad to tour the Far East in May/June 1979. Senior players Neary, Uttley and Cotton were all unavailable for the trip, but the press were not informed. This failure of communication led to the headlines focusing on the fact that three of England's top players were left out of the tour. This taught Rogers an early lesson about dealing with the media and from that moment he arranged for a press conference before every match to explain selection and provide an opportunity for questions. Now commonplace, at the time it was a ground-breaking innovation and was to pay off for Rogers in a rather unexpected way.

Rogers, as tour manager, was also the first to introduce a written tour itinerary for each player. This meant the squad knew exactly what they were doing day by day. The thinking was that if the players were treated like adults, then they would respond in kind. Unfortunately, the players took a little time to get used to this enlightened form of management. The group spent two days at the Petersham Hotel in Richmond and enjoyed the opportunity to visit Twickenham for the Middlesex Sevens prior to their departure. The squad arrived in Tokyo in late afternoon and were given the opportunity to relax and settle in after their long flight. The following morning, Budge learned that several of his squad had been arrested following some rowdy behaviour in a local bar. Maurice Colclough, sensing the danger, quickly got the miscreants out of trouble before too much damage was done. The chair of selectors was unimpressed by the players' exploits but was more concerned about how the travelling press would handle this indiscretion. Rogers called in the media and asked them to keep a lid on the whole affair, particularly as it was so early in the tour. They agreed without exception, probably grateful for this new-found openness from the tour management.

For Rogers, the most worrying thing about the incident was that coach Mike Davis was with the players on their night out. Budge had to remind Davis of his responsibilities and the importance of keeping a degree of distance between management and players. In fairness to Davis, he accepted this and the tour continued without any major incident. The coach may also have seen his role as a bridge between the players and the tour manager. Rogers himself had only been retired for a few seasons, but quickly recognised the need to stand apart from the players. Like the rest of the selectors Budge, resplendent in his England tracksuit, attended all the pre-match training sessions in his time as selector. With his slightly patrician air, the former England captain quickly gained the respect of the players and the trust of his captain.

The Far East trip was a huge success, a 'fabulous' tour, recalls Rogers. The itinerary took in Japan, Fiji and, interestingly, Tonga. The latter had a reputation for ferocious tackling and fierce will to win, but in the late 1970s the standard of the country's rugby pitches was still some way behind the rest of the world. Budge and his management team insisted that the pitch be heavily sanded before the England players were prepared to even set foot on the 'appalling' surface. Sand was quickly carted up from the beach and spread across the pitch. On a second inspection, Budge and Mike Davis noticed that in places sand had been contaminated with razor-sharp coral which would have cut the players to pieces. Thankfully, most of the coral was removed and the match went ahead. Shortly before kick-off, Budge asked the Tongan officials if the players could use a room to warm up in, given the pitch was temporarily off limits. The players were taken to a room below the stand, the door to which sported a heavy lock. An axe was summoned and the offending lock smashed off. A few rusty bicycles were removed, leaving the players a few minutes for their warm-up – that is, apart from those who were too helpless with laughter to concentrate. Further merriment ensued when the players noticed the Queen of Tonga had a special seat in the main stand designed to fit three people.

Veterans of several trips abroad as players, Rogers and Davis began to see the experience of touring in a different light on the Far East tour. They witnessed young players like John Carleton and Nigel Pomphrey laying down challenges to some of the senior players. As Bill Beaumont has said, the four-week trip gave Mike Davis an opportunity to exert his influence, never easy for a new coach, especially one with a schoolteacher background. Beaumont wrote in his book *Thanks to Rugby:* 'Mike was initially a bit too much of a school master … but he adapted his approach and soon won everybody's respect. He was able to adjust so quickly to knocking a national side into shape. There is no doubt… that the groundwork for our grand slam season was firmly laid on that Far East tour.'

Rogers, Davis and Beaumont all bemoaned the previous lack of imagination of English coaches. The England captain was particularly critical, saying: 'Coaching in England had been in a state of stagnation for a number of years, with the forwards grinding away remorselessly and the backs ploughing through a series of dull, predictable moves.'

With Rogers, Davis and Beaumont full of ideas and bonding nicely, and an encouraging blend of experience and promise among the players, England rugby at last appeared to be on the right track. The England skipper was upbeat about the forthcoming season and knew the team was in good hands: 'Budge and Mike impressed me enormously with the thoroughness of their preparations for the trip, which turned out to be one of the most enjoyable tours of my career.'

Rogers had taken his own sense of fairness and honesty into his new role – something the players appreciated – but this refreshing new spirit of openness in the England camp took time to get used to.

The summer tour to the Far East had been successful on many fronts, but the new leadership team faced a whole different challenge in November, when England faced the formidable All Blacks at Twickenham. Now in sole charge, Rogers was able to take the initiative. In an inspired example of man-management, Rogers and Davis announced that Beaumont would be captain and invited the Lancastrian to Leicester for a weekend prior to the game against the All Blacks. Beaumont relished the opportunity to discuss aspects of squad training and tactics with the new regime.

Beaumont said: 'I was pleased because I had tremendous faith in Budge and Mike. This was an entirely different working relationship. They even had the courage to appoint me captain a full month before the international. At long last the selectors had confidence in me and not only did I have confidence in the selectors, what is even more important I had confidence in myself.'

The team retained their selection practices and priorities in the build-up to the match, arguably the ultimate test in international rugby. The selectors had picked 13 of their team prior to the All Blacks's match against the Northern Division, holding back two places for outstanding performances against the tourists at Otley. In a game that has entered rugby folklore, the North beat the All Blacks 13-4 on 17 November. On that day at Cross Green, Fran Cotton was the inspiration behind the victory – the All Blacks's only defeat on the tour. Faced with the traditional pre-match *haka* routine, Cotton heard scrum-half Steve Smith whisper: 'Fran, I'm shit scared.' In response Cotton, immortalised in rugby circles by the 'mud man' photo of 1977, allegedly turned to his players and said: 'Look at the big poofs dancing.' Later, Cotton said he had the greatest respect for the All Blacks and the cultural significance of the *haka*, but that day in November 1979 his gentle debunking of the dance helped to motivate his side – and it worked.

New Zealand selected their strongest side to face the North, but that day the tourists found themselves up against one of the most dazzling displays of attacking rugby ever seen at the old ground. In front of a rain-soaked Yorkshire crowd of 8,000, Cotton's men ran in four tries and dominated the game from start to finish. Some critics argued that this was an average All Blacks side, but any rugby team that included such star names as skipper Graham Mourie, Murray Mexted, Andy Hayden and Stu Wilson was going to prove a real force. The opposition matched these star names player for player with Neary, Beaumont, Uttley, Old, Dixon, and Cotton himself all having outstanding games. The latter later described the match as 'the greatest 80 minutes I ever had in my life'. Selector Mike Weston and coach Des Seabrook had a wealth of riches at their disposal and deployed them wisely. The North decided to adopt the style of play employed by the England team on their recent tour to the Far East, playing ten-man percentage rugby and importantly taking no risks.

Bill Beaumont remembers: 'We drove at them in the set, rolled off from the mauls and picked a fast set of loose-forwards to help us dominate the open play.'

The outstanding performance of the Northern Division against the All Blacks gave the England selectors a headache, but they steadfastly refused to react to one single game and change the policy they had so carefully constructed. At Twickenham seven days after their Otley mauling, the All Blacks faced a confident, if controversial England side. In a hard-fought game, Dusty Hare's three penalties were not enough to save England from a narrow 10-9 defeat. Fran Cotton, in the England side that day, later laid the loss firmly at the door of the selectors: 'They chose Les Cusworth ahead of Alan Old at fly-half to play a kicking game, which wasn't Les's style. They also chose 5ft 9in Mike Rafter over 6ft 4in Roger Uttley, despite Uttley's excellent line-out display at Otley, where he was all over Andy Hayden. Those two decisions made a hell of a difference, especially as we lost by just one point.'

England captain Beaumont supported his North teammate. He wrote: 'While the All Blacks shrewdly strengthened their side for the England game, the new selectors made the only real mess of their first three years in office. Budge Rogers never made such a bad selection again.'

Rogers and his panel were labelled 'irresponsible' and slammed for making what some described as 'unbelievable decisions'. Criticised for inconsistency in the past, the new selection panel were damned if they did and damned if they didn't. But to be fair to Rogers, he was quick to admit his mistake. 'We got the Uttley-Smith non-selection wrong against New Zealand, but I wonder how many players, hand on heart, would have come up with Phil Blakeway at prop. As a selector, you try your best.'

As Rogers recently explained: 'In many ways, these mistakes were the product of experience which, in this case, proved to be wrong. It came about because in 1967 I played against the All Blacks for Midland Counties at Leicester and early in the game Danny Hearn broke his neck. There being no substitutes, we played on with 14 men. We played really well to keep the score to 3-3. The England selectors picked 13 or 14 of the team to play against the All Blacks a week later. This was not the best team available and we were well beaten.

'It was this experience that led me to say to the panel: "We should, but for a couple of positions, pick the England team to play the All Blacks before they played the North."'

The All Blacks made several changes for the England game and were clearly stung by the defeat at Otley – they may have won whatever team the selectors picked. Rogers conceded that in their commitment to consistency the panel made early mistakes, but as Beaumont confirmed history shows they were quick learners. The England players were encouraged by their displays at Otley and Twickenham and could look forward to the Five Nations that season with real optimism. Beaumont and his players could not wait for January. 'I was in no doubt we would win both the triple crown and the championship,' Beaumont said.

His comments were greeted with ridicule by the press, but the England captain was to have the last laugh. Rogers was desperate to introduce a root-and-branch transformation of a job that had become mired in inept decision-making and compromise. The intolerable results of the previous decade lay heavy on English rugby and the new panel were determined to be different. As the *Official History of the RFU* tells us: 'Rogers rectified his earlier mistake... by selecting Phil Blakeway at tight-head and switching Cotton to the loose-head berth and bringing in Smith and Uttley.'

The new panel had made serious errors in their team selection for the match against the All Blacks in November, but were big enough to admit it and move forward. The RFU were clearly impressed with how quickly Rogers settled into his new responsibilities, as the *History* says: 'Budge Rogers brought a certain pragmatism to the post, consulting frequently with captain Beaumont and introducing a steadfast approach to team selection.'

When he became chair of selectors, Rogers decided not to allow a vote on a particular player or position. Believing voting to be divisive, the new chairman insisted on a full discussion until the panel reached a unanimous decision. He brought John Young and John Finlan on to his panel and with Mike Davis he knew selection would be tough but fair.

Rogers and Davis sensed they might have a special team on their hands. At the heart was a tough group of forwards who began to believe they could dominate any opponent and a backline they were sure could translate possession into points. They had much to prove – no grand slam for 23 years and just three Five Nations championships in all that time. Beaumont's side were hungry for success.

Extra training sessions were organised on Monday evenings at Stourbridge – a convenient location for everyone involved. The club was run by John Jeavons-Fellows, who personally took care of all the arrangements. The facilities were excellent and the pitch first class. Jeavons-Fellows's father-in-law was a local butcher and supplied the players with the very best chops and steak for their post-training meal. Rogers believed the sessions were crucial: 'They were great fun, tremendous bonding nights. They were a very happy group on a mission.'

But was this England team ready to test the dominance of Wales and France? They were certainly well prepared for the challenge ahead. The meticulous Mike Davis led a full squad training session in the week before the first match, working on areas for improvement and building team spirit and confidence. Beaumont and his team clearly enjoyed these sessions, as the skipper says in his autobiography: 'Mike had an uncanny knack of practising the odd little forward skill with groups of three or four players. Amazingly, the opportunity to use these skills often seemed to crop up in matches.'

The England camp had a settled feel as the Five Nations approached and Beaumont's upbeat comments appeared justified. They may also have provoked his opponents. Relations between England and the other home nations had deteriorated following Phil Bennett's 'what have these bastards done for Wales' outburst in 1977. England skipper Beaumont was not prepared to tolerate this kind of provocation. Tensions were running high ahead of England's opening match against Ireland at Twickenham.

Maurice Colclough was injured and his place against the Irish was taken by line-out specialist Nigel Horton. Disagreements with his club side in France kept Horton out of any future international involvement, but his final international was his best – Horton was magnificent against the Irish. Blakeway had an outstanding debut and tries by Smith, Slemen and Scott and 12 points from the kicking sensation Dusty Hare helped the home side to an emphatic 24-9 victory. England's championship campaign was off to an impressive start and the captain's prediction remained intact. Rogers's side had played the kind of disciplined, controlled rugby they believed would bring them success. The game was won by England's pack, which drove the Irish forwards back for most of the game. As skipper Beaumont said later: 'At long last the selectors had given us the pack to carry out this demolition job, and if we all played our part we would all share in a great victory.'

Victory in the first match was overshadowed by a dreadful injury sustained by Tony Bond. A broken leg ended his season and his place in the next match – against France in Paris – was taken by his replacement at Twickenham, the fleet-footed Loughborough graduate Clive Woodward. Bond's injury kept him out of rugby for a very long time. Beaumont said: 'Tony's horrific injury spoiled what was almost a perfect day.' The selectors had more than made up for their mistakes in the All Blacks fixture earlier that season with their inspired selection of Phil Blakeway for the match against Ireland. The performance of the tight-head prop was critical to England's victory. The Gloucester man suffered a broken neck in 1978 but recovered sufficiently to be picked for the Rest team in the final trial for the 1980 Five Nations. Blakeway was a key figure that season with his celebrated scrummaging ability at tight-head. England could look forward to their second match having beaten the favourites with something to spare.

Two weeks later, England travelled to Paris to face a French team low on confidence following their first match, an 18-9 defeat to Wales in Cardiff. Rogers made two changes. Woodward replaced the stricken Bond while Colclough, now recovered from injury, was restored to the second row at the expense of Horton. England were buoyant after their great start but had not won in Paris for 16 years.

Beaumont's boys' confidence took a knock when France led through an early Jean-Pierre Rives try. But the English fought back. When a scrum broke up early in the first half, Fran Cotton floored the French prop Robert Pararemborde. Steve Smith remembers Cotton being 'psyched up to the eyebrows'. With the French fans baying for Cotton to be sent off, referee Clive Norling let it go. It was a turning point in the match. After the final whistle, Cotton sought out the chair of selectors. 'The incident cost us three points and I apologised to Budge Rogers immediately after the game, but it did give us a psychological ascendency over the French pack,' Cotton said.

England recovered from Rives's score through tries from Preston and Carleton, the first either had scored at international level. As the game developed, the red rose jerseys began to dominate the line-out and totally outscrummage their opponents. For 70 minutes, England were in total control of the match. After taking a hammering for most of the game, the French rediscovered their form in the final ten minutes when Averous went over in the corner, leaving the match in the balance. But England's belief and sound tackling enabled them to keep their 17-13 lead to the final whistle and achieve their first win in Paris for 16 years. The champagne at the Moulin Rouge that evening must have tasted particularly good.

Two down, two to go. England's next opponents were fierce rivals Wales. Festering resentment and unwelcome press hype fuelled what was always going to be a feisty encounter. In 1980, the tension between the two camps reached fever pitch. The press whipped up the occasion as a battle between the downtrodden Welsh and their cocky, oppressive English masters. It didn't help that there was an acrimonious steel strike in Wales at the time, which gave impetus to the media's divisive narrative. Bill Beaumont referred to the build-up as 'a sordid, distasteful affair, sparked off by some irresponsible comments in some sections of the press'. The *RFU Official History* also blamed the press for their irresponsible coverage of the Wales match: 'The press ... conveniently overlooked the fact that England had defeated Wales on only one occasion in the last 16 years, lit the touchpaper and retreated to a café at a safe distance to recount, with great surprise and righteous indignation, the brutality that followed.'

But away from the media hysteria Rogers, coach Mike Davis and the selection panel knew that England had not beaten their opponents for over a decade – that was the chilling reality and extent of the challenge England faced at Twickenham. Both management and captain spent a considerable time in England's pre-match preparations trying to diffuse the situation and persuade their players not to let the match develop into a brawl. 'We were better footballers than that,' argued Beaumont.

The match lived up to its pre-match hype. Nick Preston dropped out through injury and his place was taken by Paul Dodge, whose greater physical threat actually strengthened the team. Early on, the referee was forced to call the captains together and demand they restrain their players following some ferocious exchanges early in the game. The call for calm was ignored by Paul Ringer, who a few minutes later smashed into John Horton without a thought for the ball. Most observers felt the tackle was fairly innocuous compared to what had gone before. It was a foolish rather than dangerous challenge given that the referee had just warned both sides about their future conduct. His hand was forced by Ringer's stupidity. He became only the second Welshman ever to be sent off – it was a humiliating end to his career.

As often happens, Ringer's red card inspired the 14 Welshmen as they stretched every sinew to prevent an English victory – and very nearly succeeded. They were ahead at the interval but lost the game to the boot of Dusty Hare, who outkicked his opposite number Gareth Davies to hand England a narrow 9-8 win. Such was the spirit in the side that Phil Blakeway revealed at the end of the match he had played the whole 80 minutes with broken ribs. The prop had taken a kick in the France match and went for an X-ray, which proved negative. As Rogers reveals: 'Phil was determined to play and kept his injury quiet – it was the toughest game the players had ever played in.' Gareth Davies echoed the England man's words: 'It was the most violent game I ever played in,' said the Welshman. The *Daily Mirror* headline the following Monday spoke for many. It read: 'Someone will die one day'. After this most bruising of encounters both dressing rooms resembled A&E units, with blood and bandages everywhere. The England players had over 30 stitches between them – all in head wounds. The match was a brawl, with the players hammering each other to the point of exhaustion.

Despite the negativity surrounding the match, the England squad and management were jubilant. The team had showed tremendous character in the most hostile of environments. In truth, the match was a disgrace and an affront to the game of rugby. The England players were no innocent victims and gave as good as they got, but the Welsh had come prepared for a fight and went looking for one. The England captain was adamant that his players did not want an over-physical match: 'I want to emphasise that at no stage in any of our preparations was any mention of a tough, physical approach made by me, by Mike Davis, by Budge Rogers, or by any of the players.'

Rogers knew that game had been a disastrous advertisement for rugby football and done a great deal of harm to the game. He advised his players to think carefully before they spoke to reporters: 'Look, there's going to be a lot of flak flying around from the press after that game, so let's be sensible about what we say at press conferences.'

Thankful that the most difficult of games was behind them, the England party could begin to prepare for the final match of the championship. In the midst of all the celebrations, the British Lions tour manager Syd Millar asked the inspirational Beaumont if he would accept the offer to captain the Lions on the forthcoming tour to South Africa. This tremendous news capped a triumphant day for Beaumont, the England management and the players. They could enjoy their victorious evening, but knew their job was far from finished. They had overcome their most difficult hurdle but there remained a trip to Murrayfield, where the Scots were waiting.

The grand slam was a tantalising one game away. Surely Scotland could not spoil the party and prevent England's first clean sweep since 1957 and their first triple crown since 1960. Rogers's team had four weeks to recover from the Wales game and prepare for their final assault on the title. When the day came, the England team were well prepared. The newly introduced Monday evening sessions continued and there was the standard Thursday and Friday practice before the match. Bill Beaumont believes that no England team 'had ever been better prepared for such an important match'.

The nervous English supporters at Murrayfield that day need not have worried. Carefully prepared by Davis, the team stayed true to the tactics that had brought them to the brink of the grand slam. The order went out – destroy the Scottish pack, depriving Irvine and Rutherford of any loose balls, and run the second phase. A rampant England scored three tries in the first half and led

16-0 at the break. Woodward, Carleton, Slemen and Smith were unstoppable. Carleton's hat-trick of tries was the culmination of a magnificent season for the Orrell winger and the first by an Englishman for 56 years. The former schoolteacher made his debut in the match against the All Blacks earlier that season and went on to gain 26 caps and made several appearances for the British Lions. That day in March 1980, Murrayfield belonged to John Carleton. England's 30-18 victory was emphatic. The grand slam and triple crown belonged to the red rose jerseys and how they deserved their celebrations.

In addition to the team's triumph, there were personal milestones. Tony Neary surpassed John Pullin's record of 42 caps and Bill Beaumont equalled the record for the most England appearances as captain. On the morning of the match, the England captain trawled the shops of Princes Street searching for a gift to mark 'Nearos' record as the most capped player in England rugby history. Beaumont settled on a tankard that he quickly had inscribed before presenting it to the flanker after the match, which turned out to be Neary's final appearance for his country. England defeated the Scots in front of a capacity crowd of 75,000 and they did it in real style. England won the grand slam for the first time since 1957. For once, rugby took over the back pages of the newspapers from soccer – the dark deeds of the match against Wales at Twickenham had receded into a distant memory as the nation celebrated their heroes.

The 1980 side was the greatest England team for a generation. Beaumont, Neary, Colclough, Wheeler, Uttley and Cotton, along with Rogers and Davis, had all experienced the worst of the depressing results of the previous decade and must have wondered whether they would ever be part of a successful England team. Coach Mike Davis paid his own tribute to the players' commitment and motivation: 'Coaching that team was easy on match day. It was full of leaders and players on a mission. I might have a few relaxed words in the changing room in the build-up, but then I would deliberately vanish. There were so many great players that the last thing they needed was me bashing on the tables and kicking up a noise.'

Their mission accomplished, Uttley and Neary retired and a torn hamstring in the first match of the following season ended Cotton's England career. As we shall see, Beaumont continued as captain for a further two seasons, along with Rogers as chair of selectors and Mike Davis as coach. Winning the grand slam is the height of a player's rugby career and it was a fitting finale for these great players. John Scott later spoke about the combination of skill, power and experience that marked out his teammates that year: 'Colclough was an outstanding athlete while Billy was the workhorse, then we had Nigel Horton as back-up. We had guys with so much skill and ability in the pack. "Nearo" was on another planet. Uttley was a fantastic guy and Wheeler was before his time as a hooker.'

Paul Dodge reiterated his teammate's thoughts about the all-conquering England side: 'It was not all down to the forwards. Steve Smith and John Horton kicked well and Woodward's silky running was a factor in both their opening tries. I learned more from playing for three years with Uttley and Neary than with anyone.'

The grand slam was also good timing. Seven of the England team were called up for the Lions tour to South Africa, with Beaumont the first Englishman to lead the Lions for 50 years. The triumph of 1980 was also a fitting tribute to the work of coach Davis, who won the respect of the players. Success was also an endorsement of Rogers's role as chair of selectors. Like some of his players, he had experienced first hand the pain of being part of a failing England set-up in the previous ten years. The future looked bright and players, management and supporters alike could celebrate their long-awaited day in the sun.

One of the features of the 1980 success was the relationship between Rogers as chair of selectors and his captain Bill Beaumont. The pair couldn't have been more different. Rogers was a Corinthian amateur from a successful southern club, while Beaumont was the archetypal blunt northerner straight from central casting. But the pair did have several important things in common. Both had an unsurpassed love for their sport, both were totally committed on the field of play and both were desperate to see England winning again. So, along with the coach, Rogers and Beaumont were a formidable force and they swiftly hit their stride.

Rogers and Davis were determined to succeed and Beaumont took his captaincy duties very seriously. The three men worked tremendously well together in terms of selection, tactics and preparing their players for matches. As Beaumont has said, these preparations helped to get the team results that won the grand slam: 'A controlled four-hour build-up with Budge Rogers and Mike Davis beginning at 11 o'clock on the Saturday morning brought us nicely to fever pitch by three o'clock in the afternoon.'

This calmer approach to team-building and big-match preparation suited the modern player more than the ritualistic chest-thumping beloved of old-school rabble rousers – although Beaumont always delivered a 'blood-and-thunder' team talk minutes before kick-off. In 1980, the players felt comfortable with the management of the side, which allowed them their own idiosyncrasies within a clear structure. It certainly paid off in that grand slam year, when all the stars were aligned in the England rugby planet. In 1982, Bill Beaumont wrote to Budge enclosing a signed copy of his book *Thanks to Rugby*.

The former England captain wrote: 'Dear Budge, I would like you to have a copy of my book and with it is my personal thanks for all you have done for me personally, and on a wider front English rugby over the last few years. Yours, Bill.'

The relationship between captain and chair of selectors has rarely been an easy one and is often fraught, with little respect on either side. The one between Beaumont and Rogers was based on mutual respect and affection. The results speak for themselves.

At the age of 41, Rogers added the grand slam to his growing list of achievements. His role as chair of selectors was demanding of his time and energy. He was totally committed to the job and fully engaged with the players and their clubs, a commitment that required days of travel watching matches, attending committee meetings and the weekends of the matches themselves. On the

Thursday prior to an international, Budge would leave to be with the team, not returning until late Saturday night or more likely Sunday morning. There were trips around the country to watch matches and the Monday evening sessions at Stourbridge, a demanding schedule for a working man with a young family. Things were made a little easier by the selection panel sharing responsibilities, with each member concentrating on individual players in different parts of the country. The job of chair of selectors is a pretty thankless and unglamorous task, a duty rather than an exciting means to remain part of the England set-up. But Rogers is a serious man and changed the way the selectors operated. He was effectively a bridge between the old amateur days and the new era ushered in by Geoff Cooke in the late 1980s.

In the grand slam year, Budge was living and working in Manchester having accepted a new job offer from CT Bowring. Nanette and Budge had three small children and the demands on their time were considerable. But they were young and building their lives and Budge's standing in the national game could not have been higher at this time. Nanette soon joined her husband in Manchester but the couple knew the move would only be temporary so began to plan their return to Bedfordshire, which was always Budge's spiritual home. He never really wanted to be too far from Bedford.

Today, professional sport is all about winning, something Rogers has come to accept, if reluctantly. But the experience of victory in sport is fleeting before preparation for the next match, fight or tournament begins to occupy the mind. For Rogers and his team, the grand slam was a glorious memory that can never be taken from them, but the new season soon began to loom large in the minds of the selectors, coaches and players themselves. The England team members who toured South Africa with the Lions would have been physically drained by the end of the summer, but recovered in time for the Five Nations in January. England began their defence of the championship with a narrow 21-19 defeat in Cardiff, which quickly ended any hopes of them successfully defending their crown. A comfortable 23-17 victory over Scotland at Twickenham secured the Calcutta Cup and eased the selectors' minds.

There was further encouragement with a good win in Ireland before a disappointing display against France at Twickenham meant that England's campaign ended in frustration. They had won just two matches out of four. Both England and France retained hopes of sharing the title ahead of the final match at Twickenham, while their opponents remained on course for a clean sweep. France won the match and the grand slam thanks to a controversial try just before half time. It was no disgrace to lose to a very good French side captained by 'player of the year', Jean-Pierre Rives. The great Frenchman led an unchanged side throughout the championship in 1981 and such was the strength of their defence that not one try was scored against them in their four matches. Rives's side toured New Zealand in 1979, when they played two Test matches against the All Blacks.

Watching France steal their crown would have been hard to take for Beaumont and his players. The magnificent triumph of the previous season was reduced to a distant memory. Seldom can success have been so fleeting. Selection is easy when the team are winning and full of so many great players. When the side began to break up, selectors were usually tempted back into inconsistency. The mood in the England camp was lifted by the experimental tour to Argentina in May and June, with the tourists drawing the first Test in Buenos Aires before they recovered to take the second Test 12-6. On what was always going to be a tough tour, Beaumont's men were without Slemen, Colclough, Wheeler, Blakeway and full-back Marcus Rose, who all decided not to travel to South America, leaving the captain, and manager Derek Morgan, who took Rogers's place, with an inexperienced party. The group flew home just months before the two countries became engulfed by the Falklands War, which illustrated that some things are more important than sport.

The chair of selectors remained at home to focus on his work and family commitments. He also needed some time away from the game. Despite the two defeats in the Five Nations and handing the title to France, Rogers believed England played well in 1981 without reaching the heights of the previous year. Skipper Beaumont echoed his comments when he argued that after years of lacking belief England had become used to success and expected to win each time they played. In this sense at least, England had made real progress.

Beaumont appreciated the support he had been given by the selectors. England's grand slam captain wrote to his former chair of selectors in early 1980, in his neatest handwriting, thanking him for his support: 'I hope you don't mind [me] writing you a quick note thanking you for all you have done for me as captain and for the rest of the side. Your enthusiasm has been tremendous both on and off the field, and this has been a great filip to the side.'

The 1981/82 season began with a curtain-raiser against Australia, which the home team won 15-11 in a match best remembered for the topless streak across the Twickenham pitch by the infamous Erica Roe. The team began the Five Nations at Murrayfield. It was a match that Bill Beaumont remembers, mostly for the wrong reasons. It was bitterly cold in Edinburgh that January and the England team had nowhere to train. So instead of the frozen Murrayfield pitch, they ended up using the Hibernian soccer ground, where they had undersoil heating. Beaumont went to bed that night confident that his team were well prepared and ready for the new campaign. But at 2am, the England skipper was violently sick and throwing up all over his bathroom.

Beaumont recalled: 'I rang Budge Rogers and Mike Davis, who told me to spend the morning in bed. Budge said they really needed me to play and urged me not to tell anyone how sick I was feeling.'

Beaumont dutifully came down to breakfast and joined the players on the team bus. 'Sheer adrenalin got me through but we had to settle for a draw, which is just about the most frustrating result in the opening game of the championship,' said Beaumont.

The Scotland match, which England should have won, is best remembered not for Beaumont's misfortune but for the injury-time penalty scored by Andy Irvine from inside his own half.

How different this was from England's wonderful performance at Murrayfield to win the grand slam in 1980. The heart of the team had been ripped out. The superlative pack of the 1980 season had been slowly dismantled and proved irreplaceable.

As Mike Davis said later: 'We started losing the mafia – Uttley, Neary and Fran. They were the people who, if they said do it, the young players in the squad did it.'

England next faced Ireland at Twickenham without their inspirational captain. Beaumont telephoned Rogers the Sunday night before the match to say he wasn't going to make it. The team was due to meet at the usual Monday session at Stourbridge and the first thing Budge did was take Steve Smith aside to tell him he would take over as captain. Smith's reaction was typical: 'We won't miss Bill as a player but we certainly will as a captain.'

England lost to Ireland 15-16, but it was a game they should have won. In the following match in Paris, France were trounced 27-15 but the game was remembered not for England's performance but for a particular off-field incident involving one of the senior players. It was the infamous 'aftershave' incident at the post-match dinner involving Maurice Colclough and prop Colin Smart. The players had a few beers in the changing room before making their way to the hotel for dinner. During dinner, with the wine flowing, Colclough challenged Smart to drink a bottle of aftershave, one of the dinner-table gifts provided by the French. 'I'll drink mine if you drink yours,' was Colclough's challenge, which Smart accepted, if a little reluctantly. Colclough drank his bottle down in one. Smart, egged on by the others, followed.

Unbeknown to the now groggy prop-forward, Colclough had emptied his aftershave from the bottle and replaced it with champagne, while his teammate drank undiluted cologne. Feeling understandably sick, Smart headed straight for the gents. A few minutes later, Peter Wheeler approached Rogers and whispered in his ear: 'Budge, Smart's unconscious in the gents.' An ambulance was called and Smart was despatched to hospital to have his stomach pumped. Rogers went in the ambulance accompanied by

Colclough but later returned to the dinner. Later that evening, the chair of selectors went back to see his stricken prop-forward, who by now was sitting up in bed. Budge remembers: 'The whole ward reeked of aftershave pumped from Smart's stomach'. According to Mike Davis, by the end of the dinner the England players had knotted handkerchiefs on their heads and their trousers rolled up to their knees in the time-honoured way of English rugby players. The whole episode left a nasty taste in the mouth of not just Smart but the watching chair of selectors. It was a sight that left a lasting impression on Rogers.

The Five Nations ended with a comprehensive 17-7 win against Wales at Twickenham and Steve Smith ended his first season as captain with two wins, a draw and one loss, but it could have easily ended in another grand slam.

The denouement of the grand slam England team came not in an international match but in the semi-final of the County Championship in 1982 between Lancashire and the North Midlands. During the match, Bill Beaumont took a knock to the head and was advised that if it happened again it could result in permanent brain damage. The England captain was forced to withdraw from the rest of the championship. The 9-9 draw against Scotland was to be the last international in what was one of the most iconic rugby careers of the post-war era. Beaumont had proved one of England's greatest ever captains. To see just how good he was, we need only look at England's results in the four seasons following Beaumont's retirement. England won just seven of their 27 fixtures and were twice beaten by a record margin. A heavy defeat by the All Blacks is bad enough but to lose 36-3 to Scotland, as England did in 1986, shows just how far the team fell from those dizzy heights of 1980.

With Beaumont gone and Mike Davis's retirement just a few weeks away, Rogers was the last man standing of the successful management team of 1980. One of Beaumont's least public achievements was the way in which he acted as an effective bridge between Rogers, Davis and the players. When he left the scene, that important connection was broken. The life of a selector is one of never-ending decisions. Players came and went in time-honoured England fashion. Peter Winterbottom at flanker was one of the few successes, as was Rory Underwood, a direct replacement for Mike Slemen. Richard Hill and later outstanding individuals like Rob Andrew, Rory Underwood, Mike Teague and Wade Dooley worked their way into the team. If the two post-grand slam seasons represented a decent return for England, the 1983 championship was a very different matter. The season shot holes in Beaumont's argument that England's recent success had instilled a lasting winning mentality among the players.

The Rogers/Davis/Beaumont era was over almost as soon as it began. They had won the biggest prize and there is no doubt that between them they created the conditions for the triumph of 1980. All three desperately wanted England to succeed. That Rogers, Davis and Beaumont achieved their goal was tribute enough in itself. Not one of the three was troubled by ego or self-seeking. All they wanted was for English rugby to regain the respect of the world. Of course, it helped that they had a wonderful group of players at their disposal, but England had great players in the past and managed to fail. This time it was different and 1980 was a turning point in English rugby.

If English rugby turned a corner in 1980, the grand slam was not to be the beginning of a glorious dawn, with season after season of triumph and trophies. But the success in 1980 was welcome and England had clearly learned lessons and made progress. The team, though, was not at the point where it could be expected to dominate European rugby throughout the 1980s. The authors of *Behind the Rose* describe England's progress in these graphic terms: 'The dozy giants, having briefly awoken and flexed their muscles, stumbled back into the stygian gloom and promptly fell asleep for another seven-year spell.'

In the early 1980s, off-field problems began to trouble the game's administrators. For Rogers, a real blackspot in the 1983 season was the Adidas boot money scandal.

He remembers: 'The players were paid to wear the company's branded boots, with their representative Robin Money going so far as to paint three stripes on non-Adidas boots. It was only the good sense of a fellow selector that prevented me from dropping the players' ringleader.'

His friend Pat Briggs remembers the controversy over Money's 'stash', which he dished out to certain players. 'Budge maintained a highly principled stand at the time,' said the former Bedford and England under-23 coach. 'He simply told Money: "Keep your cash, I don't want it."'

In the summer of 1982, Budge managed an England tour to Canada, where the team played nine matches, winning all of them and conceding only 30 points. But for the chair of selectors, things were changing rapidly. Rogers had lost his trusted coach and captain. The tour began badly but some of the squad, who were new to international rugby, began to demonstrate real progress. Rogers began to question the loyalty and commitment of some of the England players. Within 30 minutes of arriving at the tour party hotel in Seattle, Rogers received a knock on his door from an irate hotel manager. 'Are you in charge of the England team?' he demanded. 'Yes, why do you ask?' replied Budge. 'Because your players have just thrown the wife of one of our guests into the swimming pool, and she can't swim.' The incident, coupled with the Adidas scandal, reinforced Budge's view that the players' behaviour was becoming increasingly disruptive and that the relationship he had carefully constructed with Davis and Beaumont was now irretrievably damaged. Rogers admits that three years into his spell as chair of selectors he began, unknowingly at the time, to distance himself from the players. While in the US, Budge was given unlimited use of a top-of-the-range Jaguar for the duration of the trip. This was too much for a man who once possessed a Jowett Jupiter and Budge frequently went off on his own, speeding along the quiet roads of rural America, leaving his coach and captain in charge.

Rogers very nearly gave up the position of chairman after the tour but decided to give it another season with Mike Davis. The

1982/83 season began with a 19-15 home defeat by France which, although not disastrous, was not the start England wanted. This was followed by a 13-13 draw in Cardiff, a game England should have won but for a silly off side in the last minute. Unfortunately, the draw against Wales was followed by defeats by Scotland and Ireland, handing England the dreaded wooden spoon. Rogers later reflected on a dramatic season: 'I laid much of the blame for England's poor performance at my feet. I made a number of bad selections and played people out of position. It was inevitable that, despite being offered another year, I knew I had to resign.'

The following season, when England lost to Scotland in the first match of the Five Nations series, Budge admits making one or two selection mistakes, the biggest being the axing of Mike Slemen, who had previously been regarded as untouchable. The press were merciless and called for heads to roll. To balance the decision to drop the Liverpool man, the selectors were delighted to discover the exciting Peter Winterbottom as replacement for England's world-class flanker Tony Neary. England recovered to beat Ireland in 1984 before losing to France and Wales. Selection mistakes and ill-disciplined players were playing on Rogers's mind at this time. He had been a selector for eight years and began to feel that it might be time to move on. That year, Budge and Nanette decided to move back to Bedford. The time spent travelling between Manchester, London and the rest of the country had become intolerable and something had to give. He had enjoyed his time as chairman and achieved his primary objective in returning England back to the top of international rugby. Under Rogers's guidance, the selection process was transformed from a policy of knee-jerk reaction to one of consistency and fairness. A more effective relationship was established between England selectors, the coach and the captain. Winning the grand slam was a product of this new and more transparent way of doing things. Rogers's period in office helped change the face of England rugby, as John Scott recognised: 'In 1979, when Budge Rogers took over, he laid the foundations for Geoff Cooke to take England to a higher level a decade later. As chairman, Rogers has seen the value of experience and a settled team, and his enthusiasm and planning has given momentum to the whole campaign.'

Cooke described Rogers and his coach Mike Davis as 'intelligent optimists' whose presence helped to revive the fortunes of English rugby. There is little doubt that the England team benefitted from Rogers's depth of experience as a player. But he knew when it was time to move on, to spend more time with his family and to focus on his successful, if slightly overlooked, work commitments.

Rogers's whole outlook on rugby was infused with the spirit of pure and proud amateurism. As his great friend Pat Briggs has said: 'Despite his "professional" dedication to fitness and hard work, Budge was a true Corinthian throughout his career.' There is little doubt that he did not find the brave new world of commercial rugby to his liking. The inevitable march to 'open' rugby began in the early 1980s and his grand slam skipper Bill Beaumont was at its head. The 'boot money' scandal of the 1980s was simply the rather shabby precursor of commercialism driven by sponsorship inspired by Kerry Packer's Channel 9 Australian TV company, which had players signed up ready to go, forcing the hands of the International Rugby Board. Commercial pressures had triumphed in other professional sports years before and began to creep into rugby union, slowly at first and then like an avalanche to sweep the old world away for good. Predictably, the RFU was slow to react to what it saw as an unwelcome intrusion threatening to destroy all its ancient and cherished traditions. However, the first challenge to the RFU's authority did not come from Packer but from the England players, and the 'mutiny' was not at all well received by officialdom.

Bill Beaumont and Fran Cotton both wrote autobiographies on their retirement and naturally wished to keep the royalties. Beaumont was told in no uncertain terms by the RFU that their former captain should give all the proceeds of his book *Thanks to Rugby (1982)*, ghosted by Ian Robertson, to charity or the RFU. If he retained the profits, then Beaumont would be banished from all forms of rugby. He quickly sought the advice of his grandfather

William Blackledge, whose response was wise and to the point: 'If, in ten years hence, your backside is hanging out your trousers, would the RFU buy you a new pair?' That was enough for Beaumont. He wrote to Bob Weighall at the RFU and informed him of his decision to go ahead and sign a contract with the publishers, Stanley Paul. Weighall accepted his former captain's decision and even attended the book launch – at the author's invitation. In his book, Beaumont reveals that while still England captain he handed over half his £1,200 fee for appearing on BBC's *Question of Sport* to the RFU charitable trust and the other half to Fylde RFC. Despite this act of generosity, Beaumont was duly banished by the RFU and was soon joined by Phil Bennett, Mike Burton, Gareth Edwards and Fran Cotton in a flood of rugby autobiographies in the 1980s. The floodgates were open and there was little the RFU could do to stop it happening. Beaumont had played by the rules and was banned for his trouble. In 1989, helpless to prevent the inevitable, the International Rugby Board reinstated the miscreants who had kept the proceeds of their books. As Beaumont wrote in his second autobiography: 'From being a well-respected former England captain, I was to become a pariah overnight, barred from any involvement in rugby union at any level, and all because I had the temerity to accept monetary rewards for writing my autobiography.'

All these disruptions aside, Rogers could leave the hotseat confident that he had done all he could to improve the fortunes of the England team. With Davis and Beaumont he had won the grand slam, after which results tailed off as key members of the 1980 side retired and left the arena. With all the political and commercial pressures surrounding rugby at this difficult time, the job of chair of selectors was no easy ride. Players began to assert their independence in a move to prove their financial worth to the RFU and to potential sponsors. Even the RFU finally succumbed to professionalism but that is for another time and another story, and is well documented elsewhere. The game had changed beyond recognition from Budge's time as a player and as captain of England. The year 1980 was a triumph and it was another 11 years before

England won the grand slam again. Rogers had served his country well and it was now time to step away from the game he had loved for over 30 years and concentrate more fully on other things. For now at least, rugby could look after itself.

In the years he spent away from the game, Rogers was able to focus fully on his family and business interests. The new family home in Bedford was a short distance from Goldington Road, where he made his first-team debut in 1959 as a 17-year-old. It seemed the most natural thing for the most distinguished of old Bedfordians to return to his old club as president or in some other honorary capacity. But the club had moved on since 1976, when Budge played his last game for Bedford. He had been a long time away from Goldington Road. There was also no natural role for their former captain and he never really fancied coaching. So Budge was free to enjoy his time away from the responsibilities of selection and the glare of publicity that surrounds the modern game. He would also have relished the opportunity to improve his golf handicap. Budge's business flourished, he had more time for his family, even though his golf stubbornly refused to improve. He started his own insurance brokers in 1988, DP Rogers Insurance Holdings, in premises in Dunstable, opened by his one-time England captain, TV personality and currently chairman of the International Rugby Board, Bill Beaumont.

But such was Rogers's reputation in the sport that the RFU were bound to come calling sooner or later, and the call came in the most unexpected way. But first there was real work to be done. Unlike many sporting celebrities, Budge never got a job because he was Budge Rogers. He was never tempted to play rugby league when that could have been an option. There was very little, if any, money to made from rugby, as Budge remarked on his retirement: 'The only person I can think of who could make money out of being a rugby player is Barry John. He caught the public's eye after the Lions tour to New Zealand but I bet he is the only one in 50 years.'

Of course, Budge was well known and well respected in the insurance business, but even when he was chair of selectors he continued to travel across the Home Counties to visit clients and build the business. Of course his name would have opened some doors, as he recalls in his normal self-deprecating manner: 'Sometimes it's a help and someone will recognise who I am. It means that they're rugby followers themselves, so you have a basis on which to form a relationship.'

Budge's friend Brian Marshall, who ran the family horticulture business, remembers Budge putting together attractive deals for the greenhouse industry. Budge received countless messages of congratulations at every milestone in his career from his business associates and clients. These kept coming throughout his playing days, on the occasion of his OBE and later when his England side won the grand slam. They are clearly heartfelt and genuine and are an indication of the great respect he had not only in rugby but also in his business life.

While Budge developed the business, the boys enjoyed school and the family prospered, but rugby had been such a force in his life that it was unlikely that at his relatively young age he would be lost to the game forever. The not-to-be-forgotten call from the RFU came in 1998. There was a thorny problem at the headquarters of rugby and they wanted Rogers to join a small group to look into it. There was a contention that the three members who were leading the negotiations with Sky TV had misled the RFU over parts of the contract. The accusations were led by committee members Fran Cotton and Graeme Cattermole, who argued that Jeavons-Fellows should be removed from the committee. Rogers agreed to President Brook's request and formed a group chaired by Sandy Sanders. The group met five times at the Holiday Inn on the A14 over a six-month period, when they closely examined all the facts and read all the relevant documents. Satisfied with their deliberations, they met the 'accusers' at the East India Club in London to report their findings. The meeting concluded that Jeavons-Fellows had no case to answer and that the matter was now closed.

If the case against Jeavons-Fellows was not proven, it did raise some serious questions about how rugby union was being governed.

As Rogers has said: 'These were bad times at the RFU.' The annual general meeting of 1998 initiated a complete review of its operating structure. The terms of reference were to include governance, the position of junior and senior clubs, and the relationship between management and the committee/council. The working practices between the president and the CEO were high on the list of issues the enquiry would look at. The review group, which became known as 84b, was to be chaired by Rogers, who was at this time junior vice-president of the RFU, and included representatives from all parts of the game. Feelings at the RFU were running high. Professor Mark Bailey, a Cambridge rugby Blue and senior committee member, advised Rogers that 'we are in a mess – break the mould'.

The RFU were made up of county representatives from junior or senior clubs, referees and one member each from Oxford and Cambridge universities. The Army, Navy and RAF also each had one member. Pat Briggs recalls Cambridge Blue Ian Metcalf arguing passionately for Oxbridge to retain their seats on the council. 'Just think about all the great international players Cambridge University has produced,' pleaded Metcalf. The council of 55 members was supported by a CEO and a team of professional staff. It was an archaic and ineffective structure that needed a serious overhaul. The structure was unwieldy, top-heavy and failing. Unbelievably, the terms of reference of 84b were similar to those of the 1971 Mallaby Committee, on which Rogers also served.

The president had been all-powerful in the history of the RFU and this was not a healthy model for modern sport – rugby union was being left behind. It was clear the structure needed changing, but there was also an outstanding issue that other sports had already addressed – money. The RFU had initiated the John Player Cup in 1976 and 11 years later accepted the argument for a pyramid league structure. The Heineken Cup was introduced in 1995 and many more sponsored trophies were to follow. On 26 August 1995, 'open' rugby was finally welcomed in and this time by the front door. Rugby union was now a professional sport and its players were able to earn money through salaries, sponsorship and book royalties. The way was open to introduce players' contracts, work out sponsorship deals and, importantly, align the club structure to the new professional era – which clubs could be professional and which would remain amateur?

Perhaps the first thing that needed to happen was to drastically reduce the size of the committee/council. But as Budge has said: 'The board would need to vote for their own exclusion – it would be like turkeys voting for Christmas.' Such were the vested interests. With the structure that existed in the late 1990s, the CEO was undermined at every stage by the members, who wished to continue to make the important decisions on policy, law changes, ticket prices, player release and so on. Rogers's 84b group met with the Football Association and discovered both sports were suffering from the same old traditional barriers to change. It was clear that the role of the CEO and his staff needed to be strengthened while the committee needed to accept that a delegation of its powers was best for the sport. Rogers describes the outcome of the sub-group's deliberations: 'After many weeks of deliberation the group produced a unanimous set of recommendations, which was a miracle bearing in mind the number of vested interests within the group. Our terms of reference included defining the roles of the president and the CEO. One of the most controversial decisions was to reduce the role and influence of the counties.

'Along with most of the group,' remembers Budge, 'I was disappointed and frustrated by the council's decision to adopt only a few of our recommendations. This was so reminiscent of what happened to the Mallaby Report.'

Despite the frustrations and the RFU resisting change, the game had changed forever with the decision to go professional – the rest would follow.

President of the RFU

With his experience as chair of selectors in the early 1980s, and part of the reforming tendency within the RFU in the mid-1990s, Rogers was well placed to lead the game into a new future – but the 'blazers' once again refused to reform. But his turn was to come. In 1998, the chair of the RFU nominations panel, former Oxford Blue Peter Johnson, telephoned Budge with the news that the panel were 'thinking of nominating you for the role of president'. It was Mark Bailey who originally suggested to the nominations panel that Rogers would make an ideal candidate for the presidency. The presidency is an honour given to few and Budge was flattered to be asked, but naturally wanted to know what the job entailed. He travelled down to Johnson's holiday home in Devon to discuss the offer in more detail. Of course, he accepted the honour – the culmination of a wonderful career. As is customary on such occasions, Budge was appointed junior vice-president in 1998 and senior vice-president in 1999 before accepting the presidency in 2000. As Budge was not a county representative on the council, he was appointed as a 'privileged' member, such are the arcane rules of the RFU.

Rogers cared deeply about the game of rugby and would have wanted his presidential year to be as effective as possible. In 2000, the role was largely ceremonial – a figurehead without any powers – the ambassador for English rugby, if you like. Most of the power in the organisation was in the hands of the CEO Francis Baron, a business specialist who improved the RFU's finances from a deficit of £10m when he arrived in 1998 to an operating surplus of £9m and a healthy balance of £119m when he left in 2010. The new president's job was to support the board and the CEO, lead on the club versus country issue, which remained unresolved at this time, keep an eye on the imperfect coaching structure, and ensure that the council focused on the good of rugby at all levels and left the running of the professional game to the CEO and his team.

Rogers's presidential term of office coincided with an unfortunate issue that brought English rugby into disrepute. The threatened players' strike of 2000 took the game to a new low. In November of that year, the England team refused to play in the Test against Argentina at Twickenham unless their dispute with the RFU was resolved. New contract talks had broken down on the Monday night prior to the international against the Pumas.

The players wanted £4,000 for a match fee and £2,250 for a win bonus. The RFU's original offer was slightly less – the difference was a mere few hundred pounds. The result was deadlock and a threatened strike. Coach Clive Woodward warned the players they had until 11am on the Wednesday to make themselves available for training, or he would pick an alternative squad. The players were led by skipper Martin Johnson, Lawrence Dallaglio and Matt Dawson, with the RFU side headed by Francis Baron. Woodward was clearly not happy and said at the time: 'This is the saddest day in the history of English rugby. I feel let down by the players I have done so much for over the last few years.'

For the players, Johnson was unrepentant and accused the RFU of being 'old fashioned, patronising and arrogant'. He added: 'It's not just an issue of money. It's the principle, the way the RFU have handled the situation. They are affecting the guys' livelihoods on a matter of principle.'

Dawson, never one to hold back, announced the players would ignore Woodward's ultimatum unless their demands were met. The strike was averted on the Tuesday afternoon at a meeting with the players, attended by the RFU team of Rogers as president, Baron and board member Peter Wheeler. A deal was struck, with both sides saving face. There was to be no disciplinary action against those involved and, as is often the case in these situations, both sides were able to claim victory. The additional money amounted to about £50,000 shared between the 25 squad players. Woodward called the players in for an extra training session, but he remained unhappy, insisting: 'I don't think you can use an England shirt to get what you want. This has been a waste of time. This should never happen again.'

The RFU were unhappy that the players broke away from their appointed agency to try and get more money. 'You can't run with the hares and hunt with the hounds. The difficulty occurred when the players took it on,' declared Baron. Either way, the 'strike' was a huge embarrassment for the sport. The issue was settled for good when Rob Andrew negotiated a 'player release' scheme with the major clubs, which has since been improved to suit all sides. Player power had now begun to set the agenda – how the game had changed since Rogers's emergence as a teenage prodigy at Goldington Road.

Despite the inevitable difficulties, Rogers thoroughly enjoyed his year as president. He had the opportunity to visit over 100 clubs throughout the country and remained close to the England team and management. Entertaining visiting teams and officials was a real pleasure, as were the committee dinners and lunches in the president's room prior to each match. Among the invited guests at the lunches were leading administrators from other sports, politicians and, on occasions, royalty. Princess Anne was always good company, although a dedicated Scotland supporter. Rogers remembers one special day: 'One stand-out occasion was when we invited the Prime Minister to a match. A few days before the game, we received a call saying he could not attend but would it be possible for Euan [Blair] to attend with a few friends as it was his birthday. Of course, we said yes and set up a room, gave them lunch and tickets for the match. We invited my son Mark to spend the day with the PM's party. At half time, we were surprised when Tony Blair walked into the president's room. In conversation, he told me that his schoolboy hero was Richard Sharp. I said that I knew Richard was at the match and we could arrange a meeting after the match. This we did and the Prime Minister talked to nobody else in the room but Richard.'

A few days after the match at Twickenham, Sharp, young Mark and Budge all received a handwritten letter that read:

> Dear Budge
> Thank you and your staff for the warm welcome you gave us on 2 December. We very much appreciated your hospitality and Mark was excellent in looking after me and the boys.
>
> Thank you so much.
> Yours sincerely,
> Tony Blair

One lasting legacy of Budge's presidency was meeting Phil Henry, the president of the Australian Rugby Union. He and his wife Meryl became very close friends through regular visits to Australia, while Budge twice had the opportunity to entertain the Henrys in England. This is a further example of Budge's ability to maintain long term friendships, often across the world.

Rogers's year in office passed quickly. On the field, Woodward's World Cup team was taking shape and won the grand slam, beating Ireland in the final game, which was played in the autumn because of the foot-and-mouth outbreak. At the end of 2000, Rogers's work as a national rugby figure was completed and he walked away content with a job well done. For the next few years, Budge enjoyed the privileges associated with past presidents – matches at Twickenham, attending dinners and so on. He kept in touch with the game and enjoyed trips overseas to watch England on tour and saw old friends and teammates. But it was time to hand over the reins. This great rugby figure could return to his growing family, his business interests and his golf at Royal Worlington, satisfied that he had left the English game in good shape.

Budge Rogers enjoyed a long and distinguished career at Bedford, one of the leading clubs in the 1960s and 1970s. Making his club debut at the age of 17, he made a record 485 appearances for the club. He went on to exceed the record number of caps for his country, which had stood for 25 years. He captained England on seven occasions and toured with the British Lions. When he retired in 1976 after leading his club to victory in the national knockout cup at Twickenham, Rogers was appointed chair of selectors, president of the RFU and became the first rugby player to be awarded an OBE while still playing. Rogers played with and against the world's very best players for his club, country, the Barbarians and the British Lions. During his career, he played in every country in the world where rugby is played, including Australia, New Zealand, South Africa, Japan, Singapore, Canada and Sri Lanka. His speed to the ball, tenacious tackling, and magnificent running terrified fly-halves around the world for over a decade. There is no doubt that

Budge Rogers defined the role of the England No. 7 and made it his own for years.

As chair of selectors, Rogers's England team, under the captaincy of Bill Beaumont, won the grand slam in 1980. We should never forget that the Bedford man achieved all this while qualifying as an engineer, building a career and eventually running his own successful business. We have seen from the tributes and messages of congratulations from friends, fellow players, journalists and administrators just how well-respected and immensely popular, even loved, this great man of rugby was. Given his vast experience at the top of the sport, and with such an incredible list of achievements, there are very few people in the game who can speak about rugby with such authority.

Rogers brought to rugby administration all the positive energy and drive he displayed in his playing days, imbued with an optimism and belief that things could improve – and they did. There was a complete lack of cynicism in his outlook and an acceptance that this was not just an honour, but a job to be done and done well.

Rogers's friends and colleagues testify to his personal qualities of honesty, loyalty and sheer decency. 'Straight as a gun barrel,' as one close friend described him. If Rogers had been born in 1969 instead of 1939, we can safely assume that he would have been a sporting superstar of the highest order. Instead, this dedicated rugby hero of the 1960s and 1970s remained a proud amateur throughout his career. But for all his loyal amateurism, Rogers was as 'professional' as any international rugby player before or since. He set the standard for fitness and dedication during his playing career that few players could match. A non-drinker in a time of Olympic-standard beer drinking in rugby, Rogers was a pioneer. If he was a purist, an old-style Corinthian sportsman, he was no pushover and could mix it with the toughest in the game as the All Blacks Waka Nathan and Colin Meads will testify. With his depth of experience in every facet of the game, there are very few who have earned the authority to comment on the modern game more than Budge Rogers.

When asked what made Rogers such a great player, his friend Rick Chadwick, who played in the famous final against Rosslyn Park in 1975, answered: 'The qualities that made Budge a great international player and leader were outstanding physical fitness, total commitment to the cause, a driven personality and absolute focus on his target regardless of any obstacles. Uncompromising, his strength of personality is staggering.'

The last word on one of the greatest English sportsmen of the post-war era should go to two men who knew him best: Pat Briggs, the legendary Bedford coach who led the Blues to their great victory in 1975, and David Perry, with whom Budge shared so many great rugby moments.

Pat Briggs, with the coach's trained eye, believed Budge's successful career was forged back in his early Bedford days: 'Budge was a real student of the game and thought about how he could improve. He would practise his screw kick and passing for hours. With his commitment to fitness, he built a great foundation.'

Few people knew Budge's game as well as Briggs, who said: 'Rugby was made for Budge. He had a real nose for the game and the ability to be in the right place at the right time. In this sense, he was very much like Richie McCaw. Budge was also a legendary tackler. He played every game with a never-say-die attitude and knew how far to go and what could or could not be done. He always played just on the edge.'

Briggs remembers that Budge analysed the referee before each game and passed on his knowledge to his teammates. It was just another small way his team could gain an advantage over the opposition, similar to the 'small gains' orthodoxy of today's coaches, pioneered by cycling's Dave Brailsford. The opposition used to complain that Budge was always offside and sometimes they were right, but if he did keep the referees interested, most of the time he was just very quick. He was also tactically aware and, according to Briggs, analysed every game for hours. In this, as in so many ways, Budge was ahead of his time. If he thought deeply about the game, Briggs remembers that Budge was not an easy player to coach: 'He was bloody obstinate, opinionated and didn't believe in compromise. He didn't like being told. This was another part of his strong personality and one of the things that made him such a great player.'

Today, over 50 years after they first met at Goldington Road, the two men remain close friends. Briggs said: 'On the rugby field, Budge was fearless – he would have made a brilliant fighter pilot. Off the field, he has always been the most loyal and generous friend.'

I was fortunate to speak to David Perry in 2017 a few months before his sad death. The former England captain had fond memories of his playing days with Budge, both at Bedford and for England: 'Budge was the best No. 7 of his time. He was fitter and more determined than any of us, still running around the ground when most of us were seeking refreshment in the bar. He was tough as nails, but such a nice man – a lovely bloke. He was not easy to get to know very well, but he was a good friend and a pretty remarkable player. He had all the best qualities and none of the bad. Budge was never injured – a tribute to his great fitness.'

Fearless and courageous on the field, he has been a loyal and generous friend off it. Budge Rogers enjoyed one of the most successful rugby careers of the amateur era and we should end this biography with his own thoughts on a remarkable sporting life.

Reflections on
a rugby life

WHEN Phil asked me to write a few words on what my rugby career had given me, I thought of the overriding pleasure of over 40 years of enjoyment both on and off the field. Of the 600-plus games I played, I can truthfully say I only failed to enjoy a handful, and they were not necessarily games lost. The thrill I felt when running on to the field never diminished. But it was more than just the matches, it was also the training and practice – in my case twice a week with Bedford and twice on my own. I loved it. It was only later, when talking to the fitness coach of Clive Woodward's 2003 World Cup-winning side, that I realised how unstructured, and in some cases harmful, our training had been – but, of course, we had no guidance from a coach or physio.

Playing the game was matched by the friendships and camaraderie that developed with both teammates and opposition, which created a lifelong bond. I well remember after the World Cup victory in Sydney flying to Auckland the next day and calling Wilson Whineray, who I had not seen in years, to see if we could meet up. His reply was that they were holding an All Blacks captains' lunch the next day at a hotel nearby and would I like to attend? I ended up chatting with eight former All Black captains, most of whom I knew.

My rugby career also afforded me the opportunity to travel as I would not otherwise have done. At the age of 22, to criss-cross South Africa after my first long-haul flight in a Comet was an amazing thrill. Further trips to New Zealand, Australia, America and the Far East added to my travel experience. I had a relatively sheltered, quiet home life and rugby introduced me to hotels and good food. I well remember the England team hotel in Porthcawl before the 1963 game (we practised on the beach because all the grounds were frozen). Jim Roberts persuaded me to eat whitebait when I was dubious about eating a whole fish. Also, the formal dinners at the Mayfair Hotel were a great experience, as was staying at the hotel, although the first night was not as I expected, for when I got to my room the late Dickie Jeeps expelled me because he was accompanied by his wife or girlfriend and I ended up sleeping in a room with six of my teammates.

As my career progressed, I received speaking invitations and quickly learned to articulate my thoughts into a formal speech. A very early experience sticks in my mind – I was speaking at a small Welsh club and made the mistake at the end of inviting questions. After a pause, a chap at the back in a flat cap and red and white scarf said: 'Tell me, Mr Rogers, who scored the second try for Wales against the 1935 All Blacks in the top right-hand corner of the Arms Park?'

I paused for effect and replied: 'I don't know, can you tell me?' He stretched to his full height, puffed his chest out and said: 'f*****g me!'

My time as an England selector and especially as chairman was most rewarding, with the spirit of camaraderie with the rest of the panel coming close to that of playing, although I was very disappointed with how it ended. My final direct involvement was as president of the RFU in 2000/01. It was challenging, enjoyable and exhausting, but great fun. It can be seen from these pages that rugby has been the dominant feature in my life and given me memories I will always cherish.

Budge Rogers
Chronology

1939 Born on 20 June in Bromham, Bedfordshire

1949 1st Year at Bedford School

1956 Debut for Bedford v Old Paulines

1957 Final year at Bedford School

1957 County debut at Leicester

1957 Began Electrical Engineering degree at City University and apprenticeship at WH Allens in Bedford

1961 England debut v Ireland in Dublin

1962 Toured South Africa with the British Lions

1962 Debut for British Lions v South Africa in Johannesburg

1963 Toured New Zealand and Australia with England

1965 Appointed captain of Bedford RFC

1966 Appointed England captain for the season

1967 Toured Canada with England

1968 Toured Japan and the Far East with England

1969 Recalled as England captain

1969 Broke Lord Wakefield's record number of England caps

1969 Final England appearance at Cardiff Arms Park

1969 Awarded Order of the British Empire

1971 Married Nanette in Buckinghamshire

1971 Captained England on tour to Far East and Sri Lanka

1975 Captained Bedford Blues to victory against Rosslyn Park in the RFU Cup Knockout Competition

1976 Retired as a player

1976 Appointed England selector

1979 Manager of England tour to Japan, Fiji and Tonga

1979 Appointed chair of England selectors

1980 England won Five Nations grand slam

2000 Appointed president of the Rugby Football Union

2001 England won Five Nations Championship and grand slam

Bibliography

Anderson R, *A Funny Thing Happened on my Way to Twickenham* (1970) Arthur Barker

Beaumont B, *Thanks to Rugby* (1982) Stanley Paul. *The Autobiography* (2003) Collins Willow

Clearly M and Rhys C, *100 Years of Twickenham and the Six Nations Championship 1910-2010* (2010) Twickenham Stadium

Evans A, *The Barbarians – the united nations of rugby* (2005) Penguin Books(2005)

Jones S, *Midnight Rugby: Triumph and Shambles in the Professional Era* (2000) Headline

Jones S and Cain I, *Behind the Rose* (2014) Arena Sport

Jones, English, Cain and Barnes, *Behind the Lions: Playing Rugby for the British & Irish Lions* (2012) Polaris

McLaren B, *The Voice of Rugby* (2004) Bantam Books

Palenski R, *All Blacks v Lions* (2005) Hodder Moa Beckett

Perry D, *Big Dog: The Memoirs of David Perry* (2015) Unpublished private edition

Roy N and Beard P, *125 Years of the Blues* (2011) Bedford Blues Ltd

Starmer-Smith,= N, *The Barbarians: History of the Barbarian Football Club* (1977) MacDonald and James

Thomas C and Thomas G, *125 Years of the British and Irish Lions: The Official History* (2013) Mainstream Publishing

Titley UA and McWhirter R, *Centenary History of the Rugby Football Union* (1970) Rugby Football Union

Walker J, *The Roar of the Crowd* (2016) The British Library
Woolgar J, *England: The Official RFU History* (1999) Virgin

Journals and archive material:
The Rugby Playfair Annual (1952/53 to 1970/71) Dickens Press
Rothman's Rugby Yearbook 1983/84 and *1984/85*
The British Lions Tour of South Africa 1962 The Times Publishing
    Company
The Career Scrapbooks of Derek Prior Rogers
Bedford, England, British and Irish Lions and Barbarian match
    programmes from 1958–1976

Newspapers (by courtesy of the British Library):
The Times and *Sunday Times*
The Telegraph and *Sunday Telegraph*
The Guardian
The Observer
The Daily Mirror
The Daily Mail
The Bedfordshire Times
The Daily and *Sunday Express*
The Ouzel – Bedford School journal 1969, 1970
Bedford RFC *Souvenir Booklet* (1975)

Websites:
The Barbarians FC
Bedford School
Bedford Blues RFC
ESPN: satellite sports channel and archive
Old Bedfordians Club
The England Rugby Football Union 'englandrugby'
The British and Irish Lions 'lionsrugby'
Wikipedia

Index